SPRAWLBALL

MARINER BOOKS

HOUGHTON MIFFLIN HARCOURT

BOSTON   NEW YORK

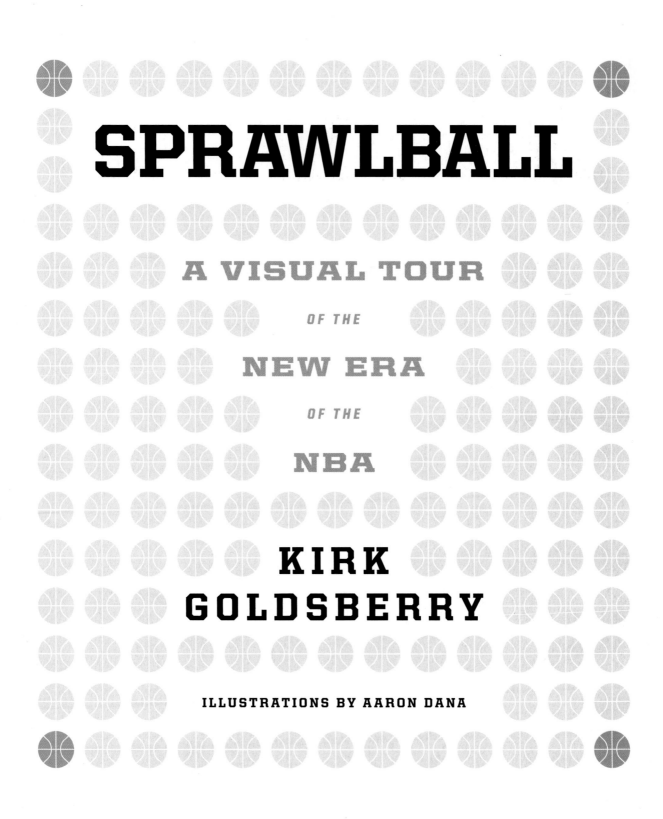

SPRAWLBALL

A VISUAL TOUR

OF THE

NEW ERA

OF THE

NBA

KIRK GOLDSBERRY

ILLUSTRATIONS BY AARON DANA

First Mariner Books edition 2020

Copyright © 2019 by Kirk Goldsberry

Illustrations copyright © 2019 by Aaron Dana

Infographics copyright © 2019 by Kirk Goldsberry

For information about permission to reproduce selections from this book, write to trade.permissions@hmhco.com or to Permissions, Houghton Mifflin Harcourt Publishing Company, 3 Park Avenue, 19th Floor, New York, New York 10016.

hmhbooks.com

Library of Congress Cataloging-in-Publication Data

Names: Goldsberry, Kirk Patrick, author.

Title: Sprawlball : a visual tour of the new era of the NBA / Kirk Goldsberry.

Description: Boston : Houghton Mifflin Harcourt, 2019. | Includes index. |

Identifiers: LCCN 2018042565 (print) | LCCN 2019004552 (ebook) |

ISBN 9781328765031 (ebook) | ISBN 9781328767516 (paper over board) |

ISBN 9780358329756 (pbk.)

Subjects: LCSH: Basketball players—United States—Statistics. |

Basketball—United States—Statistics. | Basketball—Shooting. |

Basketball—United States. | National Basketball Association.

Classification: LCC GV885.55 (ebook) | LCC GV885.55 .G65 2019 (print) |

DDC 796.323/64—dc23

LC record available at https://lccn.loc.gov/2018042565

Page composition by Kelly Dubeau Smydra

Printed in the United States of America

DOC 10 9 8 7 6 5 4 3 2 1

Illustration on p. 16 is based on an underlying work used with permission from John Costacos, Inc. Copyright © 1990 by Costacos Brothers, Inc. Photo by Bill Smith, Art Wolfe / Allstock, Greg Probst / Allstock. All rights reserved.

Excerpt on pp. 204–205 is from "Is It Time to Move the NBA 3-Point Line Back?" by Kirk Goldsberry, first published online in *Grantland,* June 23, 2014. Copyright © 2014 by ESPN. Text reprinted by permission of ESPN. All rights reserved.

*For Adrienne, Rosie, Daisy, Mom, Dad, and
the rest of my wonderful family*

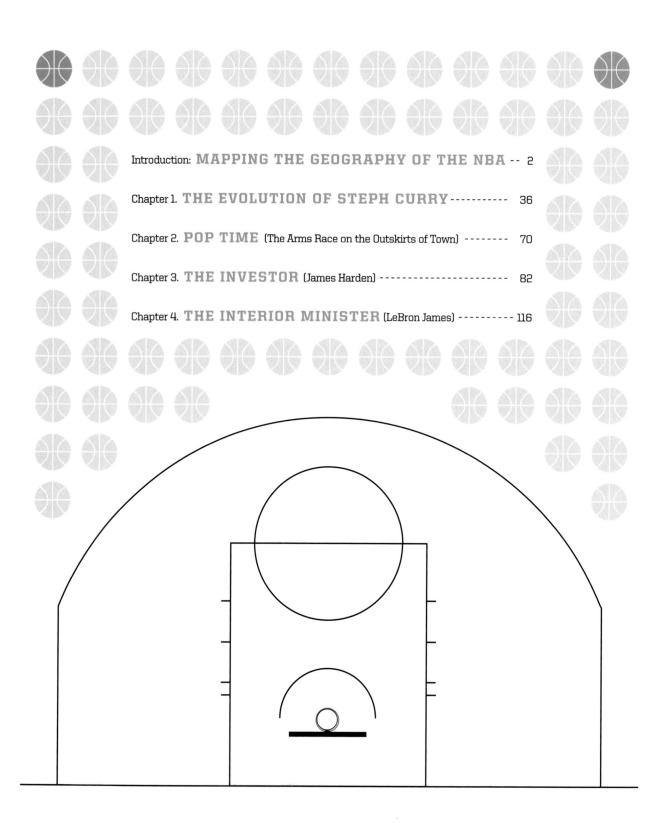

Introduction: MAPPING THE GEOGRAPHY OF THE NBA -- 2

Chapter 1. THE EVOLUTION OF STEPH CURRY ----------- 36

Chapter 2. POP TIME (The Arms Race on the Outskirts of Town) -------- 70

Chapter 3. THE INVESTOR (James Harden) ---------------------- 82

Chapter 4. THE INTERIOR MINISTER (LeBron James) ---------- 116

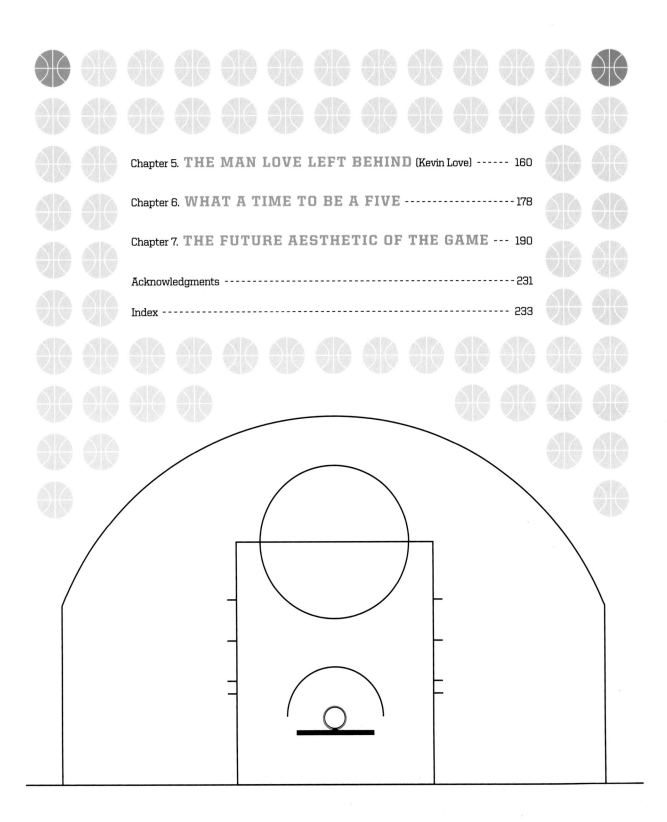

Chapter 5. THE MAN LOVE LEFT BEHIND (Kevin Love) ------ 160

Chapter 6. WHAT A TIME TO BE A FIVE -------------------- 178

Chapter 7. THE FUTURE AESTHETIC OF THE GAME --- 190

Acknowledgments -------------------------------------- 231

Index --- 233

SPRAWLBALL

MAPPING THE GEOGRAPHY OF THE NBA

GEOGRAPHY IS DESTINY. Ever since Sun Tzu talked about terrain in *The Art of War*, soldiers and generals alike have been hyper-aware of the vital interactions between spaces and strategies. The world's chess masters are not only aware of these interactions, but engineer them and relentlessly leverage them all the way to checkmate. As soon as team sports began to emerge in the late 19th century, coaches began to strategize around the playing surfaces of baseball fields, soccer pitches, and basketball courts. Vince Lombardi and John Wooden chalked out x's and o's on their chalkboards. Spatial descriptors like "power alleys," "the trenches," and "the low post" crept into the languages of these new games and eventually came to organically dominate the discourses around strategy. It took a little while, but sports observers started to understand what Sun Tzu had been saying for centuries: space matters, terrain matters.

A regulation basketball court is 94 feet long and 50 feet wide. That's 4,700 square feet, the equivalent size of a nice McMansion in Orlando. It features two goals and a bunch of painted lines and circles. The goal of the game has always been simple: put the biscuit in the basket. For a century or so, the best strategies involved big dudes getting close to the peach basket and attempting to shoot and score from as close as possible.

But only recently, with the convergence of computing, spatially referenced game data, and our culture's increasingly manic urges for quantification and efficiency, have sports truly begun to adopt analytical spatial reasoning as a strategic ally. This new ally, along with a generation of players, coaches, and executives who grew up with three-pointers and Michael Lewis books, has changed the entire aesthetic of basketball.

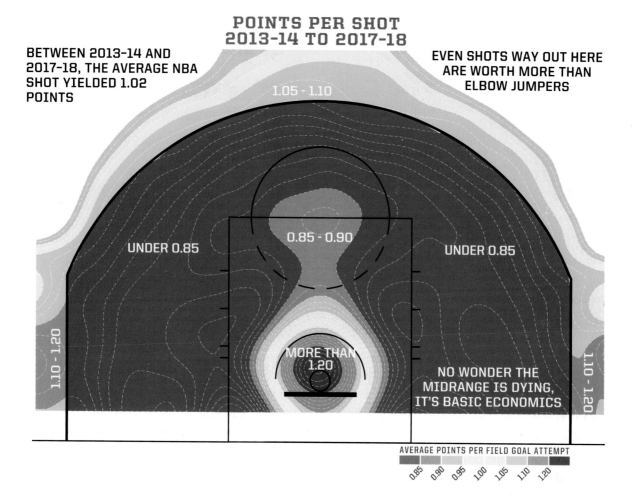

POINTS PER SHOT
2013-14 TO 2017-18

BETWEEN 2013-14 AND 2017-18, THE AVERAGE NBA SHOT YIELDED 1.02 POINTS

EVEN SHOTS WAY OUT HERE ARE WORTH MORE THAN ELBOW JUMPERS

1.05 - 1.10

0.85 - 0.90

UNDER 0.85

UNDER 0.85

1.10 - 1.20

MORE THAN 1.20

1.10 - 1.20

NO WONDER THE MIDRANGE IS DYING, IT'S BASIC ECONOMICS

AVERAGE POINTS PER FIELD GOAL ATTEMPT

0.85 0.90 0.95 1.00 1.05 1.10 1.20

This is the new efficiency landscape of the NBA.

This smoothed map visualizes the new terrain of the NBA. By running a smoothing algorithm, we can estimate the average point value for shots taken anywhere on the court. The areas in green are zones where average NBA shots yield at least 1.00 points on average. The purple areas are worth less than that. As you can see, the only green on the map is located either very close to the basket or beyond the arc. Aside from that, the color purple is everywhere.

This points-per-shot map transformed my view of the NBA. Sure, I was long aware that three-point shots were relatively good investments for players and teams, but something about seeing it laid out on this image made that point impossible to ignore. I thought about it every time I watched basketball. And I wasn't alone—a growing analytical movement in the sport was leading to an increasingly obsessive embrace of three-point shooting. The three-ball was quickly becoming associated with analytically aware basketball reasoning.

The soldiers and generals of pro basketball are charged with competing on this terrain, and the emerging aesthetic of the NBA, marked by an intensifying love affair with three-point shooting and growing distaste for midrange scoring, is simply a reflection of the topography we see in that map.

Area 31

On March 21, 2016, the San Antonio Spurs were in Charlotte taking on the Hornets. With approximately three minutes remaining in the first quarter, the Hornets had the ball and Kemba Walker dumped an entry pass down to Al Jefferson, who received the ball in his favorite spot—down near the left block. Jefferson loves the left block; he's a throwback big man in that sense. In an era when more and more bigs "stretch" the floor and shoot more and more long jumpers, he loves to post up and hates to shoot threes.

After gathering the pass, Jefferson went to work. He was closely guarded by Tim Duncan, one of the best interior defenders ever to set foot on a basketball court. After backing into Duncan, Jefferson quickly spun over his left shoulder and released a hook shot from just about eight feet away from the rim.

It was vintage NBA. This could have been Mikan versus Schayes, Russell versus Chamberlain, McHale versus Abdul-Jabbar, or Shaq versus Mutombo. We've seen this dance for generations. It is quintessential NBA basketball.

But Duncan won this battle. Jefferson missed, and LaMarcus Aldridge quickly grabbed the rebound for the Spurs.

For years, the nerdy folks familiar with the geography of an NBA basketball court claimed that the worst shot on the floor was the long two-point jump shot. This assertion was based on simple logic. After all, shooting a basketball generally becomes more difficult as distance to the hoop increases, so shooting the longest two-point shot on the floor must be the worst shot possible. High risk, low reward. If you're going to shoot that far out, you may as well shoot a three!

However, this simple line of reasoning neglects one important thing: the effect of defense. Looking at years of raw, nonsmoothed shooting data, one can discern small pockets in the two-point area that are actually more inefficient. Across the league, NBA players sink just about 38 percent of those long twos, but there is

a spot near the left block—just eight feet away from the bucket—where players make just 31 percent of their shots. Let's call this mysterious zone Area 31.

It turns out Al Jefferson loves Area 31. Between 2013–14 and 2015–16, NBA players combined to take 556 shots there, but no NBA player shot in that zone more than Big Al. As it turns out, that shot against Duncan came from there too.

The simple fact is that some of the lowest-percentage shots in the NBA happen surprisingly close to the rim. This has less to do with shooting ability and more to do with contact allowances (try manhandling a spot-up shooter the way you manhandle a post-up player) and the effects of large NBA defenders. The

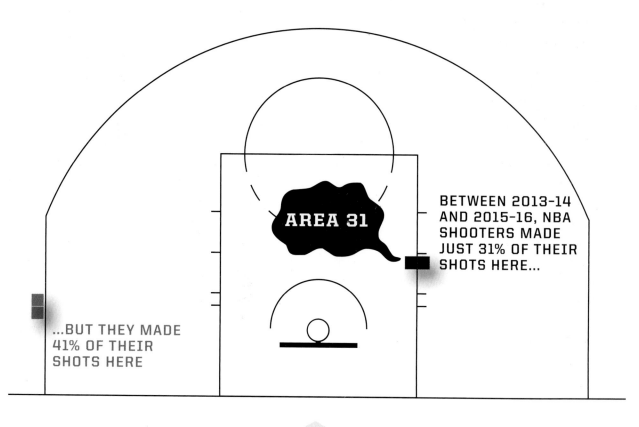

AREA 31

BETWEEN 2013-14 AND 2015-16, NBA SHOOTERS MADE JUST 31% OF THEIR SHOTS HERE...

...BUT THEY MADE 41% OF THEIR SHOTS HERE

best shot on the court is a dunk or layup; these close-range attempts almost always goes in. Not surprisingly, then, it's also among the most heavily defended shot types on the floor. Many of the core defensive principles in basketball are specifically designed to prevent offenses from getting good looks near the rim. Duh.

Still, there's something more interesting here. Given the choice, players like Big Al would dunk the ball every trip down the floor. But players like Duncan are there to take away that choice. And the only time NBA players ever even shoot four feet from the basket is when an interior defender like Duncan successfully prevents them from shooting one, two, or three feet from the basket. Any four-foot field goal attempt necessarily happens because a big fella won't let you shoot a one-footer. And chances are that big fella ain't too keen on your four-footer being very easy. Lastly, the big fella in question is allowed to be pretty physical with you as you try to shoot that four-footer—he can be handsy, he can use an arm bar, he can body you up, and, of course, he can stretch out his giant arms.

In your backyard, the relationship between shot distance and field goal percentage is very straightforward, but in the NBA it is not. Forget the fact that threes are worth more than twos: NBA players hit corner threes at higher rates than they hit shots in a lot of two-point areas!

Why is this the case? Consider that interior defenders like Duncan can be physical with close-range offensive players like Jefferson, while perimeter defenders get whistled for just looking at a spot-up shooter the wrong way, and the numbers begin to make sense.

But here's the thing: the very idea of the NBA three-point line is built in part on the foundational premise that shots from farther away are harder than closer shots. The idea is that a 24-foot shot is so difficult that it should be worth 50 percent more points than a 20-foot shot, a 15-foot shot, a 10-foot shot, or a five-foot shot. But, friends, that premise is simply hogwash—and we have the data to prove it.

I'm here to tell you that the entire basis for the three-point line is now a farce. And once you understand the nature of this farce, you'll understand why the NBA is rapidly becoming more and more obsessed with 24-foot jump shots. Meanwhile, it is becoming less and less smitten with any jumpers inside the magical arc, especially the ones that post players like Big Al Jefferson throw up from Area 31.

Between the 2013–14 and 2015–16 seasons, NBA players took over 600,000 shots from the field. The graphic on the facing page shows you how field goal percentages varied in that time span according to shot distance.

As you can see, while it's fair to say that field goal percentages decrease with shot distance, it's also fair to say that this effect is relatively slight, especially outside of the paint. During the 2017–18 season, eight-foot shots went in 39.6 percent of the time, while threes went in almost 36 percent of the time. No wonder the midrange shot is dead and it took the post game with it. It's basic economic geography.

On average, NBA jump shots are somewhere between a 35 and 45 percent proposition; however, there is a line on the court that makes some of those jump shots worth three points and others just two. And the rising

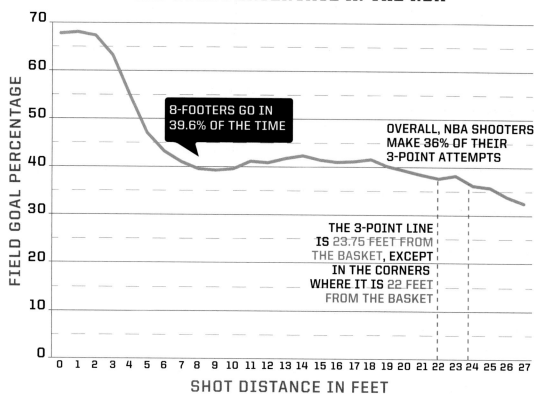

SHOT DISTANCE AND FIELD GOAL PERCENTAGE IN THE NBA

8-FOOTERS GO IN 39.6% OF THE TIME

OVERALL, NBA SHOOTERS MAKE 36% OF THEIR 3-POINT ATTEMPTS

THE 3-POINT LINE IS 23.75 FEET FROM THE BASKET, EXCEPT IN THE CORNERS WHERE IT IS 22 FEET FROM THE BASKET

FIELD GOAL PERCENTAGE

SHOT DISTANCE IN FEET

---

awareness of these basic facts is driving the biggest strategic shifts that the NBA has ever seen.

Recall that the average NBA field goal attempt (FGA)* is worth exactly 1.02 points. Shots from Area 31 are

worth just 0.62 points. In 2017–18, even an *average* NBA three-pointer was worth 1.09 points.

Through one lens, the relationship between shot distance and field goal percentage makes a lot of sense. There is a predictable decrease in the probability of a shot finding the bottom of the net as distance increases.

---

* NBA shooters combined to make over 1 million FGAs between 2013–14 and 2017–18. On average, these attempts yielded 1.02 points.

But through another lens the relationship between shot distance and points per shot is really weird. And this weirdness largely stems from one major regulatory decision in 1979, when the league painted a stripe through the jump shooting zone and declared that shots north of this dividing line were 50 percent more valuable than those south of it.

To anyone looking at the following graphic, it's very obvious why teams and players are taking more and more of their field goal attempts from beyond the arc and fewer and fewer of them in the two-point area. Points remain the ultimate currency in basketball, and teams that invest a lot in two-point jumpers do not enjoy a good return on that investment. You're much better off investing in 24-footers than in nine-footers.

In the three-season span between 2013–14 and 2015–16, the average NBA three-pointer yielded 1.07 points. The average five-foot shot yielded 0.94 points. The average six-footer yielded 0.87. The average seven-footer yielded 0.82. You get the idea; the margins are not small. With the exception of layups and dunks, two-point shots are simply dumb choices.

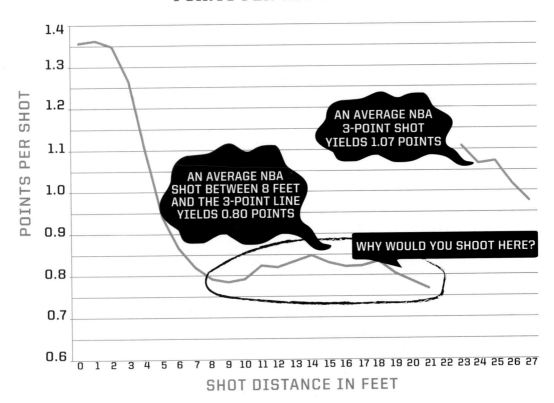

The implementation of the arc not only introduced a massive efficiency gap that cuts right through the jump shooting zone, but also inspired a generation of hoopers to practice and learn to shoot from distances that would have been considered stupid in the pre-three-point-line era. And it also made players like Al Jefferson endangered species.

Despite the fact that the shot Al took and missed that night in Charlotte requires an impressive blend of size, strength, speed, and finesse to even try, the reality of the current economics of the playing surface dictates that this shot is one of the least efficient shots in the contemporary NBA. We have legislated a version of the game that deems that shot foolish. Moreover, players who spent their entire youth becoming among the best in the world at this tried-and-true form of

hoops are having a difficult time finding jobs. Guys like Al Jefferson, who were once among the bright young prospects at their position, now bounce from team to team, with their post-up moves in their suitcase, scrounging the few minutes of playing time they can still get in a league that just wishes they could "space the floor" and let the guards and wings do their thing.

When the league added the three-pointer, it did not just massively inflate the value of the 24-footer and the sniper who can drain it, nor did it just massively deflate the value of five-footers, 10-footers, 15-footers, and 20-footers. It also rearranged the value of skill sets and the value of player types. The value of the catch-and-shoot specialist has exploded, while the value of the post player has collapsed.

Furthermore, when the NBA decided to massively subsidize those long-rangers, it also inspired its teams to invent all kinds of new tactics to create opportunities for catch-and-shoot guys beyond the arc, while also discouraging post-up actions. Coaches used to design creative ways to enter the ball down to the bigs on the block. Now they design creative ways to kick it out to catch-and-shoot guys in the sprawling suburbs. Welcome to sprawlball.

It turns out that the timeless Russell-Chamberlain waltz ain't so timeless after all. And many bigs who came of age in the NBA in the last two decades have gradually morphed from post-up guys to spot-up guys. If Chamberlain were playing today, he'd be shooting threes like Joel Embiid, DeMarcus Cousins, and the rest of the best bigs still clinging to their precious minutes in the league today.

The Ryan Anderson Contract

On November 9, 2016, the new-look Houston Rockets were in San Antonio taking on the Spurs. Earlier in the summer, the Rockets had added a slew of new faces, including head coach Mike D'Antoni and free agents Eric Gordon and Ryan Anderson. The new group had showed encouraging signs, but the game in San Antonio would provide the first real barometer of the season: would these new-look Rockets be any good?

With 8:35 remaining in the game, Houston trailed by one but had the ball. James Harden was getting the team into their offense. He used a Clint Capela screen at the top of the arc to attack the right side of the floor.

As Harden dribbled toward the right wing, the entire shape of the Spurs defense morphed accordingly; weak-side players sagged away from their men in case they needed to help their teammates protect against a Harden rim attack. But they sagged too far, and as soon as Harden noticed that, he flung the ball across the court to his new teammate, Ryan Anderson, who was standing a full yard beyond the three-point arc, deep along the left wing.

Anderson gathered the pass while his defender, the two-time Defensive Player of the Year Kawhi Leonard, raced back to try to contest Anderson's shot. But Leonard's defense was too little too late. The best defender on the planet couldn't get his hands up fast enough to prevent Anderson's three-point launch, and as Anderson's arcing shot found the net, the Rockets took a two-point lead. They would never trail again.

One reason Leonard failed to contest the shot was that Anderson was spotted up three feet beyond the arc, a few feet farther back than a normal spot-up shooter. And in a "game of inches," this slight difference made all the difference in the world. Leonard is nothing if not a finely calibrated wing defender, and Anderson's deeper-than-normal spot-up location screwed with Leonard's defensive spacing just enough to make the difference.

This play was no anomaly. Anderson and the 2016–17 Rockets were routinely spotting up farther behind the arc than any team in league history. They were placing deep-space rocket launchers like Eric Gordon and Anderson 27 or 28 feet from the rim, happy to trade the loss of a percentage point or two in shooting efficiency associated with slightly longer threes for upticks in three-point chances, wider pick-and-roll corridors for Harden, and fewer closeouts by defenders. They weren't just expanding the scoring area their opponents would have to defend, but also exacerbating the already dangerous pick-your-poison dilemma for their defenders: either stick close to the perimeter shooters and let Harden attack the paint without help, or help on Harden and allow open threes all night.

The 27-footer Anderson hit in San Antonio—and many more like it—propelled Houston past the Spurs that night; Anderson ended the game with 20 points, including 12 made on threes, and was instrumental in handing San Antonio a very rare home defeat. For Houston, the win was doubly sweet. Not only had they bested their in-state rival on the road, but the win also showed that their new players and their new deep-space shooting were quickly coalescing into one of the most efficient offenses in the league.

The Impact of the Line

The three-point line is the most influential gerrymander in sports history. Its introduction deformed the basic economics of an entire sport. But the line didn't just redistrict the playing surface: it also empowered the party of jump shooters to slowly take over the most prestigious basketball congress in the world. With the exception of the forward pass in football, no rule change in American sports history has reshaped the aesthetic of its sport more than the three-point line has deformed the NBA.

For the last few decades, the three-point line has made long-range specialists like Dennis Scott, Steve Kerr, and Anthony Morrow millionaires. And with each passing free agency season, we're learning that this particular skill set continues to steadily increase in value. In the summer of 2016, Daryl Morey and the Rockets demonstrated this idea when they gave Anderson a massive four-year, $80 million contract.

In what world is Ryan Anderson's basketball skill worth $80 million? It's a fair question on many levels. One answer involves a simple fact that lies at the heart of this book: the three-point shot has changed basketball forever. It's changed everything about basketball. And as the three-point shot has become increasingly central to NBA offenses, players like Anderson have become increasingly valuable.

It's hard to overstate how much the game has changed in the first two decades of this century. Perhaps words aren't the best approach. Instead, consider the following graphics. The first shows the league's most common shot locations during the 2001–02 NBA season.

The second shows the most common shot locations 15 years later during the 2016–17 season.

The contrast is striking, for a few reasons. First, it's remarkable just how different these two graphics are. They reveal the drastic changes in NBA scoring strategies in just a 15-year period. Second, the difference between them shows the proliferation of three-point shooting. Whereas the 2001–02 graphic includes a few patchy clusters of three-point activity, a chain of connected hexagons decorate the edge of the three-point zone in the 2016–17 graphic. Finally, the graphics expose the NBA's exodus from the midrange areas between the paint and the three-point line. Back in the

MOST COMMON
SHOT LOCATIONS
IN THE NBA 2001-02

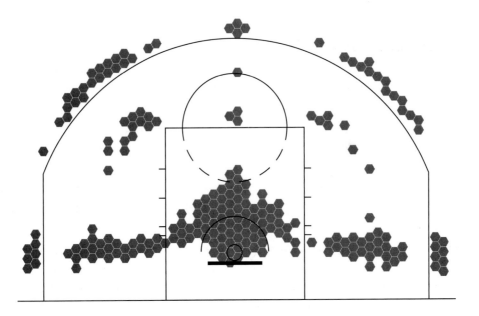

MOST COMMON
SHOT LOCATIONS
IN THE NBA 2016-17

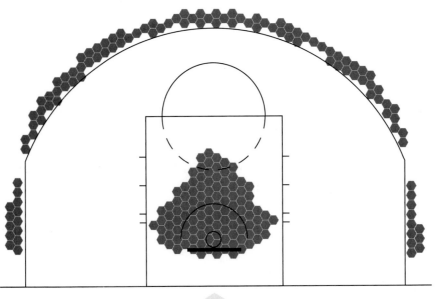

olden days of Shaquille O'Neal and Allen Iverson, two-point jump shots were a very popular way to score in the NBA. In the time of Stephen Curry, James Harden, and Ryan Anderson, that's no longer the case.

Ryan Anderson Contract Specs

Inside a July 3, 2016, *ESPN.com* article summarizing Anderson's new deal, a photo of Anderson appears with the caption, "Three-point specialist Ryan Anderson is headed to Houston after agreeing to a four-year deal worth $80 million." That's a bigger check—for a "specialist"—than Team USA's Paul George was earning.

Ten years earlier, nobody in America would have dreamed that the kid from Sacramento would turn into an $80 million NBA star. Coming out of Oak Ridge High School in 2006, Anderson was relatively unheralded for any eventual pro player, let alone one worthy of a giant contract. Back then, the recruiting mavens over at *Scout.com* had Anderson slated as only the 23rd-best power forward in his high school class.

Scouts weren't predicting this kid was the future $80 million cornerstone of an NBA roster.

But when Anderson landed at Cal, it didn't take him long to quickly establish himself as one of the most versatile and potent big men in the entire country.

Just five games into his freshman year, Anderson started turning heads. The NBA draft heads at Draft-Express lavished the freshman's game with some big early-season praise:

Equally as effective with his back to the basket as he is facing the hoop, Anderson scored at will from all over the court in the Alaska Shootout. He's incredibly precocious for a player his age, showing an incredible knack for finding the hoop and fitting into an offense that just cannot be taught. Based off what we saw here, he's certainly of the best freshman big men in the country early on at least and will probably go head to head with Chase Budinger at Arizona for Freshman of the year honors in the Pac-10.

Less than two weeks into his freshman season, the kid's reputation had transformed from 23rd-best power forward in his high school class into one of the top young bigs to watch in all of college hoops. He could do a little of everything, but by his sophomore year the Draft-Express guys were honing in on what was bound to become Anderson's signature NBA skill:

His perimeter game is a very important part of his game, as he has become an even more prolific three-point shooter, at an even better percentage, this season. His release looks excellent, with a high release point and quick release, and his range extends all the way to the NBA three-point line. However, he seems to have fallen in love with his perimeter shot to a certain extent, at nearly 4.8 attempts per game.

Anderson wasn't the only one falling in love with perimeter shooting; so was the entire National Basketball Association. Still, while those DraftExpress guys deserve credit for being so high on Anderson in college,

INTRODUCTION

with the benefit of hindsight, it's apparent that they weren't nearly high enough on him.

As he approached the 2008 NBA draft, Anderson's best-case NBA comp was thought to be Troy Murphy, a middling NBA journeyman who shuffled between six franchises during an up-and-down 12-year career. It's not that Murphy didn't have a nice career—he certainly did—it's that Anderson landed an 80-freak-ing-million-dollar deal. Nobody gave Troy Murphy one of those. One thing the DraftExpress fellas failed to account for back in 2008 was that Anderson was entering a league rapidly falling head over heels in love with bigs who could shoot threes.

Murphy was born too early; Anderson was born right on time.

The Rockets knew exactly what they were getting in Anderson, a 6'10" forward who could sink threes on offense and play adequate enough defense on the other end. That's the funny thing about a league where threes become much more important: interior defense becomes much less important. But make no mistake, it was Anderson's ability to catch and shoot basketballs through metal rings from 24+ feet that made him worth $80 million. On *ESPN.com*, Anderson is always listed as a "power forward," but in reality there's no "power" in his portfolio: Anderson will be remembered as one of the defining "stretch fours"* of his generation. And even though the programs you buy at NBA arenas still list players like Anderson as power forwards, by the middle of this decade the stretch four was overtaking

the power forward across the league. If you're looking for a reason why this happened, look 23.75 feet from the basketball hoop and you'll see a two-inch stripe where the real power in contemporary basketball rests.

The slow metamorphosis of the power forward into the stretch four could have never happened without the three-point stripe. For dudes like Anderson, the arc is the real MVP (Most Valuable Partition) in their lives. In a world without the stripe, competent interior players like Al Jefferson would be a lot more valuable than stretchy dudes like Anderson, but unfortunately for Al, that's not the world we live in.

From an economic point of view, the Anderson contract represents an interesting precedent. On the list of NBA players who made more money than Anderson in the 2016 season, you can find future Hall of Famers, some MVPs, NBA champions, Olympic gold medal winners, and a whole mess of All-Stars, but there are no other "specialists." Almost all of the other fellas in that tax bracket possess multiple elite skills: they can handle the ball, create shots for teammates, play great defense, fly through the air and land on *SportsCenter*. And of course, the most important thing of all—they can sell tickets, sneakers, and beer ads. They aren't specialists, they're superstars. They're the illuminati of the NBA.

Meanwhile the rank and file of the NBA is chock-full of roster players who specialize in things like rebounding, rim protection, or defense, but none of those fellas make more money than Ryan Anderson, who just happens to specialize in the exact right thing at the exact right time.

Daryl Morey and Houston paid Anderson $80 million

---

* "Stretch fours" are power forwards who can shoot from long range and enable their team to "stretch" the floor, keeping opposing big men far away from the basket.

to help them "space the floor" and realize their MIT Sloan Sports Analytics Conference fever dream of making three-pointers the centerpiece of their entire game plan. Less than two months into Anderson's first season in Houston, it was working. The Rockets began December 2016 by beating Golden State in a double-OT thriller, then embarking on an impressive 10-game winning streak; they had one of the most efficient offenses in the league, and Anderson was among the biggest reasons why. He was making 40 percent of his triples and spacing the floor better than any other big in the league, sucking his defenders out of their comfort zones into deep space, and widening driving lanes for James Harden, the team's superstar catalyst.

Anderson was his team's fourth-leading scorer, but that's not the point. His biggest contribution to his new team could not fit neatly into some cell on some spreadsheet. There's no "spacing" column on NBA box scores. Sure, some possessions included him setting a screen or shooting a catch-and-shoot three, but in countless more he stood around waiting, "keeping the defense honest," "spacing the floor," and keeping his pesky defender far away from Harden, one of the most valuable attack guards in the NBA.

The Rockets were paying Anderson $20 million a year to loiter. That's a lot more than John Paxson, Kerr, or Scott ever got. And nobody on the Rockets' message boards was really complaining. A great complement for Harden's ball-dominant, isolation-happy brand of offense, Anderson was a new kind of $80 million man.

Anderson is an interesting precedent, because of what he contributes not only directly but indirectly. Just as that key triple in San Antonio demonstrated, Anderson's deep-space shooting skills keep defenders hon-

est. So by simply being a spot-up threat 27 feet away from the rim, Anderson forces his defenders—players like Kawhi Leonard—to also loiter far away from the rim, eliminating their ability to help on defense or grab rebounds and thus becoming less and less valuable as players.

To fully assess Anderson's value, you have to look far beyond his box score numbers. His total contribution is just as much about making his rim-attacking teammates more dangerous as it is about weakening the opponent's defensive form. It turns out that removing Kawhi Leonard from a defensive possession can be just as valuable as inserting James Harden into an offensive one. And when you take Leonard out of defensive plays, you greatly elevate your team's chances of scoring against his team.

It's that ripple effect—how a deep-space spot-up threat like Anderson changes the entire 10-man ecology of the game—that is changing the aesthetics, the tactics, and the values of both offense and defense in the contemporary NBA. It's playing out at the possession level, at the game level, at the season level, and, as Anderson showed us in 2016, at the summertime negotiating table level.

By heightening the value of spot-up shooting, players like Anderson are simultaneously devaluing the defensive skills of all the defenders whose impacts they negate on a nightly basis. As more and more teams play like Houston does—and they will—more and more Andersons will station themselves way out in the deep-space outposts at the edges of the scoring area, dragging more and more defenders like Leonard out there with them. When that happens, an entire population of NBA defenders will be less able to demonstrate their defensive wares on a regular basis, and consequently those wares will become less valuable.

Is this good? Well, if you're 6'10" and can shoot basketballs from 27 feet, this is absolutely terrific! And if you like to watch James Harden run isolation sets over and over again, it's great. Regardless of your preference, this movement is happening. Just like the saying about how the butterfly flapping its wings in Brazil affects the price of rice in China, the league's rising infatuation with deep-space shooters will affect far more than just individual box score numbers or the number of triples we see per game.

For those of us who go to the arena in part to see great athletes like Kawhi Leonard play all-world defense, the rise of the floor-spacing spot-up shooter should give us pause. The more we see "five-out" offenses featuring every offensive player hanging out beyond the three-point line and more spacing specialists stagnantly stationed farther and farther from the basket, the less we will see the defensive prowess of elite defenders like Leonard. As players like Leonard see fewer and fewer chances to flex their defensive muscles, they will see their defensive value drop in roughly direct proportion to the explosion in offensive value of players like Anderson.

Player valuation within the cap-driven NBA marketplace is a zero-sum game: as players like Anderson get bigger and bigger deals, other kinds of players—players like Al Jefferson—will experience the opposite.

Since the quest for efficiency in post-moneyball basketball has driven the NBA's rapidly growing obsessions with spot-up shooting, floor spacing, defensive switching, and isolations sets, it's worth asking how these ob-

sessions are changing not only the product we see on the court but also the numbers thrown around on contracts and offer sheets in the free agency period.

Do we, the NBA fans, really prefer watching all of these catch-and-shoot threes and the players who take them more than the kinds of plays they are replacing? Is the spectacle of NBA basketball slowly getting better or worse?

Anderson was the Rodman or Pippen to Harden's Jordan. When I was a kid, all of my friends had posters of those Bulls stars on their walls, and some of those posters were iconic. Who can forget that poster called

"Space" that included Jordan dunking the freaking moon!

Well, today's NBA has different kinds of spacemen, and they ain't dunking the moon. They're standing around idly, waiting for a chance to shoot the moon. Do the kids watching these days want a Ryan Anderson space poster on their wall?

When Michael Lewis wrote *Moneyball*, he woke up the sports world. He used the ballad of Billy Beane to signal that the financial world's mania for quantification and efficiency could transform the reasoning processes surrounding pro sports. He forced us to rethink the core strategies and value systems at the heart of front offices. It's no coincidence that a decade after *Moneyball* came out, Lewis devoted a glowing chapter of his 2016 book *The Undoing Project* to the Billy Beane of basketball—

Houston's visionary GM, Daryl Morey, the man who gave Ryan Anderson $80 million.

More than any other figure in pro basketball history, Morey has heeded *Moneyball*'s call to arms and built an entire basketball strategy around analytical reasoning. Anyone curious to see what a fully realized data-driven basketball project looks like should look no further than Houston, Texas, where the Rockets, led by their record-breaking three-happy offense, are emerging as a new kind of NBA powerhouse. By the 2017–18 season, Houston had the most efficient offense in the NBA and, not coincidentally, won the most regular-season games that year.

Morey built his monster around three-point shooting and isolation plays for Harden. For many of us, Harden and the Rockets were a revelation: a new kind of team

playing the game in a new way, the Rockets dominated the NBA in ways we'd never seen. But for others, Houston played ugly, monocultural basketball featuring repetitive and boring games marked by endless isolation plays, too many catch-and-shoot tries, too many free throws, and not enough aesthetic diversity.

With that in mind, it's worth asking: do we really want the three-point line to be the most important feature at every NBA arena? I don't know the answer, but I can tell you this: Ryan Anderson doesn't seem to mind. Al Jefferson does. By July 2018, Jefferson couldn't even get a good job in the NBA. The Indiana Pacers let him go, and no other teams wanted him. A news release briefly summarized his next move: with his NBA career cut short, Jefferson was taking his low-post game to China:

> Jefferson is expected to sign with the Xinjiang Flying Tigers of the Chinese Basketball Association, Jordan Guskey of the Indianapolis Star reports.

> Jefferson was recently let go by the Pacers after playing just 36 games in his 14th NBA season. After failing to drum up much interest as a free agent, Jefferson has opted to head overseas where he may have received a more lucrative contract.

Al Jefferson was once a big-time player. But in the sprawlball era, he is the wrong kind of player. Just a few years before he moved to China, in 2014, he made the all-NBA third team, but by 2018 he couldn't even get a job in the NBA.

When the league added the three-point line, they obviously added a new category of field goal 50 percent more valuable than every other shot on the floor. Back in 1979, very few players could even make that shot in a game setting; it was a gimmick. But by adding the three-point line, they unknowingly set the stage for a new category of basketball player more valuable than every other. You don't need to be Michael Lewis or Billy Beane to realize that dudes who can make three-pointers on a regular basis are more valuable than those who can make two-pointers.

The 2017–18 Rockets became the first team in history to attempt more than half of their shots from beyond the arc. Think about that: over the course of an entire season, the team was more likely to shoot a three than a two. Pretty soon it'll make more sense to call it the two-point line. Why not? Of the 84.2 shots the Rockets took per game, 42.3 of them came from beyond the arc.

We can think of the three-point line in several ways. Before the 2017–18 Houston Rockets came along, we generally regarded it as a mechanism that increased the value of long-range shooting. However, as we enter a world where teams are shooting more shots beyond the arc than inside it, maybe it's time to conceive of the three-point line as a way to deflate the value of two-point scoring, or the line that helped kill Al Jefferson's career. Forty years into the three-point era, it's clear that the truth is found in both conceptions: the line has done just as much to heighten the value of perimeter scoring as it has done to reduce the value of interior play.

In this sense, three-point shooting defines the game today in the same way post play defined it in the last century.

For those of us who grew up watching the Olajuwon, Ewing, and Malone teams thrive in the 1990s NBA, it's a bit jarring to see players like Anderson becoming the most highly paid bigs in the NBA, while more traditional big players like Jefferson are left to play in China. Even though Morey and the Rockets ended up trading Anderson and his massive contract to the Phoenix Suns in the summer of 2018, the deal they signed in 2016 still represents a turning point in the valuation of big men in the NBA. Twenty-five years ago, bigs could still get paid if they couldn't shoot, but those days are fading fast. Morey was one of the first to see it: spotting up is more valuable than posting up.

The guys who played the power forward spot alongside Jordan were players like Horace Grant and Dennis Rodman, physically frenetic competitors who elbowed and leaped their way to their money. They didn't loiter. They didn't space. They made hay in the paint and on the glass. They couldn't shoot threes. Hell, Rodman couldn't shoot twos or even ones for that matter. But in the same way that Anderson was born right on time to take advantage of the current era, so was Rodman.

If Rodman or Grant were in their prime right now, they wouldn't be worth as much as Anderson. Nowadays it's more important for our fours to shoot like Kerr than it is for them to rebound like Rodman. Morey would have much less interest in those dudes. Maybe they could play in China or even North Korea. They wouldn't be nearly as good at standing around 27 feet from the basket as Anderson is. Space matters.

NBA Geography

The NBA began tracking the spatial location of every shot taken in 1996–97, but it didn't become reliable until 2001. Every time Tim Duncan or Kobe Bryant re-

leased a field goal attempt, one of the official scorers over at the scorer's table would record where on the court the shot occurred and whether it went in or not. For decades we obsessed over the "did it go in" part, and stats like field goal percentage and three-point percentage became standard fodder for even the most basic basketball conversations. But while the shot location stuff had a chance to make us smarter, it didn't neatly fit into the established set of spreadsheet formulas we'd built to evaluate NBA players and teams.

Aside from crude considerations like the shooter's location (Was he beyond or in front of the three-point line? Was he in the paint?), the spatial components of scoring in the NBA were generally ignored. The daily newspapers would plot league leaders in primitive metrics like field goal percentage, and inevitably these leaders would be big players like Shaq or DeAndre Jordan. While it's true that these guys were very likely to make field goal attempts, it's also true that this was the case because they were also unlikely to ever shoot more than a few feet from the basket. And their status at the top of the FG percentage leaderboard had just as much to do with their interior prowess as it did with their utter impotence away from the rim.

Basketball is a spatial sport. The structure and dynamics of court space influence every second of every game ever played, and any analytical framework that glosses over this fact is not very good. For years, analysts didn't have a choice—the only stats collected by the league were nonspatial tallies of the most basic events that fed the daily box scores. By the early 21st century, however, basketball discourse had established its analytical branch. And like baseball analysts, we pored over all the stats we had, looking for clever ways to calculate new metrics. In the early part of this century, pioneer-

O'NEAL, SHAQUILLE – $X=250, Y=0$
FIELD GOAL MADE

ing analysts like Dean Oliver, Ken Pomeroy, and John Hollinger came up with great new ways to characterize performance. They gave us things like points per possession, true shooting percentage, and, of course, player efficiency rating. In doing so, they elevated the discussion around the sport and made everyone around the NBA a bit smarter.

Well, not everyone . . .

Basketball analytics still has its skeptics. While it's true that many of the most important elements of basketball performance remain hard to measure, thanks to the hard work of many analysts earlier in this century, our ability to quantitatively separate the great from the good in the NBA is undeniably stronger now than it was two decades ago. Still, this progress is largely ignored by many top coaches, media personalities, and fans. Some skeptics, including the great Charles Bar-

I've always believed that analytics was *CRAP!*

kley, seem to harbor personal animosity toward those achieving 21st-century NBA success via analytical approaches.

Back in February 2015, Barkley used his bully pulpit on TNT's *Inside the NBA* to let the world know analytics are stupid:

"I've always believed that analytics was crap . . . I never mention the Rockets as a legitimate contender 'cause they're not. And, listen, I wouldn't know Daryl Morey if he walked into this room right now."

"The NBA is about talent," Barkley added. "All these guys who run these organizations who talk about analytics, they have one thing in common—they're a bunch of guys who ain't never played the game, and they never got the girls in high school, and they just want to get in the game."

Barkley is not alone. Even the world's most prominent NBA media analysts of the early 21st century turned a blind eye to the massive new opportunities in NBA analyses. They treated these opportunities to study and learn about the game in exciting new ways the same way girls treated me in high school.

Even as a teenager with a crooked jumper, I was always hyper-aware that the accuracy of my shot depended on where I was on the court. Like a shitty version of La-Marcus Aldridge, I preferred the left side of the court so I could threaten the center of the court by driving with my dominant dribbling hand. As a relatively tall kid, I experimented with the post. Back in the 1990s when I was a teenager, post moves were a prerequisite for winning the NBA MVP Award.

All the MVPs of the 1990s had their own signature post-up moves. Hakeem had the Dream Shake. Karl Malone had his unstoppable half-hook. David Robinson was so strong and fast that, when he didn't just dunk on you, he rose up for an easy uncontested short hook. Even Michael Jordan, the best shooting guard God ever made, had an infinite repertoire on the block. To watch the NBA in the 1990s was to watch superstars outwit, outmuscle, or outjump basic bros in the post. Simply put, post play was the dominant tactic of the most dominant players in the league.

Those guys were the masters, and millions of kids like me were taking notes when they taught master classes on national TV, or when they played the Hawks on TBS, or when their highlights showed up on *SportsCenter*.

I fell in love with the left block. I developed my favorite move at my favorite park when I was about 14. With my posterior backing against my defender, I would fake a spin move toward the center of the paint, before quickly spinning back over my right shoulder, rising, and attempting a fadeaway shot off the backboard. If I timed it just right, I knew I could get this shot almost anytime I wanted; only really smart, really fast defenders could stop me from getting this shot off, so if I could just learn to knock it down reliably, I could become a more dangerous scoring threat. I practiced and practiced it. I got really good at faking the spin and reversing my shoulders. I got comfortable with elevating a little bit away from the basket to provide myself with a little more space for shooting. And I started to be

able to hit the eight-foot bank shot almost every time I practiced it. I pinpointed the exact spot on the backboard where I knew the shot could kiss so it would then fall right through the net. In my head I was like Mike; in reality, I was just another teenage hack with big dreams. And girls definitely didn't talk to me.

Regardless, I started to get the shot to translate to game environments, and on good days my teammates would encourage me to post up on that sweet left block and go to work.

As I aged into my teens I wanted to expand my game. I practiced longer and longer shots, and as I grew stronger I was pleased that I could shoot from farther and farther away. At that time the three-point line was painted on most playgrounds, but not all of them. I strengthened my left-handed dribble and started to get more comfortable on the right block. But a funny thing happened when I tried to develop a mirror-image of my left block move over on the right block: I got the footwork down, I got the spin fake down, but I could never make the shot. I would make nine of 10 from the left side, but could only ever make five or six of 10 from the right side.

I practiced and practiced, but it just didn't come naturally. The shot just wouldn't fall. Even undefended, I couldn't hit the right spot on the backboard on a regular basis. I was so confused. I would go back to the left block and hit nine of 10. Then go to the right block and miss three or four straight. The same exact shot from the same exact spot on the other side of the court was yielding completely different results.

So I went back to the masters. I started watching their post-ups more closely than I'd done before. And even though they made it all look so easy, I noticed something weird. I noticed that even these guys all loved to post up on one side more than the other. Many of them set up camp on the left block. It's not that they only shot from the left side, but most of them would post up on the left a lot more than the right. Location, location, location.

This realization stuck with me for years. I embraced the asymmetry at the heart of my own shitty post game. I made peace with the fact that I was better from one side than the other. Like LaMarcus Aldridge, I would almost exclusively post up on the left block. Forget the right one—if you need me, you can find me camped out down on the left block.

One of the greatest things about basketball is that different players have different strengths and weaknesses. It's an effect that rings true and affects all games at all levels of play. We all have our own basketball DNA. From my pickup games in central Pennsylvania to the Olympic gold medal game in Barcelona, every team on the planet consists of players with unique skill sets. Basketball players are snowflakes: each one is different in his or her own special way. And one main point of analyzing basketball statistics is to help us identify and sort out these differences.

Even after the remarkable analytical contributions of folks like Hollinger, Oliver, and Pomeroy, however, our ability to really understand some of the biggest differences that separate the best players on the planet remained fairly primitive early in this century, especially when it came to shooting, the most important skill in the sport right now.

For years official scorers were logging stats like points, rebounds, assists, blocks, and steals, but at the outset of a new technological century, the league added *x,y*

coordinates to the mix. Every time Ray Allen rose up and fired off a three-point shot, not only would scorekeepers log the event as a field goal attempt and note whether it turned into a make or a miss, but they would also record the specific place on the court from which Allen released the shot.

Chances are, the league did not know it was about to change basketball analytics forever. In fact, even though by the early 2000s the league was doing a good job of logging and cataloging the precise location of every NBA shot by every NBA player, it would be years before these data sets revealed their true power: helping us map the NBA shooting genome.

Mapping the NBA Genome

Every year NBA players take about 200,000 shots. Each season 30 teams combine to play 1,230 games, and at the end of the regular season you can bet the sum total of shots taken will be very close to 200,000. In the hands of a cartographer, a season's worth of this shooting data is a veritable treasure trove of information. But here's the thing: in the first decade of this century, there weren't many cartographers working in the NBA league office or for analytics departments in any of the team front offices.

Back then, basketball analytics was still in its infancy; it was all about spreadsheets and linear regression, not spatial and visual reasoning. Still, whether the league knew it or not, by adding these little spatial references to their game data, basketball analytics was about to become a lot more than spreadsheets. Things like data visualization and spatial analyses were going to be very important.

Unfortunately, there weren't many folks with those skills working in pro basketball, and even though countless analysts had access to all the data the league was collecting—including all of the shot data—nobody was applying a spatial treatment. Nobody was mapping the NBA.

When I first got my hands on these massive haystacks of shooting data, I was teaching cartography at Harvard. I'd found a way to retrieve five seasons' worth of shooting data from the web, and I built a database that included over 1 million NBA field goal attempts, who shot them, and where they shot them from. As an analyst, I knew there was amazing intelligence waiting to be revealed within the database. As a mapmaker, I was confident I could visualize some of it in cool new ways. And as a huge NBA fan, I couldn't wait to see the results.

Although I was desperate to chart out the shooting abilities of players like Kobe Bryant and Dirk Nowitzki, the first thing I wanted to see was the basic shooting patterns of the entire league. When you plot an entire season's worth of shot data, some interesting patterns quickly emerge:

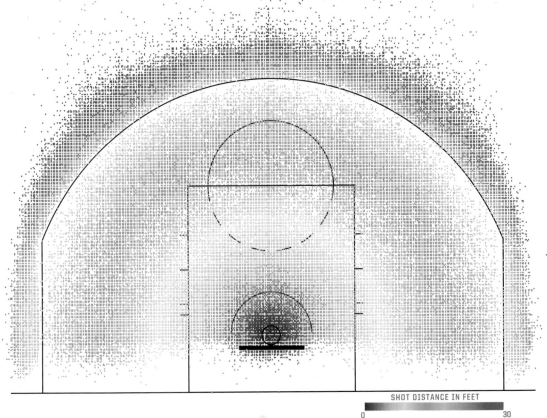

NBA SHOT LOCATIONS
2014-15

SHOT DISTANCE IN FEET

0   30

The graphic is more than just a shitload of dots. This basic plot shows us where on the floor the most important concentrations of field goal attempts occurred in 2014–15. We can see that there was a major hub of shooting activity near the basket and another band of activity out beyond the three-point arc. We can also see that the league's shooters were generally less active in the two-point jump shooting areas between the arc and the paint, but this plot says nothing about the relative values or successes of shots in different areas.

Each one of these dots has a backstory. Each one has a shooter attached, a team attached, and an outcome attached. We know who took each shot and whether it went in or not. And we can smooth out these dots statistically and map out the overall field goal percentage of the NBA as a collective.

Aha. Now we're getting somewhere. Now we can see that the probability of a shot going through the net greatly depends on where that shot came from. This insight is not surprising on its own, but it does reveal specifics about the basic relationships between distance, direction, and field goal percentage. What did surprise me when I first studied this chart was learning that outside of six feet there is no place on the court where shooters make more than 45 percent of their shots. I'd

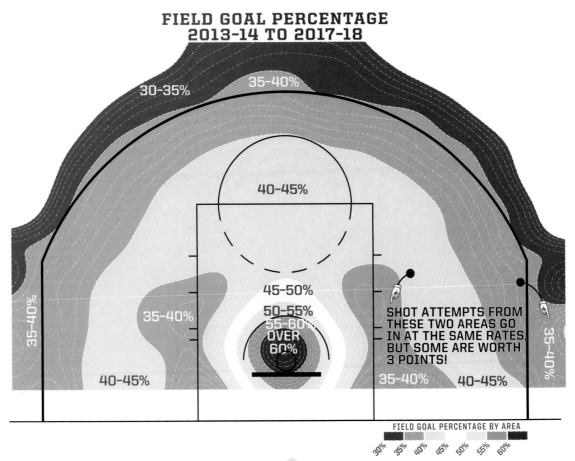

FIELD GOAL PERCENTAGE
2013-14 TO 2017-18

30-35%

35-40%

40-45%

45-50%

50-55%

55-60%

OVER 60%

35-40%

35-40%

40-45%

35-40%

35-40%

40-45%

35-40%

SHOT ATTEMPTS FROM THESE TWO AREAS GO IN AT THE SAME RATES, BUT SOME ARE WORTH 3 POINTS!

FIELD GOAL PERCENTAGE BY AREA

30% 35% 40% 45% 50% 55% 60%

always thought that 50 percent was the magic field goal percentage threshold, but this graphic shows that the only place on the floor where players exceed that magic number is the tiny swath of space just in front of the basket.

The next thing I noticed was even more surprising. When you look at league-wide shooting numbers between six and 25 feet, the league is strangely consistent. I expected to see a marked decrease in field goal percentage with greater distance: I thought shorter jump shots would go in at higher rates than longer jump shots. While this is true, the effect is much more subtle than I would have expected.

As it turns out, NBA players make only 40 percent of their shots between eight and nine feet of the rim, and that number drops to only 35 percent between 25 and 26 feet of the rim. When it comes to field goal percentage on jump shots, the effect of shot distance is pretty minor. It was a revelation, and it drove me to quickly build the following map, which would forever change the way I viewed scoring in the NBA.

Field goal percentage is only part of the story, and in a league with a three-point line, it is a very misleading part of the story. After all, points are the ultimate currency in the NBA.

When we visualize the average points per shot ac-

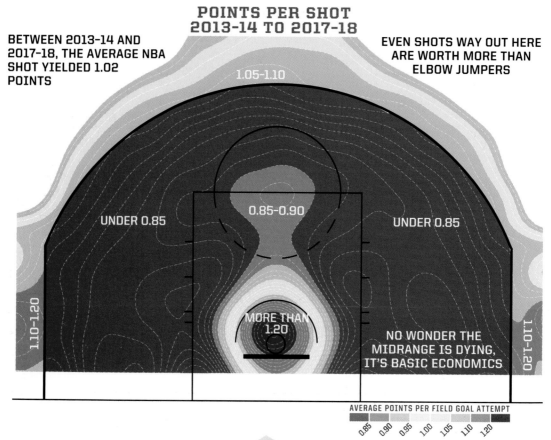

POINTS PER SHOT
2013-14 TO 2017-18

BETWEEN 2013-14 AND 2017-18, THE AVERAGE NBA SHOT YIELDED 1.02 POINTS

EVEN SHOTS WAY OUT HERE ARE WORTH MORE THAN ELBOW JUMPERS

1.05-1.10

UNDER 0.85

0.85-0.90

UNDER 0.85

1.10-1.20

MORE THAN 1.20

1.10-1.20

NO WONDER THE MIDRANGE IS DYING, IT'S BASIC ECONOMICS

AVERAGE POINTS PER FIELD GOAL ATTEMPT

0.85 0.90 0.95 1.00 1.05 1.10 1.20

cording to shot location, only then does the true economic landscape of the contemporary NBA reveal itself. Only then does Daryl Morey's economic vision become clear. Only then do we see the massive economic subsidy represented by the three-point line. And when we compare the points-per-shot map with the field goal percentage map, we are left with a troubling thought about the contemporary geography of NBA basketball.

If it's true that three-point shots go in 36 percent of the time and 10-foot shots go in just 40 percent of the time, then why are we assigning 50 percent more value to shots from beyond that magical little arc?

The natural landscape depicted in the field goal percentage map demonstrates that jump shooting in the NBA is essentially a 35 to 45 percent proposition; however, some of those shots are worth three and some are worth two. Naturally, as basic economics would predict, the behavior of players and teams has reacted in the form of shot selection. When we overlay the most common 200 shot locations in today's NBA, we see that shot selection and economic efficiency are aligned.

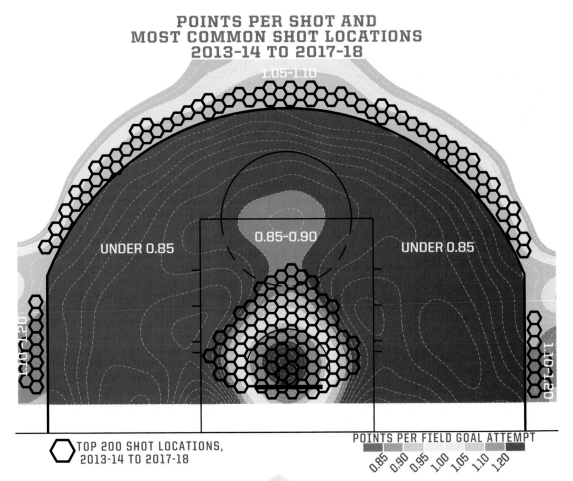

POINTS PER SHOT AND MOST COMMON SHOT LOCATIONS 2013-14 TO 2017-18

1.05-1.10

UNDER 0.85   0.85-0.90   UNDER 0.85

TOP 200 SHOT LOCATIONS, 2013-14 TO 2017-18

POINTS PER FIELD GOAL ATTEMPT

0.85 0.90 0.95 1.00 1.05 1.10 1.20

No wonder two-point jump shooting is dying.

From an analytical perspective, the position of the arc does not make much sense. It's virtually impossible to justify its location. League-wide, shots between 21 and 22 feet go in 39 percent of the time; these shots are all worth two points. Meanwhile, shots between 22 and 23 feet go in 38 percent of the time. And along the baselines of the current NBA playing surface, those shots are magically worth three points. Some people call the "corner three" the smartest shot on the court, and while that's pretty true from a competitive standpoint, from a regulatory perspective, it might be the stupidest shot the league has ever legislated into existence.

From a competitive perspective, the position of the arc and the associated economic realities it imposes on the league compel teams, coaches, and players to react. The shot selection of the contemporary NBA is a reaction to this man-made economic landscape. If the NBA scoring area is a marketplace that includes a ridiculously steep subsidy incentive near its outer edge, should we be surprised to see the league's smartest investors endlessly exploiting it? Should we be surprised that the analytics era of the NBA has begotten both a major uptick in three-point shooting and a major downtick in two-point jump shooting and post play? Should we be surprised that some of the most valuable components of current NBA rosters are guys who can shoot from 24 feet, even though they don't do much else?

Should we be surprised that the entire look and feel of the sport has changed since 1979?

The rise in three-point shooting has been accompanied by other changes a lot bigger than just shot selection. The arc has changed everything, from how teams create offense to how they build rosters. Looking at this map, it's no wonder that three-point shooting ability is now among the most important skills they look for in draft picks or free agents. The arc has even changed how we value the sport's holiest superstar players. With a few exceptions, just a decade or two ago, a post game was a prerequisite asset for any player hoping to win the NBA's MVP Award, but by 2016 the league's first-ever unanimous MVP was a skinny point guard with the best three-point shot on the planet. Steph Curry is no post player, and neither is James Harden. Today's MVPs look and play a lot differently than those from just a few years ago.

Simply put, the league's increasing love affair with threes has changed the look of the game. And just as the league didn't realize that basketball analytics would be transformed when it started charting shot locations, it also didn't realize that, in a much bigger way, adding the three-point line was also going to transform the sport.

Even in the smartest corners of basketball discourse, this transformation is almost always framed as "an increasing love affair with threes." The smart teams are finding ways to take and make more threes and finding players who help them do that. You can see the trends in the graphic "The Rise of the 3 in the NBA, 1979–2018."

But now that I'm a grown-up version of the teenager with the asymmetric turnaround jumper and no girlfriend, I see another story revealed in that points-

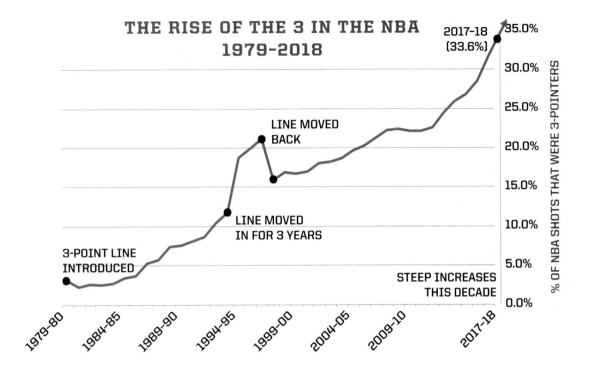

THE RISE OF THE 3 IN THE NBA
1979-2018

2017-18
(33.6%)

% OF NBA SHOTS THAT WERE 3-POINTERS

35.0%
30.0%
25.0%
20.0%
15.0%
10.0%
5.0%
0.0%

LINE MOVED
BACK

LINE MOVED
IN FOR 3 YEARS

3-POINT LINE
INTRODUCED

STEEP INCREASES
THIS DECADE

1979-80   1984-85   1989-90   1994-95   1999-00   2004-05   2009-10   2017-18

per-shot map—a story that's equally important but not told nearly as much as the love story about the three-pointer. Sure, the map makes it painfully clear that three-point shots are the best jump shots on the floor, but the sadder tale embedded in that conclusion is this: jump shots anywhere inside the three-point line are foolish investments. You don't have to be Warren Buffet to understand the decrease in popularity of the two-point shot.

NBA shot selection is a zero-sum game, and any league obsessed with taking more and more triples must necessarily also be a league obsessed with taking fewer and fewer of something else. After all, only about 200,000 shots per season are made, and if a higher share of them are coming from beyond the arc each year, there must

be an exact opposite effect on the other shot locations. In short, the rise of analytical thinking in the NBA has produced a big rise in three-point shooting—at the cost of two-point shooting, particularly two-point jump shooting.

We've recorded several albums lauding the rise of the three, but almost no singles lamenting the demise of the two—especially the ol' midrange jumper.*

During the 2001–02 season, which was marked by Shaq

---

* There is no formal definition of "midrange." Here I define midrange areas as two-point locations between 7½ feet from the basket and the three-point line. Depending on where you delineate that boundary, these shot location numbers change slightly, but the overall trends do not.

and his Lakers winning their third consecutive championship, NBA shooters attempted just 18.1 percent of their shots from three-point range; they shot 42.9 percent of them from the midrange. Shooters were more than twice as likely to take a shot in the midrange than from beyond the arc. But by 2017–18, which was marked by Steph Curry and his Warriors winning their third championship, NBA shooters were taking more threes than midrangers. That year NBA shooters tried just 27.1 percent of their shots from the midrange areas, while attempting 33.6 percent from three-point land.

But shot types are just the symptoms. *Sprawlball* is a story about the personnel, the tactics, and the spacing that beget those shot types. The last two decades have seen the league gradually ramp up three-point production by also gradually ramping up certain lineup types, tactical sequences, and personnel that are more likely to lead to threes.

Simultaneously, the league is systematically ramping down certain lineup types, tactical sequences, and personnel more likely to take midrange shots. It's a metamorphosis, to be sure, but when it emerges from its co-

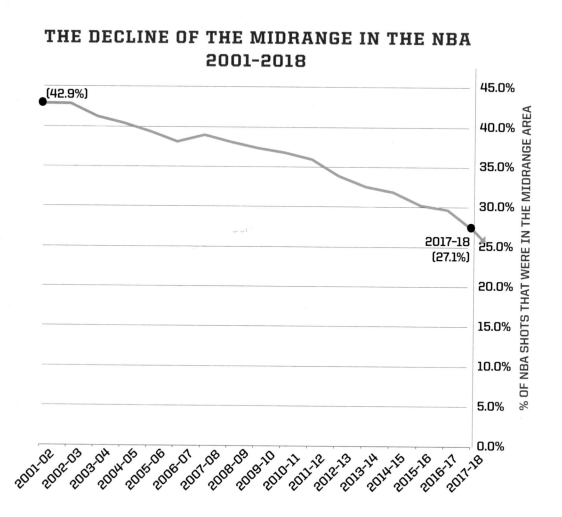

THE DECLINE OF THE MIDRANGE IN THE NBA
2001-2018

coon, a butterfly immediately flies to Ryan Anderson's house and drops off $80 million.

The recent change in the NBA isn't from large ball to smallball. It's from large ball to sprawlball. Many of the most powerful areas on the court are now sprawling out from the interior, decorating the edges. And the men who thrive there are now the game's most powerful players.

We've gone from MVPs named Shaq and Duncan who couldn't shoot from deep to MVPs named Harden and Curry who shatter records with three-point shots. We've gone from "dump it down to the big fella" to "drive it in so you can kick it out to the catch-and-shoot fella in the corner." NBA players used to race to the basket on fast breaks; now they race to the unattended edges of three-point range. It hasn't happened overnight, but the trends are undeniable, and the look and feel of contemporary NBA basketball is vastly different than it was just 15 years ago.

The magnitude of the shift is remarkable, but it's been disguised a bit by its gradual nature. Like Pangea slowly disintegrating into a set of discrete continents, the league has undergone a tectonic transition. But just like continental drift, the changes have been almost impossible to detect from one year to the next. Still, they're as clear as day when you compare the NBA's geological eras.

Both the outward migration of NBA jump shooters and the death of the post player have happened slowly and steadily. Each year the effect increases by a few degrees. Human beings are really good at detecting drastic and sudden changes, but like the old frog in slowly warming stove-top water, we're much less able to detect those that happen slowly and gradually. If you gain three pounds in a year, that's not a big deal, but if you gain three pounds a year for 20 years in a row, one day you wake up and realize you can no longer see your toes. Just ask Charles Barkley.

Imagine for a minute that the changes in these shooting patterns had occurred in back-to-back seasons. People would have been shocked. The sports radio preachers and the fellas at *PTI* would be all over it. They would take turns lamenting how these changes were distorting the very nature of the sport. They would decry the sudden death of big men, post play, and the art and athleticism of midrange scoring while sounding alarm bells about the league's sudden infatuation with spot-up shooters. How could the league let this happen? When did the Craig Hodgeses and John Paxsons of the world suddenly turn from role players to superstars? When did the Kevin McHales of the world get dethroned? They would demand that the league office acknowledge and intervene before the game became unrecognizable.

In response, just as they have done with the "Hack-a-Shaq" crisis and issues of instant replay, the regulators at the NBA office would urgently review the situation and evaluate potential interventions, and the Competition Committee would banter back and forth about "getting it right" and restoring balance to our beloved sport.

But the drastic transformation we're talking about here didn't happen in a tidy two-year window. It's taken decades, and as a result, it has lacked the abrupt imme-

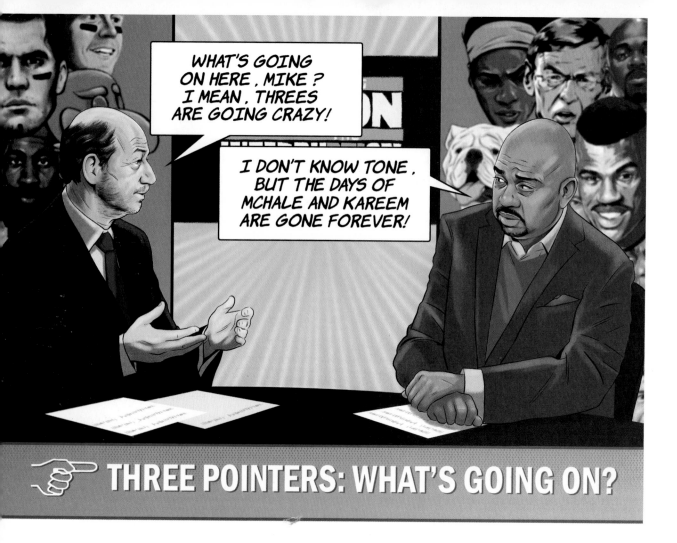

WHAT'S GOING ON HERE, MIKE? I MEAN, THREES ARE GOING CRAZY!

I DON'T KNOW TONE, BUT THE DAYS OF MCHALE AND KAREEM ARE GONE FOREVER!

☞ THREE POINTERS: WHAT'S GOING ON?

INTRODUCTION

diacy of daily news cycles, talking head segments, and contemporary national conversations.

But should the longer-term nature of the change determine our general reaction to it? Should we be less alarmed? Should we embrace this massive change in pro basketball simply because it's unfolding slowly? Should we not intervene? Should we not at least consider intervening? Perhaps. But by that logic, we should also just ignore the slowly warming and consistently rising sea levels or the slowly shrinking and consistently melting ice caps. By that logic, we should ignore the slow yet remarkable deaths of forests in the American Southwest. Oh, we do ignore those things? Never mind, everything's FAN-tastic.

To understand the NBA right now is an exercise in morphology. It always has been, but ever since the league laid down the new magic three-point stripe at the outer edge of its shooting zone, all bets are off and now the post-up game and the art of the midrange are going the way of the polar ice caps.

The addition of the three-point shot is the biggest rule change in any major sport in my lifetime. Imagine for a moment if FIFA suddenly ruled that any goals shot from beyond the 18-yard line are worth one and a half goals, or if MLB suddenly said that homers that reach the upper deck are worth one and a half runs. Fans would revolt. Teams would be irate. These proposals would be laughed at.

Well, that is pretty much what the NBA did back in 1979 when it declared that 24-foot jumpers were suddenly going to count for 50 percent more points that 21-foot jumpers. Yet back when the line was new, it wasn't a big deal; few players could shoot from that far out, and the first year it was a part of the league, players took only 3 percent of their shots out beyond the arc. By 2018, that number was 34 percent and rising—and rising fast.

Whether we love the changes or hate them, we at least should acknowledge their existence. If you have been watching the league for the last few decades, you haven't just been seeing the best basketball on the planet, you have been witness to unprecedented stylistic shifts in game play.

And these shifts are by no means complete.

Unless something changes soon, you're going to see these same trends persist if you plan on following the NBA in the coming decades. That 34 percent may reach 40 percent by 2022; it could be 50 percent by 2030; hell, it already is in Houston, where Morey, Harden, and his space force are running the most efficient offense in the league.

If you claim that the NBA looks and feels great right now, you're in a strange place. You may love the look and feel of today's game, but it's important to recognize that the game is at a halfway point between two massively different aesthetics. The form of the NBA in 2019 is not static. *Sprawlball* is not about taking a snapshot of the league in 2019 and holding a referendum on its current modus operandi. Rather, this book is an evaluation of the course the league is on—the places it's been and the places it's heading.

If you love the way the league looks right now, then, however counterintuitively, you better figure out a way to change some things, because according to the evidence, it's nowhere near an equilibrium.

The NBA is heading toward a version of basketball that values perimeter tactics and long-range shooting much more than it values interior tactics and fadeaways. It's heading for a future when centers and power forwards who cannot shoot from beyond the holy arc—or defend those who can—need not apply for jobs in the best basketball league in the world.

Just ask Andrew Bogut, the cagey starting center and key defensive stalwart of the 2015–16 Golden State Warriors. Bogut barely set foot on the court as his team tried to win the 2016 Finals. Before he suffered a knee injury in Game 5, the former number-one pick in the NBA draft was logging just 13 minutes per game as the Warriors decided that their best chance was to play "smallball." Or you can ask Timofey Mozgov, Bogut's counterpart in Cleveland; despite starting over half of the games for the Cavs during the regular season,

Mozgov appeared in only five of the seven Finals contests, averaging just five minutes per game when he did manage get off the bench. Or ask Roy Hibbert, the two-time All-Star and 7'2" defensive monster who was out of the league by the time he was 31. Or ask Al Jefferson, the All-NBA third-team center from 2014 who was playing in China by 2018 at 33.

We aren't heading toward a version of the game that has forsaken centers and compelled power forwards to turn into stretch fours. We're already there. Just ask Kevin Love, the last forward to ever average over 15 rebounds per game in the NBA and the man who currently holds the post-merger record for most consecutive double-doubles in league history. Love is a "power forward" if there ever was one. But those feats were years ago, back when Love was content to be a power forward. He's a stretch big now, and he takes more threes per game than his fellow Bruin, the great jump shooter Reggie Miller, ever did.

Many old NBA-heads think of Miller as one of the most prolific three-point shooters ever, but his productivity would make him simply average in today's game. In the five-season span between 2013–14 and 2017–18, Love averaged at least 6.5 three-point shots per 36 minutes four times. Uncle Reg reached that threshold only one time in his 18-year career.

We're not heading toward a version of basketball where the ability to create and make long-range jump shots is by far the most sacred skill in the league. We're already there. It's no coincidence that the best jump-shooting team of all time quickly became the most successful regular-season team ever. It's no surprise that the best three-point shooter in the league quickly became the NBA's first-ever unanimous MVP. Jordan never did that. Kareem never did that. But Steph Curry did it, and if current trends continue, his skill set's unprecedented "value" is only going to go higher and higher—at the cost of other skill sets, like rebounding, passing, and defense.

It's no coincidence that the first team to ever shoot over half of its shots from downtown led the NBA in offensive efficiency and winning percentage in 2017–18.

Sprawlball explores the past, present, and future of a league in transition and attempts to capture the nature of this surreal time in the NBA.

THE EVOLUTION OF STEPH CURRY

STEPH CURRY
MADE 402 3S
2015-16

ON SATURDAY, FEBRUARY 27, 2016, Stephen Curry broke Twitter. In a nationally televised game, Curry rose up and drained an impossible 37-foot buzzer-beating bomb that tore out the hearts of the Oklahoma City Thunder on their home floor. It was a breathtaking shot that won an incredible game, and it was yet another symbolic data point in an on-going series of observations pointing to one simple fact: Curry was doing things nobody else had ever done—and irreversibly changing NBA scoring in the process.

That night in OKC, Curry's Warriors were not just defending champs, but were also closing in on break-ing one of the most sacred records in pro hoops: a little more than six weeks later, they would win their 73rd game of the 2015–16 season, surpassing Michael Jordan's iconic 72-win Bulls of 1995–96. No easy feat, it had taken a season's worth of execution and bril-liance. On the road to 73, the margins for error were tiny, and this prime-time tilt against OKC might've been the most intense hurdle on the way to the new record.

With 30 seconds left in OT, Klay Thompson converted an "and-one" that tied the game at 118; the Thunder called a time-out to draw up a game-winning play to seal the win—but that wouldn't happen. When Russell Westbrook missed a tough 14-footer with eight seconds on the clock, the Warriors' Andre Iguodala grabbed the board and immediately passed the ball to Curry (good idea, Andre).

STEPH CURRY BREAKS TWITTER
FEBRUARY 27, 2016

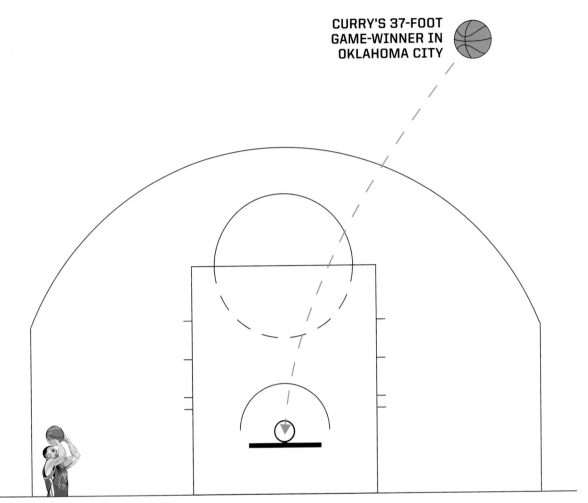

CURRY'S 37-FOOT
GAME-WINNER IN
OKLAHOMA CITY

There were just five seconds left in overtime, and Curry now held the ball 70 feet from the basket. 118–118. National TV.

Three dribbles later, Curry was barely across half-court. A normal team and a normal player might've called time-out to draw up a play. But this was the 2015–16 Warriors, and conventional wisdom did not apply. Mike

Breen was calling the action for ABC, and he struggled to keep pace with the play: "They do have a time-out . . ." Just then Breen's vocal pace sped up as he realized Curry had no plan to use that time-out: ". . . decide not to use it! . . . *Curry! WAY DOWNTOWN!* . . ."

It was Saturday night in America. Folks were out at bars, chilling on their couches at home with friends, or just zoning out watching the game before bed. The ball hung in the air for 2.6 seconds before Breen shouted out his trademark phrase:

"BANG!"

WTF just happened? Seriously, what the heck just happened? Not only did that dude not call that time-out, he then proceeded to calmly rise up 37 freaking feet from the basket and hit the shot of the year. The craziest thing was, it wasn't crazy. As the ball hovered above the court, we all knew that 37-footer had a good chance of going in. Because it was Steph Curry.

The shot melted the faces of millions of fans tuning in across America and beyond. Because this was no desperation heave: this was a poised and measured jumper that just happened to occur 37 feet from the rim. After the game, Curry revealed his thought process:

"Honestly, I don't know exactly where I am, so it's not like I'm calibrating in my head, all right, 38 feet, 37, 36," he said. "Just literally, you've got a sense of—I've shot the shot plenty of times, you're coming across half-court and timing up your dribbles, and you want to shoot before the defense goes in. And that was pretty much my only thought."

You're not supposed to be able to do that. James Naismith never intended for players to be able to shoot that far from the peach basket. But Curry can do that. Curry did do that, and in doing so he staked his flag in the idea that the traditional "scoring area" on a basketball court was bigger than ever and still expanding. If the three-point era needed a flagship moment, the

CURRY IS THE KING OF DEEP 3s

Shooter	Made Shots	FG %
Stephen Curry	66	41.8
Damian Lillard	56	32.6
Ryan Anderson	13	27.1
Kyle Lowry	12	30.0
Aaron Brooks	11	26.8
Lou Williams	11	20.0
J. R. Smith	9	20.5
Jamal Crawford	9	17.3
C. J. Miles	8	16.7
Kobe Bryant	8	17.4
LeBron James	7	14.9
Reggie Jackson	7	17.1

Between opening night of 2014-15 and that magical night in OKC, NBA players made just 19 percent of 3,348 shots from areas more than four feet beyond the arc; Curry converted 41.8 percent of 158 such attempts.

reigning MVP of the league just provided one. Curry was not only becoming the face of the best basketball league in the world but expanding the sweet land of three-point range too.

Let threedom ring!

In that same time period, 12 NBA players attempted at least 40 shots from at least four feet beyond the three-point arc. None of them made more than a third of those shots—except for our new overlord, who led the league in both made buckets and shooting percentage in the uncharted tee boxes way beyond the black tees. Curry was blending volume, efficiency, and distance in ways that no other player had ever done.

As a team, the Warriors were demoting Jordan's Bulls in the record books, but as an individual, Curry was

STEPH CURRY FROM DEEP

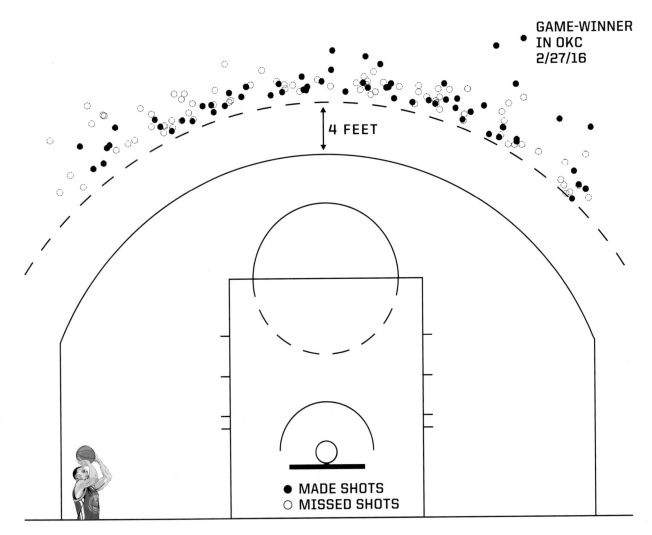

GAME-WINNER IN OKC 2/27/16

4 FEET

● MADE SHOTS
○ MISSED SHOTS

S
P
R
A
W
L
B
A
L
L

The NBA three-point line is 23.75 feet from the basket (except in the corners, where it's 22 feet away). Between opening night of 2014-15 and that magical game in the middle of the 2015-16 season, NBA players made just 19 percent of 3,348 shots from areas more than four feet beyond the three-point line. And lest you think he got lucky that night in OKC, Curry himself was 66 of 158 on such attempts—that's nearly 42 percent, folks, or 1.25 points per shot. That's not just good—this strategy by itself, just Curry hoisting *very* long triples, would make for the most efficient offense in the history of the NBA. And at some point in the 2015-16 season, Curry's swagger swelled to the point where he felt comfortable taking a lot more of these "ridiculous" long-rangers.

also deforming the economic geography of the game by rerouting the familiar Jordanesque path to NBA dominance. He was mapping a new route to stardom for a generation of wide-eyed kids who all wanted to be like Steph.

Curry was rebuilding the point guard position, and the three-point shot was his favorite tool.

For years, the hub of the NBA economy was down in the densely packed core, in the restricted area. Those days were now waning. Curry became the league's first-ever unanimous MVP, a scoring champ, and an era-defining star whose performance on the basketball court that night in OKC could have been the thesis statement in a dissertation entitled "Reimagining the Economic

Geography of Basketball." But unlike many of his fellow megastars, the author of this dissertation kind of came out of nowhere. It's hard to fathom now, but a decade before he became the first-ever unanimous MVP in NBA history, Curry couldn't even get a scholarship from a top-tier college program.

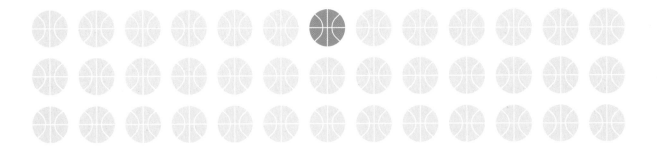

Part I:

THE ORIGIN STORY

As a youngster in North Carolina, little Wardell Stephen Curry II was a jump-shooting wunderkind. Growing up in the Dell Curry household will do that to a kid. Not only was Dell one of the best spot-up shooters of the 1990s, but Steph's mom, Sonya, was a versatile athlete who played high school hoops and volleyball at Virginia Tech, where she met Dell. So it's fair to say that from the get-go Steph was blessed with both natural gifts and elite athletic supervision.

He spent a lot of time in NBA arenas as a kid, hoisting up shots with basketball illuminati. One archived photo shows three-year-old Stephen sitting on his dad's lap at a 1992 three-point contest during All-Star weekend in Orlando, mucking it up with Mitch Richmond and Dražen Petrović. This was his childhood.

Still, even though it sounds like Curry was born into greatness, basketball greatness is never preordained. There is no Dalai Lama in the AAU; there is no Prince

Harry at the NBA Combine. At any given time, the NBA contains about 450 of the best basketball players in the world. Pro hoops is about as close as the world gets to a plain meritocracy: if you can ball, you get paid; if you can't, you don't. Basketball history is littered with great players' talented sons who never made the pros.

Sure, Curry's story involves some major blessings, but its key component, like any good American parable, was grit, grind, and a willingness to push himself. The seminal example came when Curry intentionally tore down his entire jump shot and rebuilt it from scratch. As a high schooler, Steph had already become an incredible jump shooter, but he was slight and skinny, and like a lot of slight and skinny high school players, his shooting form was childish. He wasn't strong enough to shoot the ball properly, and he knew that his immature mechanics wouldn't work going forward.

As a freshman and sophomore, Curry was a marksman who shot from the torso, making the release point of his jumper way too low. Shots released that low get easily blocked by the exact kind of longer and more athletic defenders he would face in AAU and college hoops. So, with one of the best shooters in the NBA as his guide, Steph spent an emotional and unhappy summer unlearning how to shoot and relearning how to shoot differently. As pointed out by David Fleming in *ESPN: The Magazine*, "It was a frustrating, tense few months for everyone. Stephen, who loves his craft so much that he often takes 1,000 shots *before* practice, says it was the only time in his life he flat-out hated shooting."

But it worked, and just as Robert Johnson went to the crossroads and sold his soul to the devil in return for guitar techniques that would change the world, Curry went to the backyard court and traded in his jumper. He reemerged with a shot possessed by demonic greatness, a shot that would eventually change the NBA. But not right away.

Blake Griffin, Hasheem Thabeet, James Harden, Tyreke Evans, Ricky Rubio, and Jonny Flynn. Those were the six names David Stern read on June 25, 2009, before he announced that Golden State had selected Stephen Curry. Curry wasn't just the seventh pick of that draft; he was the third point guard taken—fourth if you count Harden, who was listed as a shooting guard back then. Of course, hindsight is 20/20, and history is unkind to draft night fuckups, but looking back at that summer night in 2009, it's hard to believe that Curry went after Thabeet, Evans, Rubio, and Flynn. A quick review of some 2009 NBA draft preview discourse reminds us how and why this happened.

Revisiting the history of that draft, it's not hard to uncover real concerns and uncertainty surrounding Curry's ability to thrive in the NBA. At the time, many draft experts expressed doubt that a player barely recruited

to Division I could thrive among the fastest, biggest, and baddest ballers in pro hoops.

Sure, he was a consensus first-team All-American who had broken NCAA three-point shooting records, had a few hot weekends in the big dance, and tore up the Southern Conference, but so what? The Southern Conference isn't exactly the Western Conference, and as we've seen time and again, accolades like that do not guarantee anything at the next level.

NBA point guards need to make plays against other NBA point guards, and there aren't a lot of guys like Chris Paul, Kyrie Irving, Russell Westbrook, or Tony Parker suiting up in the Southern Conference. Curry did about as well as anyone could do at Davidson, but even that couldn't erase the uncertainty surrounding how he'd fare in the league.

The Nostradamuses of the basketball internet weren't sold.

A look back at the archives shows some hedging in the Curry scouting report on DraftExpress:

> Projecting him to the next level, Curry is an interesting case. He's likely to do a lot of his damage in spot-up situations in the NBA, but got only 8.9 percent of his possessions off of spot ups last seasons. He's not likely to use a lot of one-on-one possessions, but he used 8.6 per game last season (1st). Averaging 8.3 isolations per game (68.3 percent Left), Curry probably won't sniff half that number next season. In terms of guard play, his 41 percent shooting in transition ranks second to last, showing how hard he was pressing to

score, but his 1.3 PPP on the pick and roll is excellent—which leaves a lot of room for optimism. He did use 2.6 possessions per game as a jump shooter running off of screens, so he does have a nice base of experience there, but it is notable how far apart Curry's role in the NCAA was from the role he is likely to play in the NBA.

Whoops.

Writing in a draft preview piece for *Bleacher Report*, Joe Slowik exemplified the overall sentiment toward the 2009 cohort of point guard prospects: "Rubio is easily the best pure PG in the draft because of his passing ability and court vision." Oopsies. But to be fair to Slowik, almost all the projections had Curry slated below Rubio. Curry's frame was slight by NBA standards, and his résumé, while impressive, was built against questionable amateur opponents. Slowik explained: "He's

been highly productive in college, but a lot of people still aren't convinced he's a difference maker in the NBA. Few players with his size and athletic profile have been successful at the NBA level. However, he is an elite shooter and someone will take a chance on him fitting into their system. He'll improve his chances of making an impact if he keeps developing his point guard skills."

But one thing that these projections all failed to consider was that the league was in transition: the stylistic plate tectonics were slowly moving toward a league that would be very kind to Curry's skill set. In 2009, shooting was quickly increasing in importance, but the NBA was still waking up to the idea that three-point shots are among the best scoring options on the floor. Year after year, threes were growing in popularity, and the same abilities that made Rubio the best "pure PG in the draft" were becoming less important. Rubio couldn't shoot. Curry had the best jumper on planet earth.

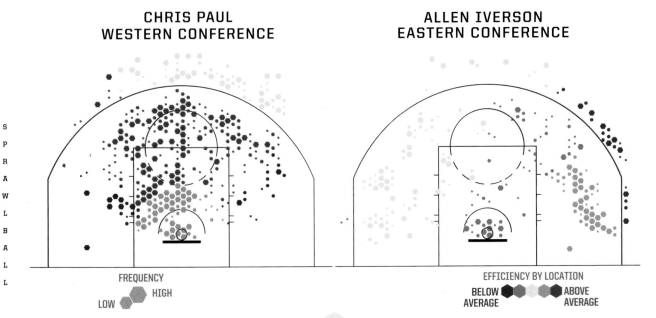

THE STARTING ALL-STAR POINT GUARDS OF 2009

CHRIS PAUL
WESTERN CONFERENCE

ALLEN IVERSON
EASTERN CONFERENCE

S P R A W L B A L L

FREQUENCY

LOW HIGH

EFFICIENCY BY LOCATION

BELOW AVERAGE ABOVE AVERAGE

In 2009, the operating manual for NBA point guards looked different than it does now. Entering Curry's rookie year, the reigning All-Star starters at the point guard position were Chris Paul, who was already widely regarded as the best point guard in the league, and Allen Iverson, who was at the tail end of his career. Paul and Iverson both dabbled in threes, but they were both much more comfortable in the two-point areas. The best point guards relied on speed and playmaking and for the most part played inside the arc. Curry would shatter that mold, but not as a rookie.

Curry made his NBA debut on October 28, 2009. He didn't take long to get his first shot up. Just 35 seconds into his first-ever NBA game, Curry launched an errant 27-footer. It was a harbinger of shots to come. Shots that wouldn't miss.

During his rookie season, Curry appeared in 80 of 82 games, started 77, and averaged 36 minutes per contest. He scored an impressive 17.5 points per game and

STEPH CURRY
FIRST SHOT IN THE NBA

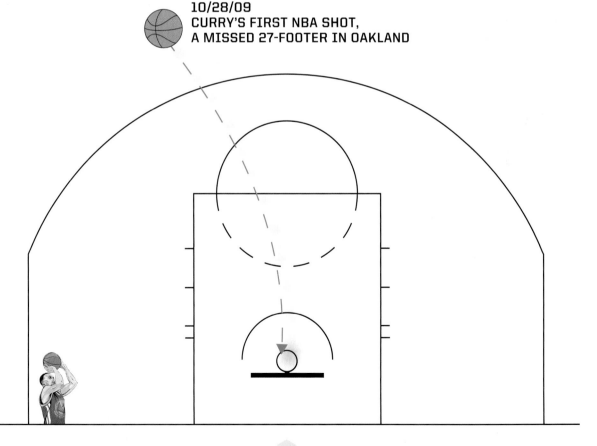

10/28/09
CURRY'S FIRST NBA SHOT,
A MISSED 27-FOOTER IN OAKLAND

averaged—foreshadowing the efficiency monster he would become—a freakishly efficient 1.22 points per shot attempt. He wasn't Rookie of the Year—that award went to Tyreke Evans, who averaged over 20 points per game—but Curry was already among the most efficient scoring point guards in the league.

Of those 17.5 points per game Curry scored his rookie year, only 6.2 came from beyond the arc, and he took fewer than a third of his shots from three-point range. When he won his first scoring title six seasons later, in 2015–16, he yielded 15.2 points per game beyond the arc, and over 55 percent of his shots came from three-point range. Between his rookie campaign and his first scoring title, Curry became much more active beyond the arc, and much less active in the midrange.

Even as a first-year player, Curry exhibited the shooting efficiency we would come to expect from him—he hit nearly 44 percent of his triples. But the nature of his offensive game was pretty different. His shot selection was a fairly traditional expression of a pick-and-roll point guard. Sure, he shot a bunch of threes, but most of his jumpers came inside the arc. He took a lot of elbow jumpers and long twos, and while these remain a small part of his game now, back then they were his bread and butter. When you compare his shot selection from his rookie year and from his scoring championship year, it's like you're looking at two different players.

In his rookie season, Curry took 42 percent of his shots in the midrange. That's a lot, considering that the league as a whole takes only about a third of its shots in that area. He took 487 two-point jumpers and 380 threes. Curry was tadpole swimming, spending most of his time in the shallow end of the jump-shooting pool.

THE EVOLUTION OF STEPH CURRY

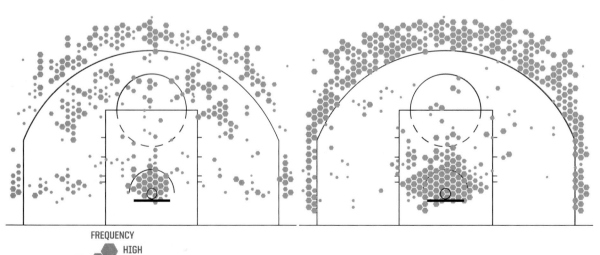

ROOKIE YEAR, 2009-10

UNANIMOUS MVP SEASON, 2015-16

S P R A W L B A L L

FREQUENCY
LOW HIGH

STEPH CURRY
ROOKIE YEAR
2009-10

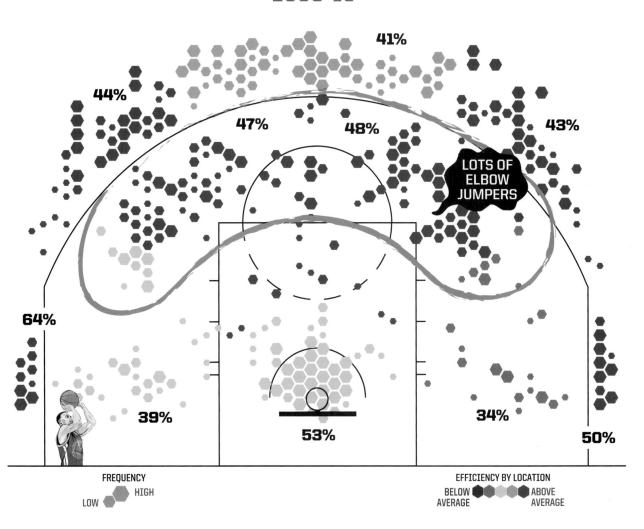

44%

41%

47%   48%

43%

LOTS OF
ELBOW
JUMPERS

64%

39%

53%

34%

50%

FREQUENCY

LOW   HIGH

EFFICIENCY BY LOCATION

BELOW
AVERAGE   ABOVE
AVERAGE

The evolution of Curry is both a study in the best jump shooter in the world finding his way within the best basketball league in the world and an examination of the rapid deformation of the point guard position. Before Curry came into the NBA, point guards were largely in charge of running plays and distributing assists. As a young NBA player, Curry fit that mold, but by the time he won his MVP, he did not.

He became a scoring machine who could also create shots for others. His transformation was all about shot volume and shot selection. As a rookie, and the son of Dell Curry, the accuracy was already established: he hit nearly 44 percent of his threes, which translated to a value of 1.31 points per shot. For Curry to become a more valuable player, all he needed to do was find ways to get more of those hyper-efficient threes. To become the most valuable player in the league, all he needed was to find ways to shoot more threes than anyone else ever had. The rise of Curry is a lesson in finding ways to do exactly that.

Stephen Curry became the most terrifying shooter in NBA history by (1) massively increasing his three-point volume and (2) hugely decreasing his activity in the midrange areas. Whereas the young Curry took 42 percent of his shots in the midrange, the first time he won the scoring title a mere 15 percent of his shots came from that area.

Through the first years of his career, Curry was immature as an NBA player. His rookie year shot chart reveals a fairly conventional jump-shooting point guard and fails to foretell the three-point messiah he would blossom into.

From a statistical perspective, Curry looked great in his first two seasons. Unfortunately, from an orthopedic perspective, he looked terrible. Early in his career, it was crystal clear that as a player Curry could compete in the NBA, but it was less clear whether his ankles would let him. In the spring of 2011, less than two years after his draft day, Curry had his first major ankle surgery.

THE EVOLUTION OF STEPH CURRY

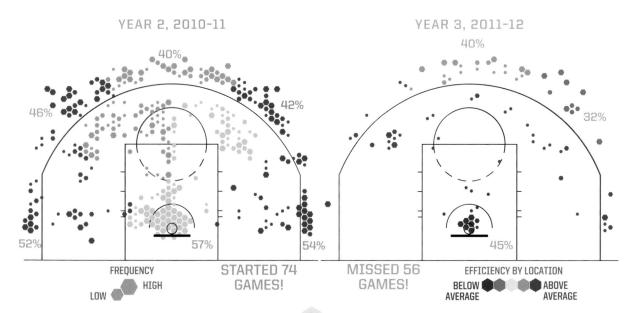

YEAR 2, 2010-11

40%

46%   42%

52%   57%   54%

FREQUENCY   STARTED 74
                   GAMES!
LOW   HIGH

YEAR 3, 2011-12

40%

32%

45%

MISSED 56   EFFICIENCY BY LOCATION
GAMES!   BELOW   ABOVE
                   AVERAGE   AVERAGE

SPRAWLBALL

The hope was that by rebuilding two ligaments in his right ankle, Curry would become a sturdier, more sustainable player. It didn't work, and the year after that first surgery, Curry endured five ankle sprains. It was fair to say that the surgery didn't help, and Curry missed a vast majority of games. Meanwhile, observers were beginning to wonder if his fragile ankles would hold up to the grueling nature of the NBA.

In the spring of 2012, Curry underwent a second, more aggressive procedure that almost included the insertion of new ankle tendons from a cadaver. Fortunately, that wasn't needed, but still, it was a make-or-break procedure, a huge inflection point in Curry's NBA career. And there was no guarantee that the second surgery would have a better outcome than the first one.

But it did. To say the least. As Curry and his ankle tendons stood for the National Anthem that opened the 2012–13 season, he was a new player. Nobody knew it yet, not even Curry, but the kid from Davidson was about to break out and some old records were about to fall.

Going into that season, Ray Allen held the NBA record for most threes in a single season. Allen, aka Jesus Shuttlesworth, was a phenomenal shooter. But while his singular masterpiece as a three-master came at the tail end of his career in the 2013 NBA Finals, his seasonal masterwork came back in his prime, during the 2005–06 season. Playing for the Sonics, Allen knocked down 269 threes, barely usurping Dennis Scott, who knocked down 267 in the 1995–96 season. But Scott's 267 mark was aided in part by the fact that it came in one of the three seasons when the NBA was experimenting with a shorter three-point line.

RECORD FOR MOST MADE THREES IN A SINGLE NBA SEASON PRIOR TO THE 2012-13 SEASON

1. Ray Allen	2005-2006	269
2. Dennis Scott	1995-1996	267
3. George McCloud	1995-1996	257

In that record-breaking season, Allen sunk 41.2 percent of his threes, but as great as he was, he was still pretty much a catch-and-shoot specialist. Over 75 percent of his triples that year involved an assist from a teammate: of Allen's 269 threes, 202 were assisted and only 67 were unassisted.

That's the tricky thing about three-point shots in the NBA: they are among the most assist-dependent shot on the floor. Traditionally, triples are the punctuation mark at the end of a long tactical sentence; they have as much to do with the coaches and playmakers who create them as they do with the spot-up shooters who drain them. As a result, ramping up three-point shooting activity is almost always a team effort. Even the best three-point shooters of all time, players like Allen, Reggie Miller, and Dennis Scott, relied heavily on coaching and cooperative teammates to set up their threes. As a general rule, almost 85 percent of NBA triples involve

RAY ALLEN'S RECORD YEAR!
2005-06 SEASON

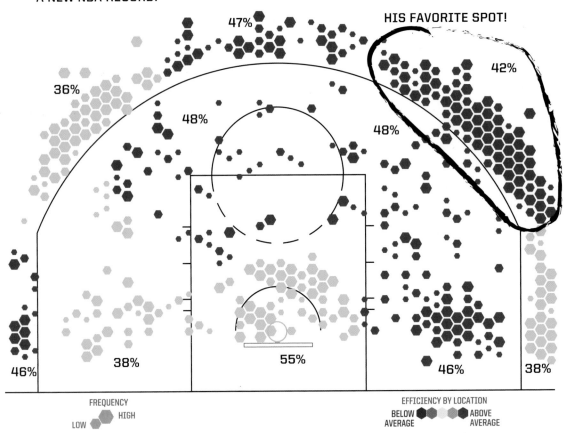

MADE 269 3S
A NEW NBA RECORD!

47%

HIS FAVORITE SPOT!

36%

42%

48%

48%

46%

38%

55%

46%

38%

FREQUENCY

HIGH

LOW

EFFICIENCY BY LOCATION

BELOW
AVERAGE

ABOVE
AVERAGE

S
P
R
A
W
L
B
A
L
L

an assist, and one reason bad teams find it difficult to "make threes" is that they struggle to work in concert to create them. Conversely, open catch-and-shoot threes are a key indicator species in the NBA: they thrive within good offensive ecosystems, but fail to take hold in bad ones.

Unassisted three-pointers are rare, largely because 24-foot basketball shots are really difficult to make, period.

For most of us, NBA threes are nearly impossible to sink in an empty gym, and even most NBA shooters find it pretty hard to make a three without being wide open. Typically unassisted jumpers are more contested than their catch-and-shoot counterparts. For years, we'd see just a few unassisted threes per game, often in transition when players would race up the floor, find themselves unguarded as they arrived at the arc, and fire away. Other than that, it's fair to say that conventional three-pointers are almost always preceded by a pass.

These conventions don't really apply to Stephen Curry.

During the 2012–13 season, Curry broke Allen's three-point shooting record in part by supplementing traditional catch-and-shoot approaches with unprecedented numbers of unassisted triples. It's not that Curry wasn't an elite catch-and-shoot guy at that time—he definitely was. But he became the most prolific three-point threat in league history by finding innovative ways to create space and get up good looks without the help of his teammates. He integrated his incredible ball-handling skills with his lightning-fast release to

generate a truly unprecedented quantity of unassisted three-point shots.

Unassisted threes became Curry's signature weapon.

Curry knocked down a total of 272 threes during the 2012–13 season, but a remarkable 38.6 percent, 105 of them, were unassisted. It was a sign that the 24-year-old kid was paving his own way to greatness. Still, as great as that 2012–13 season was, we hadn't seen anything yet. Like pole vaulters barely eclipsing each other's world records, Curry had only narrowly surpassed Allen's record in the same way Allen had narrowly surpassed Dennis Scott. The bar was getting raised a quarter-inch at a time.

CURRY BREAKS RAY ALLEN'S RECORD!

Made 272 3s
A new NBA record!

41%

40%

52%

41%

44%

59%

But relatively
ineffective near
the basket

43%

45%

50%

48%

2012-13

FREQUENCY

HIGH

LOW

EFFICIENCY BY LOCATION

BELOW
AVERAGE

ABOVE
AVERAGE

As Curry entered his prime years, he was about to raise that bar up a country mile.

When most people think of the act of jump shooting, they picture it beginning with a person elevating his feet off the ground and then releasing the basketball near the apex of his jump. But Curry didn't become the greatest shooter ever by thumbing through Bob Cousy's old jump-shooting manual. He wrote his own damn manual. To "Be Like Steph," you need to (1) seamlessly transition from all-world ball handling to illuminati-level shooting, (2) release your shot at lightning-quick speed, and (3) produce an unusually steep parabolic arc that is both deadly accurate and much more difficult to block.

Curry couldn't have broken Allen's record without all of those unassisted threes. And he couldn't have made all of those unassisted threes without some of the best handles in the NBA. Curry is not just the best shooter on the planet—he's also among its best dribblers. Along with Kyrie Irving, Curry can do things with the ball that are not just aesthetically breathtaking but that, from a tactical perspective, create space and allow him to get off the prettiest jump shot in the world. All of those unassisted threes have featured a vast array of ball-handling foreplay (yes, that's right) that effortlessly blends the dribble and gather into the more traditional rise-and-fire stage.

In other words, Curry reinvented the way point guards get their three-point shots by perfecting an independent substitute for the conventional, codependent preamble of pass-to-catch-to-shoot. Make no mistake, Curry didn't invent the step-back—but he adopted it and attached it to the wettest jumper the league has ever seen.

Even though by 2013 Curry triples were already breaking records and were already among the most efficient shots in the NBA, as we would come to learn, they were still vastly underused. The following season, at a time in his career when we'd expect his productivity to increase, we saw the opposite. Curry's perimeter productivity ebbed: he hit 272 threes in the 2012–13 season and "only" 261 in the 2013–14 season, which concluded with the Warriors losing to the Los Angeles Clippers in the first round of the playoffs. It was a

RECORD FOR MOST MADE THREES IN A SINGLE NBA SEASON AFTER THE 2012-13 SEASON

1. Stephen Curry	2012-2013	272
2. Ray Allen	2005-2006	269
3. Dennis Scott	1995-1996	267

plateau of sorts. The good news was that Curry's ankles were holding up better than ever; the bad news was that many folks around the team were unhappy with the year-to-year direction of the organization as a whole.

Part II:
THE KERR ERA

That summer the Warriors fired head coach Mark Jackson. It was a controversial move. Jackson had just led the young team to the franchise's most successful season in years. The Dubs had improved their regular-season record every year under Jackson, and the team's young core, including Curry, seemed to be developing just fine under his leadership. Jackson had played 17 years in the NBA. He was a point guard on some of the most physical Eastern Conference teams of the 1990s. But his Eastern Conference résumé and vision manifested in the team's vanilla offensive approach. Sure, Curry was breaking records, but many people felt that Jackson was incapable of designing schemes that could totally unleash the hellhounds that Curry and Klay Thompson could become. On the heels of the loss to the Clippers and a breathtaking pace-and-space Finals victory by the Spurs, few people believed that old-school Jackson could lead a championship contender that would get past the likes of the Spurs, Clippers, Heat, and Thunder.

Enter Steve Kerr. While Jackson made NBA hay as one of the game's most brutish point guards at the height of one of the league's most physical eras, Kerr made his hay avoiding the paint and spacing the floor. Both played the guard position, but they played it in very different ways. Jackson grew up dominating the playgrounds of Brooklyn before starring for St. John's. Kerr went to Palisades Charter High School in Los Angeles prior to starring at Arizona.

Many of us remember the 1998 NBA Finals as being Michael Jordan's sixth and last championship appearance; however, fewer folks recall that Jordan and the Bulls almost didn't even make the Finals that year. And their toughest series of the entire playoff run was a rough, back-and-forth, seven-game series against a ferocious and hungry Indiana Pacers squad in the Eastern Conference Finals.

Jackson was the starting point guard for those Pacers; Kerr was a rotation spot-up threat for the Bulls. In the late 1990s, sharpshooting spot-up dudes like Kerr were considered role players or specialists, while many of the league's best guards were tough, physical players.

They had to be. The late '90s were a violent time for the world's best basketball players. Back then, the focus of the scoring economy was on the two-point area, and the league was full of personnel and tactics that reflected this orientation. In the 1998 season, NBA shooters took only 16 percent of their field goal attempts beyond the arc. That's fewer than one in six. In the 2016 playoffs, the Warriors took over 37 percent of their shots beyond the arc, and their Finals opponents from Cleveland also took 37 percent of their shots from three-point range.

The lives of perimeter players were vastly different in 1998. Simply put, life was harder and a lot more physical. Back then, perimeter players were allowed to hand-check one another a lot more than they are now as a means to prevent the kind of dribble penetration we take for granted in today's action. What is hand-checking? It's the act of an on-ball defender using his hand to "check" the location and help control the direction of his man. It was a fundamental cornerstone of NBA defense until the summer of 2004. In the 2004 NBA Finals, the Detroit Pistons upset the Lakers, largely by playing incredible defense. They were able to control Kobe Bryant, who managed to make just 38 percent of his shots in the series. The Pistons got physical. They muddied up the game. It was ugly, but it worked. The Pistons used great physical defense to upset the star-studded Lakers.

Later that summer, the league curtailed hand-checking. It was a major decision that would greatly reduce the ability of NBA defenders to prevent guards and wings from attacking the paint. In other words, it would liberate dribble drivers like Kobe Bryant from the pesky hands of their defenders. According to Stu Jackson, who was a league executive at the time, the goal was simple: "Our objective was to allow for more offensive freedom by not allowing defenders to hand-, forearm- or body-check ball handlers. By doing so, we encouraged more dribble penetration. As players penetrated more, it produced higher quality shots for the ball handler as well as shots for teammates on passes back out to perimeter. When NBA players get higher quality shots—having more time to shoot—they tend to make more of them."

It turns out that it's a lot easier to defend quick but relatively slight guards like Steve Nash or Steph Curry when you can extend your hand and check them. A fella like that isn't so nifty when Tony Allen gets a claw on his hip. Following the league's decision to curtail hand-checking, Nash seemingly came out of nowhere and won two consecutive MVP Awards. In 2006, Dwyane Wade dribble-drove his way to an NBA championship. And in 2007, Tony Parker won the Finals MVP on a team that featured Tim Duncan. Suddenly guards were dominating the league.

Was this a tactical awakening or simply an underreported legislative deformation of the league?

Back in 1998, for a guard to get into the paint, he had to combine strength (to overcome the physicality of his defender), speed (to get by him), and bravery. Jordan was both strong and fast, but when a guard like MJ somehow managed to attack the paint, he would often be greeted with types of fouls we don't see very often anymore. And many of the league's best teams had players who specialized in doling out these fouls. Hockey had goons, hoops had Rick Mahorn and Bill Laimbeer. Nobody knew this better than Michael Jordan, who absorbed hundreds of "hard fouls" each season. This is what guards had to endure to win the MVP in Jordan's era.

No wonder Jordan retired so many times! Despite the brutality of that era, those 1998 Eastern Conference Finals between Jordan's Bulls and Jackson's Pacers also featured a remarkable perimeter shooting performance by Reggie Miller, who raced around brutal screens to find little crevasses of space for his catch-and-shoot threes. Miller arguably did this better than anyone in his generation, and in that seven-game series he drained 17 of 39 threes. Nobody else for either team even made more than 25 attempts. Still, in the context of today's sprawling perimeter economy, Miller's numbers from that series look downright juvenile. In the epic 2016 Western Conference Finals against OKC, which also spanned seven games, Thompson tried 72 threes and Curry launched 79—about twice as many as Miller did in 1998.

The Warriors replaced Jackson with Kerr in part to try to ignite the team's middling offense. But for those of us who remember the '98 ECF, the replacement was symbolic, taking the keys to one of the best young backcourts in the league away from the brooding point guard of the '90s and handing them to a three-point specialist who lived beyond the arc and off the ball.

While it's true that Curry broke Allen's record within the confines of Jackson's offense, it's also true that the team was an average NBA offense. Kerr was going to change that.

In early November 2014, just 10 games into Kerr's tenure in Oakland, it was clear that things were different, and it didn't take long for folks to realize that these differences were going to be good for the Warriors—and great for Curry. Writing for *Grantland* just about a week into Kerr's first year as head coach, I published a piece called "Golden Start" that attempted to capture the early-season excitement surrounding Kerr's new offense along with some of the tactical differences that differentiated the team's new look from the one it had the previous year under Jackson.

The piece started with a basic sentence: "The Golden State Warriors look awesome."

The main revelation of the early Kerr era involved the idea that his jump-shooting guards could be more effective chess pieces if they were handling the ball less and running off screens more. In the preseason of 2014, Kerr hinted that Andrew Bogut, the team's cagey Australian center, would be a big presence in the team's new offensive philosophy: "Andrew's one of the best passing centers in the league. He's one of the best I've ever seen, and so for us to get him the ball on the elbows as a dribble-handoff guy, backdoor-pass guy, that will be emphasized."

Early in the regular season, it was clear that Kerr's guards were moving a lot more off the ball, especially when the bigs held it in the high post. The backdoor stuff was working. There were fewer pick-and-rolls and more dribble handoffs. Kerr's sets made the Dubs look more like the 2013 Spurs than the 1998 Pacers. By December 2014, the NBA already knew that Curry and Thompson were a giant pain in the ass to defend, but Kerr was concocting schemes that were only going to make it more difficult. He was about to set Curry loose, and Curry was about to take over the NBA.

Kerr's arrival coincided with the third year of good health for Curry. After missing 40 of 66 games in the lockout-shortened 2011–12 campaign, Curry missed only four games in each of the next two seasons. Not only was he entering his prime as a player, but he could also trust his ankles in ways that had seemed impossible just a few years earlier. Between his good health, his rising confidence in his game, and the arrival of a savvy new coaching staff, all the ingredients were there. Curry and the Warriors had a new ceiling.

The Warriors won their first five games, and 18 of their first 20. On December 15, 2014, the world woke up to see the Dubs were 21-2. Sure, it was early, but holy moly, the Dubs looked great. They were killing teams on both sides, scoring 107.6 points per game, while giving up just 96.8 on defense. Exactly one year earlier, on December 15, 2013, this team with virtually the same roster was 13-12, scoring 103 points per game, and giving up 100.5 on defense. This was a different animal.

And so was Curry. While everyone already knew that Curry was the best three-point shooter in the league, by the 2014–15 season he'd also managed to erase the one big weakness in his scoring portfolio: his struggle to score near the basket.

The year he broke Allen's three-point record, Curry was able to convert only 49 percent of his shots within eight feet of the basket. That was not just below average (the league shoots 55 percent in this zone)—it was bad. Out of a group of 168 NBA players who attempted at least 200 shots inside of eight feet that season, *Curry ranked 151st in field goal percentage.* The kid was spitting hot fire beyond the arc, but he was as cold as ice near the rim.

In perhaps the most unheralded development of his game, Curry didn't just improve that weakness, going from bad to merely adequate; by the end of Kerr's first

season, he was simply one of the most active and efficient scoring guards in that exact same zone. Out of 50 players who attempted at least 350 shots within eight feet during the 2014–15 regular season, Curry ranked eighth in field goal percentage, converting a whopping 63 percent of those attempts. That number wasn't just good for a guard—it was a better rate than Dwight Howard, Marc Gasol, or Blake Griffin had. Curry went from being a "soft" perimeter specialist to a versatile terror able to blend volume and efficiency in the paint as well as any point guard on earth. Kerr's newfangled offense was getting Curry better looks near the basket, but Curry himself worked hard to develop an arsenal of quick and quirky releases that enabled him to outwit or outmaneuver bigger defenders. Nobody in the league had better floaters or higher-arcing bank shots. Oh, and he trusted his ankles to survive all those drives to the basket.

It was a remarkable shift. If the point of a story is the transformation of its characters, then the point of the Stephen Curry story has a lot to do with a guy intentionally turning weaknesses into strengths. Whether it was his immature jump-shooting form as a high schooler, his flimsy ankles, or his struggle to get buckets near the rim, by 2014–15 the ongoing pattern had emerged: Curry was ascendant.

At the dawn of Kerr's first season, the old draft prognostications about his starting point guard were already starting to look silly. By the end of it, they looked downright idiotic. "Few players with his size and athletic profile have been successful at the NBA level." Haha.

Curry won the NBA MVP Award in 2014–15. Yet this isn't a story about a few writers guessing wrong; it's the story of a guy ramping up his game in remarkable ways,

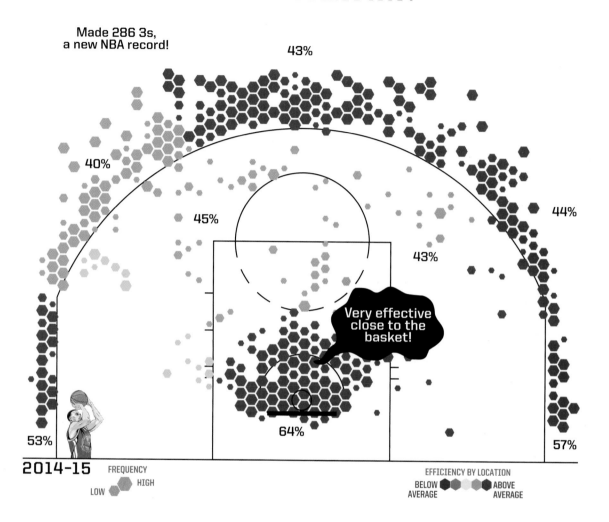

Made 286 3s,
a new NBA record!

43%

40%

44%

45%

43%

Very effective
close to the
basket!

53%

64%

57%

2014-15

FREQUENCY
HIGH
LOW

EFFICIENCY BY LOCATION
BELOW
AVERAGE
ABOVE
AVERAGE

reimagining the very idea of great point guard play and making a lot of smart people look stupid. But it wasn't just the media left looking foolish.

In the summer of 2013, right after becoming the record-breaking three-point maestro, Curry famously left Nike in favor of Under Armour. A few years later, that move had made Nike look dumb and Under Armour brilliant. It made for a convenient story. But

it also goes to show that as recently as 2013 even the league's smartest and best-funded marketing outfit truly doubted that Curry was a legit superstar. In 2013 at Nike, it was LeBron's league. It was Kevin Durant's league. It was still Kobe's league. And the biggest shoe retailer in the world had the retail figures to prove it.

The Under Armour deal was a chance for Curry to be the face of an upstart shoe company and get out from

THE EVOLUTION OF STEPH CURRY

under the shadow of those other superstars, who were Nike's priority athletes at the time. For good reason, by the way: those dudes sold a boatload of sneakers. Under Armour did what underdogs do: they weren't going to get LeBron, Kobe, or Durant to leave Nike, so they took a chance on the shooter with questionable ankles. Needing a new guy, they threw the bank at Curry, but even Under Armour didn't forecast the greatness Curry would soon demonstrate.

Anybody who ridicules Nike for massively underestimating the value of Curry in 2013 must also then ridicule Curry himself. See, in the middle of the season leading up to the Under Armour deal, Curry also signed a new NBA contract with Golden State. But it wasn't the "max deal" we would all associate with any kind of superstar player, let alone a future MVP or scoring champ or demigod. In December 2012, Curry signed a four-year, $44 million contract extension to stay with Golden State. That's not LeBron money; that's not KD money; that's not Kobe money. Hell, that's not even Chandler Parsons money. Folks, that's Tyreke Evans money. Curry signed almost the exact same contract at the exact same time as Evans, who has never won an MVP or a scoring title and never been the face of a marketing campaign.

By the 2015–16 season, the whole world knew Curry was a superstar. He was a champion, an MVP, and a media darling, but he was also the fifth-highest-paid player on his own team. Curry was the most underpaid pro athlete in the world, and he did it to himself. While it's easy to look back and say that we could see this coming, we just couldn't. The draft experts couldn't. Nike couldn't. And Curry's own camp couldn't.

In the fall of 2012, Curry was approaching the end of his rookie contract. He was playing great, but he had missed a ton of games and undergone two scary ankle procedures. Early into the 2012–13 season, he had a simple choice: sign the contract extension with its guaranteed $44 million or wait until the end of the season and test free agency, where he could make as much as $64 million. It was a classic risk assessment, and Curry chose the $44 million in part because of those ankles, the surgeries, and all the legitimate uncertainty swirling around his ability to stay on the court.

The midseason contract extension appealed to a smart guy with a family and an uncertain future, but it's a decision he was still wrestling with years later, as Curry himself told Adrian Wojnarowski in December 2015:

"'Oh, I should've done this, or that. [But] at the time, the counsel that I got from my family, my agent, myself, was that it was the right decision to make. With that, I could take care of my family and be good. And hopefully anything that happened after that would just be icing on the cake."

There would be icing.

The 2014–15 Warriors finished the season just the way they had started it: wins were very common, losses were not. They won 67 games, 11 more than anybody else on their side of the playoff bracket.

Still, this team had never made a deep playoff run, and at the outset of the 2015 playoffs the West was loaded with teams that had. Just a year earlier, the mighty Spurs had torched LeBron James and the Heat in the Finals. It was the Spurs' fifth championship, and with

55 regular-season wins in 2014–15, they looked like they had another run in store. But to give you an idea of how clogged the West was heading into the '15 playoffs, the defending champion Spurs were the sixth seed. The West was loaded.

Five Western Conference teams won at least 55 games that year, and each of those teams had a legitimate shot to win it all. The Eastern Conference had one. The Western bracket was stacked, and to even get to the Finals it looked like any Western Conference team would have to overcome an unprecedented difficulty level along the way. In addition to the Spurs and Dubs, there were the Grizzlies, the Rockets, and the Clippers, who had eliminated the Dubs a year earlier.

Everybody knew the Warriors were the best team in the league during the regular season, but the playoffs were different, and Golden State was unproven at the most intense levels.

On April 18, 2015, the Dubs kicked off their playoff run against the New Orleans Pelicans, who had narrowly made the playoffs and were clearly the weakest team in the Western bracket. But to the victor go the spoils, and Golden State earned this draw. Curry and his team easily dispatched the Pelicans. It was a four-game sweep, and Curry led his team in scoring in three of the four wins. He put up 40 in Game 3 in New Orleans and added 39 in the Game 4 clincher.

Curry was sensational, and he was doing it by showcasing both threes and his new proficiencies near the basket. After the final game, the Pelicans phenom Anthony Davis reflected on the pick-your-poison threat Curry had become: "I knew he was crafty, I mean, a great shooter," Davis said of Curry, who put up nearly 34

points per game in the series. "There's nothing you can do. You try to pressure him and run him off the (three-point) line and he'll hit incredible shots in the lane. You back off so he won't drive, he's going to hit a three. So you've got to pick your poison, and he's a tough player to guard. That's why he's [a candidate] for MVP."

Curry's new ability to score in the paint had not only erased the biggest weakness in his scoring portfolio but also made him virtually impossible to guard. Just a few years earlier, Curry was a deadly shooter who couldn't get it done in the lane, but by the spring of 2015 he'd become a sturdier two-point threat who could also kick your ass with dribble drives. Defenders could no longer afford to cheat and overplay his perimeter shooting; if they did, he'd just dribble by them and score in the paint. As a consequence, Curry started to see more honest perimeter defending, which was easier to punish with his ridiculously quick and deadly release.

In other words, by becoming a better interior scorer, Curry also became an even scarier perimeter threat.

After besting Davis and the Pelicans, the Warriors faced the Memphis Grizzlies in the second round of the playoffs. The "Grit-and-Grind" Grizz were led by Marc Gasol and Zach Randolph and featured perhaps the best defensive backcourt in the entire league, Mike Conley and Tony Allen, both terrific defenders who had already shown that they could get it done in the playoffs.

After winning the first game by 15, the Warriors seemed set to breeze through another series, but in Games 2 and 3 the Grizzlies bore down on defense and flipped the script: they smothered Curry and held the Dubs to 90 in Game 2 and 89 in Game 3. Games got physical, and points got hard to find. Suddenly the most efficient offense in the NBA looked sloppy. In Game 2, Curry was seven of 19 and just two of 11 from beyond the arc. In Game 3, he was eight of 21 and two of 10 from three-point range.

On the morning of May 10, the Warriors were down 2–1 and things seemed bleak. The Grizz looked like they had cracked the Curry code. Golden State faced a must-win game on the road in Memphis the next night, since a loss would put them on the brink. So like any good MVP, Curry made sure they won. He found his missing jumper, and by putting up 33 huge points, he led all scorers and led his team to a huge 17-point win that reasserted his team's dominance. As goes Curry, so go the Dubs. They went on to easily win the following two games and advance to the Western Conference Finals.

Kerr, Curry, and the Warriors had survived their first real playoff test against a real Western Conference foe, but two big series remained. Fortunately, the Dubs avoided any clashes with Gregg Popovich and the defending champion Spurs, who had lost a brutal seven-gamer against Chris Paul, Blake Griffin, and the Clippers in round 1.

The Clippers looked like a real threat. They had great players and a championship coach in Doc Rivers, and they had eliminated the Dubs a year earlier. But after besting the mighty Spurs in round 1, they collapsed in round 2. They won three of the first four games in their series against Houston, before losing the last three games to a team that was relying on wildly questionable NBA players in crunch time. The Clips didn't just squander a huge chance to advance to their first-ever

Conference Finals; they did so against a team that gave major roles to Josh Smith and Corey Brewer, two players picked off the NBA scrap heap before the All-Star break. It was an embarrassing loss for the Clippers, but it also meant that Curry and the Warriors suddenly had a flawed opponent standing between them and the NBA Finals.

Golden State coasted past the Rockets in just five games. Curry was phenomenal, putting up 31 points per game and sinking most of his shots. Those cold games against Memphis were a distant memory and Curry was raining down threes. Over half of his shots came from three-point range, and he converted over 49 percent of them. You can't beat Golden State when he does that. As goes Curry, so goes Golden State.

In Steve Kerr's first season, the team won 67 games, Curry won the MVP, and the Dubs made the Finals. Now all they had to do was beat LeBron James and the Cleveland Cavaliers.

2015 Finals

The 2015 NBA Finals pitted a team from Cleveland against one from the Bay Area. Cleveland, the capital of the Rust Belt, has come to symbolize a bygone period of American industrialism. The city's basketball team was led by LeBron James, who is by far the NBA's most dominant interior producer. For almost a decade, James has been not only among the league's most proficient paint scorers but among its most efficient.

LeBron's prime has included many seasons of leading the league in both volume and efficiency in the paint.

Sure, King James has always had a mediocre perimeter game, but he's won championships and MVPs by dominating the game in a familiar way: as a true disciple of past champs, he blends power, speed, and size to overwhelm the interior defenses of his opponents.

In 2015, the Warriors, the pride of the tech bros in the Bay Area, brought a vastly more newfangled offensive approach that depended on the perimeter production of their jump-shooting icons. The 2015 Finals were more than a basketball contest: as the game's most dominant interior force was pitted against its most dominant perimeter producers, the Finals were also a referendum on the state of the NBA.

Unfortunately, the 2015 Finals didn't quite live up to expectations. Kyrie Irving, the Cavs' phenomenal point guard, got hurt in Game 1 and didn't play the rest of the series. In addition, Kevin Love missed the entire series with an injury he suffered earlier in the playoffs. Cleveland's Big Three was downgraded to a Big One, and perhaps unsurprisingly, the Warriors won in six games. But it was an ugly six games. Curry didn't flourish as he had against Houston. He scored 26 points per game, but his shooting numbers were subpar for his outrageous standards. He wasn't terrible by any means, but at the end of the series the writers awarded the Series MVP to his teammate Andre Iguodala, who defended James for most of the series.

But who cares? For the first time in 40 years, the Warriors were NBA champs. It was a remarkable season, and the Warriors were clearly the league's best team all year. They nearly led the league in offensive efficiency, and they did lead the league in defensive efficiency. Any team that does that is almost assuredly the best team in the league. They won 67 games, and they won the Finals.

Still, that off-season the haters came out. Many people argued that the Warriors' playoff run was too easy. They lucked into an easy sequence of opponents. They never played the Spurs. They never played the Clippers. And they played a banged-up version of the Cavs. Perhaps the loudest version of this sentiment was offered up by Doc Rivers, the president and head coach of the Clippers. "You need luck in the West," Rivers told *Grantland*'s Zach Lowe in the summer following the Dubs' championship run. "Look at Golden State. They didn't have to play us or the Spurs."

It was a telling quote. Nobody would have dared say that about the Spurs when they won in 2014, but plenty of folks were saying stuff like this about the 2015 Warriors. Despite the fact that nobody took them to seven games, despite the fact that they dominated both ends of the floor all year long, and despite the fact that they won 67 freaking games in the regular season. That's a lot of luck, man.

At the beginning of the following season, Curry was one of the best players in the NBA, and it was clear that he was doing things nobody else had ever done. While those interior improvements were nice, Curry was also still building his record-breaking perimeter résumé. And make no mistake, it wasn't cute little floaters off the glass that propelled him to superstardom.

In the same way that Michael Jordan will be remembered for breathtaking rim attacks, Curry will always

RECORD FOR MOST MADE THREES IN A SINGLE NBA SEASON AS OF 2015

1. Stephen Curry	2014-2015	286
2. Stephen Curry	2012-2013	272
3. Ray Allen	2005-2006	269

be remembered for his triples. He won his first scoring title in 2015–16 by shattering his own three-point shooting records. Heading into that season, no NBA player, including Curry, had ever drained more than 286 threes in a season. Dozens of incredible shooters had made between 200 and 300, but nobody had ever eclipsed 300. Not Ray Allen. Not Dennis Scott. Not Reggie Miller.

Think about that. Heading into the 2015–16 season, the league had had a three-point line for 35 years, but in all

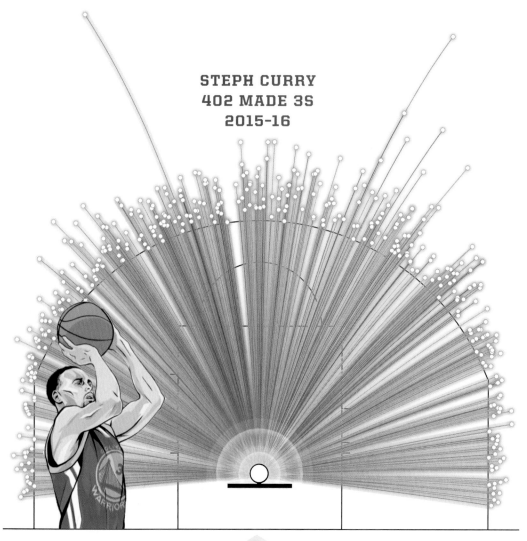

STEPH CURRY
402 MADE 3S
2015-16

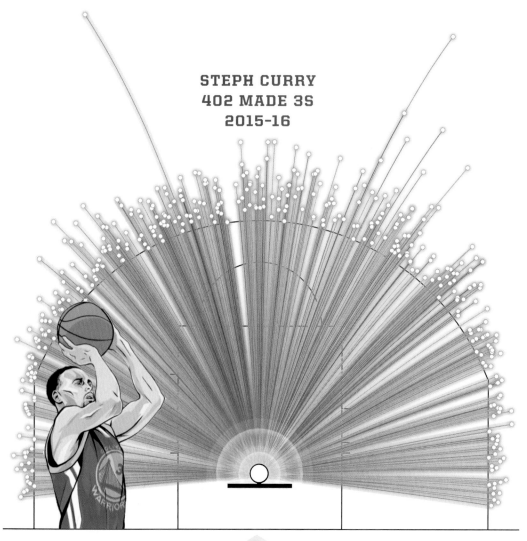

that time nobody had made more than 300 threes in a season.

Now think about this: Curry made 402 threes in the 2015–16 regular season. Holy cow, guys.

If you had to explain the 2014–16 Warriors to a stranger but could only use three facts, you might use those three numbers at right. They blew the lid off the all-time NBA wins record by blowing the lid off of three-point scoring. They became the craziest show on *League Pass*

RECORD FOR MOST MADE THREES IN A SINGLE NBA SEASON AS OF JULY 2016

1. Stephen Curry	2015-2016	402
2. Stephen Curry	2014-2015	286
3. Klay Thompson	2015-2016	276

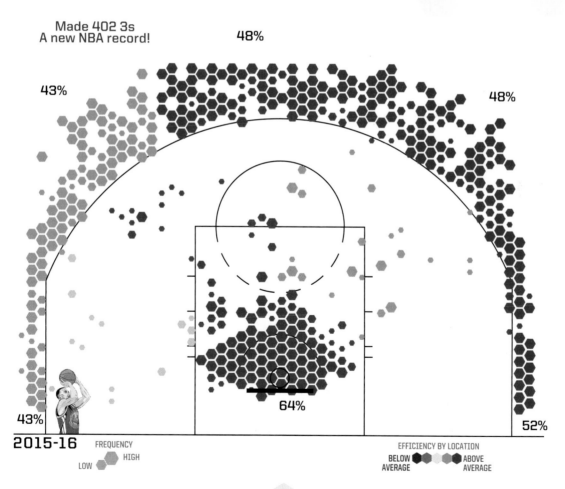

CURRY SHATTERS HIS OWN RECORD!

Made 402 3s
A new NBA record!

48%

43%

48%

43%

64%

52%

2015-16

FREQUENCY
LOW · HIGH

EFFICIENCY BY LOCATION
BELOW AVERAGE · ABOVE AVERAGE

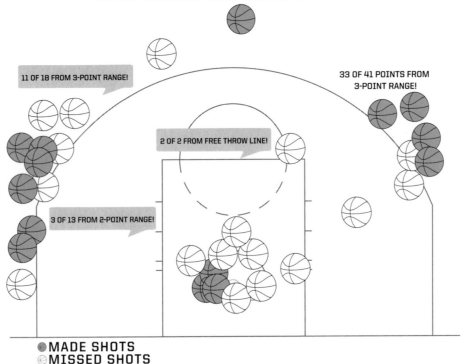

KLAY THOMPSON
GAME 6, 2016 WESTERN CONFERENCE FINALS
14 OF 31 FROM THE FIELD, 41 POINTS

11 OF 18 FROM 3-POINT RANGE!

33 OF 41 POINTS FROM 3-POINT RANGE!

2 OF 2 FROM FREE THROW LINE!

3 OF 13 FROM 2-POINT RANGE!

● MADE SHOTS
◉ MISSED SHOTS

by raining fire from beyond the arc. In 2015–16, Curry won the scoring title; he put up 30.1 points per game, over half of them coming on triples. Klay Thompson was the team's second-leading scorer; 10.5 of his 22.1 points per game came from beyond the arc. It's fair to say that the 2015–16 Warriors harnessed the power of the three-point shot better than any other team to ever step foot on an NBA court.

Speaking of Thompson, it was May 28, 2016, and the Warriors were playing the biggest game of their season to date. Down three games to two in the Western Conference Finals, the Dubs had their backs against the wall in Oklahoma City. A loss would not only eliminate them from the playoffs but also wash away the relevance of winning 73 games in the regular season. They didn't lose.

A quick glance at the box score shows us that Klay Thompson was on fire. That night he set an NBA playoff record by draining 11 threes. He nailed 11 of his 18 three-point attempts and ended up with 41 huge points in a massive must-win situation for his team. That game was arguably the most important performance of Golden State's run to history, a road win in an elimination game.

Closer inspection of the box score from that night shows us just how important the three-point line has become in the sprawlball era. That night the Warriors scored a ridiculous 63 of their 108 points from beyond the arc. As a team, they were 21 of 45 (47 percent) on triples, while just 15 of 43 (35 percent) on two-point shots. Fifty-one percent of their shots came from beyond the three-point line. This is crazy; recall that the league as a whole set a new record in 2015–16 when 28.5 percent of its field goal attempts came from three-point range. In the biggest game of the entire season, the league's defending champs made that 29 percent look minuscule. That night the Warriors not only took, and scored, a majority of their points from beyond the arc but also demonstrated something even crazier. They pretty much sucked inside the arc and still beat a very good opponent.

When we talk about the evolving aesthetic of the contemporary NBA, we often talk about the rapid rise in three-point shooting. That's fine, but what gets lost in that frame is that this rapid rise has to be accompanied by a rapid decrease elsewhere; after all, there are only so many shots in an NBA game, and if we're seeing a much higher share of threes, we must also be seeing a much lower share of twos. It's not rocket science, but one could easily argue that the most important game of the 2016 NBA Western Conference playoffs is exhibit A in the case against the future relevance of two-point shooting.

Looking at the Thunder's numbers from that night, we see a losing formula. While the Warriors rained down 21 threes and 63 points from beyond the arc, the Thunder made only three of their 23 triples (13 percent), resulting in nine lowly points. In short, through the lens

POINT DISTRIBUTION, GAME 6, 2016, WCF

Scoring Range	Points– Golden State Warriors	Points– Oklahoma City Thunder
Two-point area	30	70
Free throws	15	22
Three-point area	63	9
Total	108	101

Final score: Golden State 108, Oklahoma City 101; final score without the three-point line: Oklahoma City 98, Golden State 87.

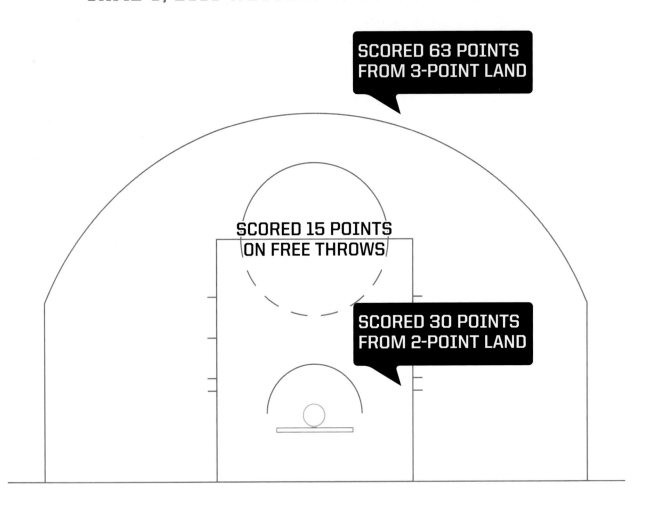

of the three-point shot, the Warriors were amazing and the Thunder were bad. It's no wonder OKC lost, right?

Well, looking inside the arc we see a very different set of performances. That night, in a losing effort, the Thunder converted 35 of 67 two-point shots (52 percent), and they racked up 52 points in the paint. Meanwhile, the Warriors were just 15 of 43 on two-pointers (35 percent) and ended up with only 28 points in the paint. In addition, the Thunder made seven more free throws than the Warriors.

Through the two-point lens, the Thunder seems to have had a much better night. But if Game 6 of the 2016 WCF showed us anything, it's that the two-point lens is a black-and-white TV in the time of the iPad. It's antiquated: just because you kick a team's ass in the paint and inside the arc, you're not necessarily going to win. Those days are gone. Just ask Klay Thompson—or maybe ask the 2015–16 Oklahoma City Thunder, who not only watched Curry break Twitter and steal a huge win from 37 feet in February 2016 but also watched Thompson rain holy hell and steal Game 6, and the Thunder's championship hopes, in May 2016.

As if those two episodes weren't bad enough, the Warriors weren't done stealing from the Thunder yet. In the summer of 2016, like thieves in the night, they stole Kevin Durant, the Thunder's best player, effectively ending the championship hopes of the Thunder franchise while all but cementing their own dynasty status. By the end of 2016, Durant's move to Oakland had taken the balance of power in the NBA with him; meanwhile, the balance of power on the NBA's playing surface had moved to the suburbs, beyond the arc.

Thirty-seven years after the NBA introduced its three-point arc, the 2015–16 Warriors reinvented the way to win games. Thompson's stellar performance from long range in Game 6 was followed by Curry and Thompson combining to drain 13 threes in Game 7 in Oakland, propelling the Warriors past the Thunder and into the NBA Finals for the second straight year.

They'd already won 73 games and shot their way back to the Finals. Now all they had to do to become one of the greatest teams ever was beat LeBron James again.

POP TIME

THE ARMS RACE ON THE OUTSKIRTS OF TOWN

AS SHOOTING HAS BECOME more and more important in the NBA, 3-point shots have become a mandatory skill for today's shooting guards. By 2018, NBA shooting guards were taking over 40 percent of their shots from three-point range. That's a lot, and it means that any young player who wants to be a starting shooting guard in the sprawlball era absolutely must be skilled when it comes to the era's most holy act: the catch-and-shoot three. For years, shooting guards just had to sink their jumpers, but with the three-ball's rising importance, much more is at stake: now the best shooting guards in the NBA aren't just the most accurate—they're really fast shooters too.

On April 5, 2017, the Cavs were in Boston playing the Celtics. The two teams were battling for the top seed in the Eastern Conference playoffs, which were set to start 10 days later. It was a big game for the upstart Celts, and their hometown fans were fired up. But the Cavs built an early lead and were up 10 just 16 minutes into the contest; the fans were already fading when the Cavs had the ball with a chance to build the lead even bigger. With 18 seconds on the shot clock, Deron Williams caught a swing pass from Iman Shumpert near the top of the arc. But Williams didn't hold the ball long, because he saw something he really liked—a future assist about to get its wings. Williams barely even caught the pass before redirecting the ball down to the left corner, where one of the world's most terrifying catch-and-shoot threats was eagerly awaiting the pass.

By the time Kyle Korver caught the ball, his defender, the half-man/half–golden retriever Kelly Olynyk, knew what he had to do: stop Korver from releasing his world-class jumper. The oafy Olynyk hurried his goofy seven-foot frame toward the corner, his long brown hair flying in the wind, and flailed up toward Korver. But he arrived a hair too late: Korver was too fast, and Olynyk was too slow. The rest was a formality. The Cavs went up by 13, and the Celtics called a time-out. The crowd fell silent. The game was never close after that. The Cavs didn't just win that game in Boston—they sent an obvious late-season reminder of who was the top dog in the Eastern Conference.

It's no secret that LeBron James, the chess master, loves to surround himself with great shooters; his best chess sets in Miami had rooks like Ray Allen, Mike Miller, and Shane Battier decorating the edges of his chess-board. When I interviewed James in 2013 for a *Grant-land* feature, he described his cadre of sharpshooting Heat teammates as "snipers." That's certainly evocative, but it may be more apt to describe them as "pistoleros" or "gunslingers"—the best shooters in the league aren't just hyper-precise snipers, but the fastest on the draw too. When James and the Cavs landed Korver in a mid-season trade in January 2017, they landed not only one of the most accurate sharpshooters on the planet, but one of the fastest.

That night in Boston, Korver's entire catch-and-shoot sequence against Olynyk lasted just a fraction of a second. From the moment he caught the ball to the mo-

ment he released his jumper, only 0.52 seconds elapsed. Olynyk never had a chance. Korver was Aaron Burr, and Olynyk was Alexander Hamilton.

"Bang!" exclaimed Mike Breen, the ESPN commentator. Had that corner shooter been somebody else, Olynyk might have successfully prevented the shot, but it was Korver, who just happens to be the fastest draw in the NBA.

When we talk about shooting effectiveness, we're quick to talk about accuracy, but we also need to consider speed. As threes become more and more important in our sport, the ability of guys to catch and shoot quickly will become increasingly prominent in our conversations about shooting ability.

The ability to make catch-and-shoot threes is hugely valuable in the NBA right now. Just ask J. J. Redick, who signed a $23 million, one-year contract in the summer of 2017. Redick is a fantastically skilled shooter, but only competent in other aspects of his game. But he represents a prototypical shooting guard right now. He's a player who can regularly win the duels out on the edge of the court that are increasingly determining the outcomes of NBA games. And for that reason, he's worth the money.

In a game-within-a-game scenario that plays out dozens of times per game in the sprawlball era, a catch-and-shoot specialist receives a pass, a nearby defender races at him, and either the shooter has time to get the shot off or he doesn't. Some shooters are simply much faster than others, which translates into more victories in the battles against closeout defenders. That, in turn, translates into the holiest of grails in the three-point era: heightened offensive efficiency.

It may seem trivial, but those moments—those close-out-defender versus spot-up shooter duels on the outskirts of town—often determine who wins a possession and who wins a basketball game. The best shooters not only make shots at a higher rate; they also, by being the quickest draws in the league, *get more of these lucrative opportunities* for their teams. As teams race to figure out new ways to increase three-point volume, they're going to wake up to an idea that baseball and football teams have known for years: stopwatches matter.

Most people, when they think of "open shooters," visualize the space separating a jump shooter and the nearest defender. In the catch-and-shoot era, however, it's not that simple. Being open involves both space and time as well as the individual shooting speed of the shooter. Thanks to his lightning-fast shot release, Korver is "open" in scenarios where slower shooters would not be. So defenders can stray only so far from Korver because they have less time to close out on him.

Paul Millsap

The Hawks traded Korver to Cleveland in January 2017, but they remained competitive and a few months later earned a first-round playoff matchup with the Washington Wizards.

It was a hard-fought series. The teams split the first four games before facing off in a pivotal Game 5 on April 26, 2017, at the Verizon Center in D.C. It's tough to win big road games in the NBA playoffs. It requires great players making big shots in big moments. Paul Millsap was the clearly the best player on the Hawks, and after he made a 12-foot jumper, he'd pulled his team within three points with 5:52 remaining in Game 5. Millsap and the Hawks had a chance to steal the game and take a 3–2 advantage back to Atlanta.

But Washington called a time-out, regrouped, and a couple of possessions later were up by seven with just under five minutes left. Atlanta needed a big bucket, and as Millsap caught a pass at the top of the arc, a three would be perfect. He was open and in one of his favorite spots. His defender, Otto Porter Jr., was out of position, caught napping at the free throw line. To stop Millsap's three, Porter would have to cover 10 feet by the time Millsap turned from pass catcher to jump shooter. It was almost the same predicament that Olynyk had found himself in a few months earlier in Boston.

But here's the thing: Millsap is one of the slowest shooters in the league. On average, it takes him about a third of a second longer than it takes Korver to get off his jumper. And in this case, he was too slow. By the time he got into his shot, Porter had arrived on the scene. Millsap's shot pocket is too clumsy for these high-speed challenges. In this race against time, Millsap lost and Porter's closeout won. The Hawks failed to score on that possession, and the Wizards went on to win by four points.

Now, there's no telling what would've happened if Millsap had gotten that shot off. He's not exactly Klay Thompson out there. But the point is that he didn't. In a league where clean catch-and-shoot threes are now an ideal outcome of a half-court possession, the fact that some of the league's shooters are much faster than others is a huge deal. Not only is Korver more accurate than Millsap, but he's so much faster that he'd probably have been able to turn that exact same catch-and-shoot

chance that Millsap had in Washington into a clean look. And not just any clean look—a Kyle Korver three-point catch-and-shoot attempt.

On the one hand, comparing Millsap to Korver is unfair. Millsap wasn't drafted into the NBA to be a catch-and-shoot threat. Korver was. However, times have changed since Millsap arrived in the NBA, and like most "power forwards" these days, he is obliged to stretch the floor and shoot threes. Hell, everybody has to do that now. It's another instance of the three-point line continuing to redefine the entire evaluative framework of pro hoops. Catch-and-release times never mattered 30 years ago. They do now.

In his first seven years in the NBA, Millsap didn't really shoot the three-ball. He didn't have to. He was a power forward, for crying out loud. Nowadays he has to. It's a story that has played out in frontcourts all over the NBA in the past decade. You can't be a traditional big anymore. You have to space the floor, and you have to learn to shoot threes. In his last year in Utah, the 2012–13 season, Millsap attempted only 0.5 threes per game; the following season, his first year in Atlanta, he tried 2.9 a game, and by 2016–17 that figure was up to 3.5 per game. For reference, Steve Kerr, the shooting specialist on one of the greatest teams of all time, never tried more than 2.9 per game. So much for being a power forward. In the time of the catch-and-shoot three, everyone has to be Steve Kerr—or at least do a Steve Kerr impression. Like Chris Bosh, Kevin Love, and Serge Ibaka, Millsap is just another power forward trying to transform his game in the midst of the three-ball era.

But while it's impressive that Millsap has become even a passable NBA three-point shooter on the fly, in the middle of his career, it's also unsurprising that his slothlike shooting mechanics lag far behind those of the catch-and-shoot specialists, like Korver, who have been practicing these shots their entire basketball lives.

Three-point shooting greatness is about a lot more than the ability to make 24-foot-jumpers. As the three-ball takes over the NBA, we need to consider a lot more than just three-point percentage when analyzing the league's most valuable skill set. And once again, when basketball needs to turn over a new analytical leaf, the best thing to do is to steal from baseball.

Pop Time from Baseball

Speaking of stealing, stolen bases remain one of baseball's most fascinating game-within-a-game scenarios. In 2012, J. J. Cooper published a fantastic piece in *Baseball America* that explores the difference between success and failure in the run game in baseball. It comes down to a trio of timing issues.

Cooper's analysis starts with the three main characters in the run game: the runner, the pitcher, and the catcher. While each of these players individually can determine the success of a stolen base attempt, the end result is usually a blend of their combined abilities.

A stolen base attempt is a race with three different kinds of racers, and you can't understand the run game without studying each of them. Some runners are faster than others, of course, but some pitchers are faster throwing to home plate than others, and some catchers are faster throwing to second base than others.

This isn't rocket science, but for years the roles played by pitchers and catchers were overlooked and stolen bases were a stat largely associated with runners. However, with advances in player tracking, baseball analysts are now able to dissect the run game with much greater depth and precision. In the last decade, analysts have enriched our understanding of which runners, pitchers, and catchers are good and bad in the run game.

With the new baseball tracking data shedding new light on the microeconomics of stolen bases, baseball analysts started to understand excellence in cool new ways, and perhaps nobody has earned more new-found appreciation than Iván "Pudge" Rodríguez. Rodríguez was inducted into the Baseball Hall of Fame in the summer of 2017, a few years after completing a remarkable 21-year career playing his sport's most difficult position. In addition to being coaches on the diamond, catchers have a defensive role that is by far the most grueling and most important in the game.

Simply put, Rodríguez was one of the best defensive catchers in the long history of baseball. Very few catchers have lasted long enough to catch 13 seasons in major league baseball; Pudge won 13 Gold Glove Awards and is also the all-time MLB leader in games caught, with 2,427. Make no mistake, he was a great offensive player too, but his defensive excellence is criminally underappreciated. He was Kawhi with a catcher's mitt. To win one Gold Glove as a catcher in major league baseball, you have to be adept at a laundry list of defensive tasks. You can't allow many passed balls, you have to be able to field bunts, you have to be able to chase down foul balls, and you have to be able to shut down the opponent's run game. Pudge won this award 13 times.

The baseball diamond is an immaculately designed playing surface. The basic geometry of the infield has withstood the test of time far better than the geometry of the basketball court has. Basketball is constantly adding new circles, delineating new areas, widening lanes, defining coaching boxes, and, of course, suddenly adding a three-point shot. Baseball has never added a new base or changed the shape of the diamond. As Cooper writes, "When Alexander Cartwright—or whoever first laid out a baseball diamond—put the bases 90 feet apart, he put them at an ideal distance to make the battle between base-stealers and batteries a fair fight."

But just as the greatest base stealers of all time are able to turn this into an unfair fight, so are the greatest catchers.

Although catchers are only one part of the trio of run game participants, they are arguably the most important; after all, everyday catchers like Rodríguez participate in more base-stealing episodes than any runner or pitcher ever will. So over the course of a season, the impact of a catcher's ability to throw out runners becomes greater than the individual impacts of runners and pitchers.

This is no secret, and for years we judged catchers according to the rate at which they were able to throw out base stealers. "Caught stealing percentage" is a commonly cited stat for MLB catchers that simply reports the rate at which they throw out potential base stealers. That's intuitive and useful to know, but it's not that insightful. Even though Rodríguez regularly led the league in this metric, it doesn't really explain his ability. Caught stealing percentage overlooks the abilities of two of the three participants in the run game. Some runners are faster than others, and some pitchers are slower than others. It's unwise to assign success and blame entirely to catchers.

Once a runner takes off and the pitcher hurls his pitch, it's up to the catcher to receive the pitch, pop out of his crouch, and fire the ball down to second base as fast as he can. Like Korver on a basketball court, catchers have to receive a ball and rapidly transition from catching mode to throwing mode before firing the ball the whole way across the diamond as hard and as accurately as they can. Naturally, some catchers are much faster than others at different parts of this process.

"Pop time" refers to the length of time from the instant a pitch hits a catcher's glove (and makes a popping sound) to the moment it strikes the glove of the infielder down at second base (and makes another popping sound). Pop time measures the time between the two pops. Catchers with the shortest pop times are the ones with the best footwork and the strongest arms. Generally speaking, a decent pop time at the big-league level is about two seconds. The best catchers clock in at around 1.85. In his prime, Pudge Rodríguez's pop time was consistently between 1.75 and 1.8 seconds.

At first glance, a difference of just fractions of a second in pop time may seem trivial, but it's not—it's the difference between a really good catcher and a poor one. The truth is that the sports we love aren't just "games of inches" but also "games of split-seconds," and these tiny timing differences often manifest in big differences between winning and losing. Just ask Usain Bolt or Michael Phelps.

Although his moniker doesn't evoke images of lightning-quickness, the truth is that Pudge was to catchers what Bolt was to sprinters and Phelps was to swimmers. Night after night after night throughout his long career, his pop time enabled his teams to greatly suppress the opponent's run game and keep base runners out of scoring position.

The introduction of timing metrics like pop time has significantly elevated baseball's understanding of the run game, and basketball is now ready for the same elevator ride. If the catch-and-shoot game is basketball's version of the run game, Kyle Korver is the Pudge Rodríguez of the NBA.

Pop Time in Hoops

Catch-and-shoot threes—the stolen bases of the three-ball era—have three main ingredients. The pass to the shooter is akin to the pitch, the shooter's ability to catch and shoot is akin to the pop time of the catcher, and the closeout of the defender is akin to the base runner taking off.

According to the NBA's player tracking data, between 2013 and 2017, NBA shooters attempted just under 110,000 pure catch-and-shoot threes. By "pure" we mean that the shooter simply received a pass from a teammate and immediately rose up and shot without relocating his feet. In other words, these were attempts

where the shooter could focus on catching and shooting, and his feet were already set.

On average, it took shooters 0.831 seconds between the moment the ball reached their hands and the instant they released their shots. Of course, some of these shots were more urgent than others—wide-open shooters and taller shooters can take a bit more time than contested ones can. Although over the course of hundreds of attempts, some shooters exhibited much faster or much slower times, on aggregate, that 0.831 represents a meaningful baseline. Between 2013 and 2017, nobody was as fast as Korver in catch-and-shoot scenarios.

The Rise of Catch-and-Shoot

In the three-ball era, the catch-and-shoot three is now one of the most common and most coveted outcomes for an offensive possession in the NBA. It's not hard to figure out why. As opposed to unassisted off-the-dribble threes, which normally involve a guarded player using a step-back move to create space from a nearby opponent, the catch-and-shoot three generally allows more balanced and open shooters a chance to be their best selves. The proof is in the numbers. Between 2013–14 and 2016–17, catch-and-shoot threes went in 37.6 percent of the time and were worth 1.13 points. They also increased in popularity in each of those four seasons: there were 20 pure catch-and-shoot threes per game in 2013–14, but by 2016–17 that number had ballooned to 25. Teams were chasing efficiency, and these threes were one of the best ways to catch it.

Keep in mind that after adding Kevin Durant to an already historically great offense, the 2016–17 Warriors averaged 1.13 points per possession; in other words, even an *average* NBA catch-and-shoot try over the past four seasons returns points at the exact same rate as one of the best NBA offenses we'll ever see. No wonder the catch-and-shoot triple is rapidly becoming the ideal outcome for many NBA offensive sets. In turn, the tactics and lineups we see on NBA floors are rapidly adapting to heighten the chances of this most highly valued outcome.

Over the past decade, coaches have increasingly designed schemes to increase catch-and-shoot threes. They "spread the floor" with shooters, they run more pick-and-rolls to collapse the edges of the defense, they post up less, and they strive to create transition and drive-and-kick situations. Not only do these tactics represent big departures from "old-school" hoops—in which teams designed plays to get good looks near the basket—but they are a direct by-product of the three-point stripe that the league suddenly added to its playing surface in 1979. Along with the forward pass in football, which was added in 1906, the addition of the three-point line is one of the most significant rule changes in American sports history.

As the league has slowly recognized the greatness of the catch-and-shoot three, general managers and front offices are adjusting their analytical assessments of personnel, placing a greater importance on anything and everything that can help them sink more of those almighty catch-and-shoot triples. Shooters like Korver and Redick are getting paid in ways that old-school specialists like Kerr or John Paxson never did.

In the early part of this decade, shooters who could drain 40 percent of their threes or more got paid increasingly high salaries. But now that all 30 teams have caught on to that basic idea, the next big thing in the NBA's catch-and-shoot arms race will have less to do with field goal percentage and more to do with speed.

Kyle Korver is an incredible shooter for two reasons. Everybody knows that he's got pinpoint accuracy, but his greatness extends beyond that: he's also one of the fastest shooters in the league. Korver's average pop time during the four-season span between 2013–14 and 2016–17 was 0.680 seconds. The league average was 0.831. Think about that: Korver can receive a passed basketball, bring it through his shot pocket, and release one of the world's most reliable 24-foot jumpers in the time it takes you to take a sip of a cappuccino.

Basketball is about to learn and value something that baseball and football have already known for years: speed matters.

Back when the NBA first installed the player tracking system, speed was one of the first things analysts started investigating. But those pioneering initial investigations concentrated almost entirely on the speed of ball handlers and transition defenders. To extend the baseball analogy, these early analyses were obsessing over the speed of base runners. That is obviously important, but to fully understand the successes and failures of the run game, you need to measure the speeds of the pitchers and catchers too.

In that first-round series against Washington, the 2016–17 Atlanta Hawks could have used a few more threes—not just the one Millsap couldn't get off in time, but many others like it. But Atlanta traded Korver to Cleveland midway through that season, and in doing so, they gave up not only their best shooter but their fastest shooter.

Like the run game in baseball, the catch-and-shoot game in the NBA essentially involves three characters: the assister, the shooter, and the shot defender. Virtually all catch-and-shoot tries are assisted, and obviously some players create better shots for their teammates than others. The best three-point creators not only collapse defenses and throw good passes but also exhibit great court vision, which enables them to detect defensive weaknesses. They can accurately project whether a potential pass can be caught and released by a good shooter before the shooter's defender arrives and tries to prevent it.

After the assister makes a good pass to a teammate, it's the skill of the shooter that propels a ho-hum perimeter catch into a three-point yield. Guys like Korver can do this both more reliably and more frequently than guys like Millsap. We know that the reliability comes from shot accuracy, but the frequency comes from speed. Each time a catch-and-shoot threat receives a potential assist from someone like LeBron, the race between the shooter and the shot defender begins. Can the shooter gather the pass, bring it through his shot pocket, raise it up to his release point, and get it off before his defender recovers and stops or blocks the attempt?

Kyle Korver is a lot more likely to do that than Millsap. Recall the average NBA catch-and-shoot release takes 0.831 seconds. If we consider fast attempts as ones that take less than 0.75 seconds, normal releases as ones that take between 0.75 and 0.9 seconds, and slow releases

as ones that take longer than 0.9 seconds, we can start to understand catch-and-shoot performances in new ways.

Between 2013–14 and 2016–17, 72 percent of Korver's 468 pure catch-and-shoot tries were fast, 20 percent were normal, and just 8 percent were slow. Moreover, he made at least 50 percent of his tries in each of those categories. His pistol is both one of the fastest and one of the most accurate in the world.

Meanwhile, only 6 percent of Millsap's 561 catch-and-shoot attempts qualified as fast, while 19 percent were normal and 75 percent were slow. And he made only 30 percent of his faster tries; he couldn't hold a candle to Korver in terms of either accuracy or speed.

By adding pop time into our shooting evaluations, we can start to see which NBA players can and can't get shots off in tighter quarters. Looking back at that Millsap opportunity in Game 5 against the Hawks, it's not just that Korver would have been more likely to make that shot—he also would have been more likely to *take* that shot. If Korver had caught the exact same pass as Millsap in that exact same place with Otto Porter Jr. out of position, he probably would have turned that catch into a clean release before Porter recovered. Millsap couldn't and didn't.

That kind of game-within-a-game race happens dozens of times per game in the sprawlball era. Those miniature battles determine the outcomes of possessions and games more and more these days, but incredibly, five years or more into the NBA's player tracking revolution, the pop time of our league's spot-up threats remains largely ignored. I guess this means that the bas-

THE QUICK AND THE DEADLY

Pure* catch-and-shoot numbers for the fastest and most accurate shooters between 2013–14 and 2016–17.

Shooter	3PM	3PA	3P%	Average Pop Time (in Seconds)	%3PA under 0.75 seconds
Kyle Korver	244	468	52.1	0.680	72.2
Klay Thompson	355	758	46.8	0.726	62.0
Khris Middleton	235	504	46.6	0.727	59.5
Evan Fournier	198	453	43.7	0.724	63.8
Allen Crabbe	148	344	43.0	0.739	59.9
Patty Mills	159	373	42.6	0.712	63.0
Channing Frye	357	841	42.4	0.728	63.3
Anthony Morrow	203	483	42.0	0.678	67.9
George Hill	171	414	41.3	0.740	59.9
C. J. Miles	251	613	40.9	0.738	58.7
Kent Bazemore	145	358	40.5	0.746	55.3
Hollis Thompson	179	444	40.3	0.740	56.8

* By "pure" we mean that the shooter simply received a pass from a teammate and immediately rose up and shot without relocating his feet.

ketball analytics community is a little more like Millsap than Korver.

Regardless, as shooting becomes by far the most valuable skill in the NBA, and as catch-and-shoot threes become the centerpiece of more and more offenses, our assessments of shooting ability will evolve to evaluate a lot more than whether or not a guy can make shots.

Three-point shooting in the NBA is an arms race, both literally and figuratively. As teams race to find ways to ramp up their three-point tries, the league's most valuable shooters will be the ones who combine speed and accuracy, and the league's litmus tests for three-point ability will expand.

Between 2013–14 and 2016–17, 140 NBA shooters attempted at least 300 pure catch-and-shoot tries. Of that

POP TIME

group, the 11 shooters listed in the table (previous page) combined accuracy and speed at the highest levels: they had an average pop time of less than 0.75 seconds, and they made at least 40 percent of their catch-and-shoot tries. As you can see, Korver is at the top of the list, being both the most accurate, making a whopping 52.1 percent of his catch-and-shoot threes, and the most likely to get his shot off in under 0.75 seconds.

Now, if you're anything like me, you're asking yourself, *What about Steph Curry?* Isn't he the fastest shooter in the NBA?

Well, he just barely missed the cut here because his average pop time during the study period was 0.77 seconds. Like Korver, he's crazy accurate. In the four-year study period, out of the 140 guys who had at least 300 catch-and-shoot tries, only Korver (52.1 percent) and Curry (54.0 percent) made over half of those shots, which is insane. But while fewer than 30 percent of Korver's tries took longer than 0.75 seconds to release, almost half of Curry's did.

It's not that Curry is slow: his average pop time is way quicker than the league average, and he made a ridiculous 50.6 percent of the attempts that he did manage to get off in less than 0.75 seconds. It's that, compared to Korver, he's more likely to be a hair slower on the trigger, and given the chance to be a tad more deliberate with his shot, he's more likely to take that chance than Korver is. And for good reason. Of the 89 catch-and-shoot threes on which Curry took between 0.75 and 0.9 seconds, he converted an absolutely ridiculous 60.7 percent. People aren't supposed to make 60.7 percent of their threes in a practice environment, let alone in a game environment. But Curry is the best shooter ever,

and part of that is the ability to shoot incredibly well at different speeds.

Those extra split-seconds only make him more dangerous, so why not take them if they're there?

This is where the analogy with baseball's pop time begins to break down. Catchers generally get the ball off to second base as fast as they can every time. Spot-up shooters may take a beat longer if they're wide open, and one of the perks of playing with the Golden State Warriors recently is a lot of wide-open shots, even for sharpshooters like Thompson and Curry.

Great three-point numbers are a by-product of both great individual shooters and great shooting environments. For the last few years, thanks to great tactics, great passing, and multiple threats around the court, the Warriors have had the best jump-shooting environment in the NBA. And that can get lost if we simply apply average pop time to individual shooters and assume that it is a useful proxy for a shooter's ability to be fast. Sometimes a longer pop time simply reflects a better shooting situation and a shorter time a more contested situation.

Still, when Curry needs to be fast, he can be—and he can still convert at great rates too. Many other shooters can't say that. In fact, the ability to shoot fast when you need to is an increasingly important skill, and one that many of the game's other top stars simply don't possess. Between 2013–14 and 2016–17, LeBron James had an average pop time of 1.03 seconds, a quarter of a second slower than Curry. John Wall's was at 1.03 too. Chris Paul was even slower still, at 1.07. That means that by the time Korver has let his shot go, players like Wall,

Shooter	3PM	3PA	3P%	Average Pop Time (in Seconds)	%3PA under 0.75 seconds
Jared Sullinger	102	358	28.5	1.092	1.4
DeMarcus Cousins	130	356	36.5	1.028	2.8
John Wall	163	426	38.3	1.027	3.3
Paul Millsap	191	549	34.8	1.014	6.0

Paul, and James are still in the middle of their shot. And that means that Korver will turn more of his potential three-point attempts into actual three-point attempts than almost anyone else. He's "open" when other guys aren't—other guys like Korver's old teammate Paul Millsap, who was one of the four slowest shooters in the study.

Not only are these guys slow as molasses, but they aren't very accurate either. As catch-and-shoot threes become more and more important to NBA success, our ability to evaluate the skills associated with them will also become more important. To that end, it's clear that while accuracy is probably the most valuable trait of a shooter, speed is very important too.

THE INVESTOR

JAMES HARDEN

ON DECEMBER 26, 2013, the Rockets were at home playing the Grizzlies. Houston was tired. 'Twas the night after Christmas and the second night of a back-to-back. The Rockets were in San Antonio a day earlier beating the defending Western Conference champs. But that's life in the NBA. Another day. Another city. Another game. It doesn't matter that you're gassed or that you're sad you spent Christmas on an airplane or in a River Walk hotel—there's a game to play.

So the weary Rockets laced them up and took the floor. They looked like shit. All of their top players were struggling from the field. Dwight Howard was only one-for-five and ended up with two points. Jeremy Lin was five-for-13, and Chandler Parsons was five-for-12. Nobody was making buckets, especially the team's superstar offensive force, James Harden, who was just two-for-nine.

During that season, Harden was emerging as a scoring wunderkind. In an average game that year, Harden would be eight of 17 and put up 25 points. But that night in Memphis, Harden made just two of his nine shot attempts. He looked tired, and his shot just wasn't falling. It was not his night.

Or was it? A quick review of the box score from that night reveals that Harden still ended up with 27 points, more than his season average. Twenty-seven points on just two made field goals?! How in the heck does that even happen?

Well, it doesn't happen very often, and that's an understatement. That night in Memphis, Harden became the first player in NBA history to register 27 points on two or fewer made field goals. And he led his team to a victory in the process. The Rockets somehow overcame poor shooting from all their top players and won the game 100–92. Here's a snippet from the Associated Press summarizing the game:

> HOUSTON—James Harden and the Houston Rockets found their legs in time to get another big win.
>
> Harden scored 11 of his 27 points in the fourth quarter, helping Houston rally for a 100–92 victory over the Memphis Grizzlies on Thursday night.
>
> Coming off an impressive 111–98 win at San Antonio on Christmas, coach Kevin McHale

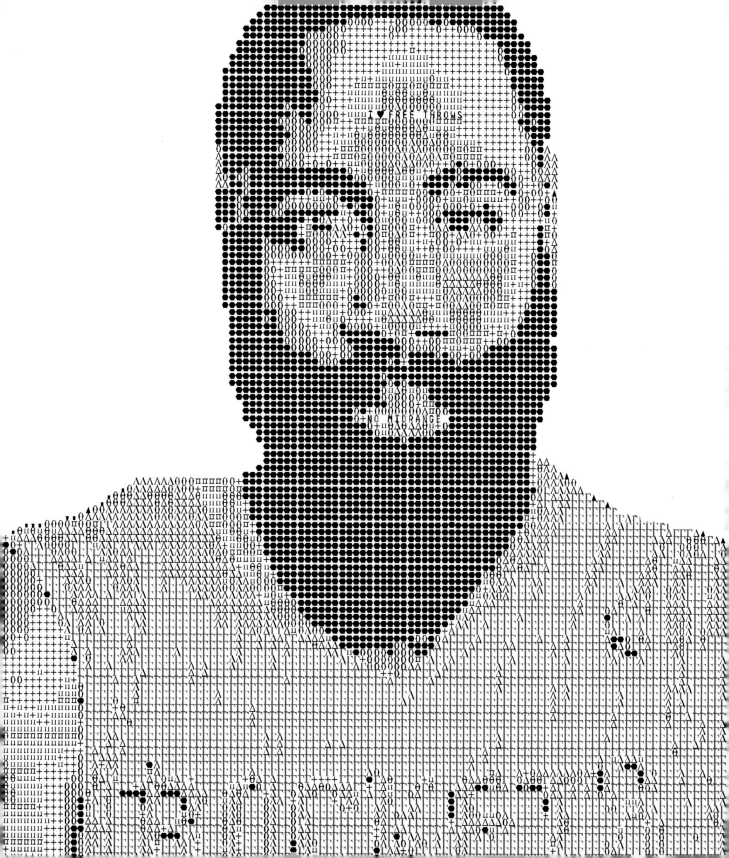

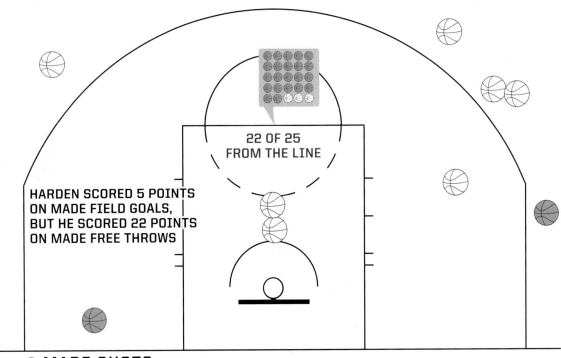

22 OF 25
FROM THE LINE

HARDEN SCORED 5 POINTS
ON MADE FIELD GOALS,
BUT HE SCORED 22 POINTS
ON MADE FREE THROWS

MADE SHOTS
MISSED SHOTS

said he could tell the Rockets were "draggy" during the pregame shootaround. But they still managed to outscore the Grizzlies 34–20 in the final period of their third victory in four games.

Harden struggled from the field, going 2 for 9, but was a career-best 22 of 25 from the free throw line. He made 9 of 11 foul shots in the final quarter while matching a Rockets sin-gle-game record for made free throws set by Sleepy Floyd in 1991.

How do you turn two made field goals into 27 total points? Easy, you make 22 free throws.

Harden earned five points from the field, and 22 points from the line. It wasn't pretty, but it worked. Just go ahead and engrave that phrase on Harden's tombstone now: IT WASN'T PRETTY, BUT IT WORKED.

Harden as Investor

Harden is one of the savviest players in the game, a 21st-century fox outwitting everyone playing 20th-century hoops. More than any other scorer in the league, his scoring portfolio skews toward the most analytically efficient scoring options available and away from high-risk, low-reward options. He thinks like a great investor; he is the Gordon Gecko of the NBA.

More than any other great scorer playing ball right now, Harden is keenly aware that the "charity stripe" is simply the cheapest place to buy points in the NBA marketplace.

Although many NBA fans hate to admit it, drawing a foul, particularly a shooting foul, is an extremely effective basketball play. On the playground, fouls are less common and free throws don't exist. Playground fanta-

sies rarely include trips to the line. But within the reality of the NBA, fouls are among the most potent stratagems in the league. Drawing personal fouls threatens to sideline or disqualify opponents, and drawing shooting fouls—the holy grail of Harden's offensive game—generates points at freakishly high rates: the average shot in the NBA is worth exactly 1.02 points, but the average two-shot trip to the line in the NBA is worth 1.5 points. For Harden, who happens to be a very good free throw shooter, that figure swells to 1.7 points.

By shooting 85 percent from the line, when Harden earns a two-shot foul, he essentially creates one of the most valuable possible outcomes on the floor. To the chagrin of some, here is one of the NBA's ugly truths: an offensive possession that ends in a shooting foul is one of the best events an offense could hope for, especially when the free throw shooter is competent. FAN-tastic!!

The numbers are startling.

Consider this: between 2013–14 and 2015–16, 61 NBA shooters attempted at least 150 wide-open three-point shots (threes where the closest defender was at least eight feet away from the shooter at the time of the shot), and unsurprisingly, of that group, nobody made a higher share of those wide-open triples than Steph Curry. During that three-year span, Curry was the most terrifying offensive force in the league in part because he drained a whopping 52.9 percent of 189 wide-open threes. That translates to 1.59 points per shot. Incredible.

We all know that leaving the best shooter in the game wide open from beyond the arc is never a good idea, but leaving Curry wide open from behind the three-

point line is still a better defensive strategy than hacking Harden and sending him to the free throw line, which happens a lot more per game than wide-open Curry threes do.

Crime and Punishment

Crime and punishment are huge tropes in popular culture for a reason. How a society defines crimes says a lot about its values; how a society punishes violators says more. There's a reason why so many of the shows on primetime television explore law and order. Laws and law enforcement provide very convenient windows into the soul of a culture, and sports is another arena reflecting the zeitgeist of a place and time. Naismith engineered basketball as a new sport that would maximize action while minimizing physical contact. He wanted to create a venue for young men to be very athletic but not to roughhouse. As a result, many of the sport's violations have to do with players "creating contact" with others in the game.

In virtually every game and every sport, "fair play" is paramount—and those who violate the sacred principle of fairness must face the consequences. As a result, the world's sports all have their own penal codes, and their systems of law and law enforcement are the most important mechanisms to achieve fair play.

Take FIFA (Fédération Internationale de Football Association), which not only is the biggest sports organization on the planet but also has one of the most thorough and standardized rulebooks anywhere. And it has to, because soccer is the most popular sport in the world. It's a beautiful game enjoyed by billions of people (and gamblers) around the globe.

Back in the summer of 2014, I was just another casual American soccer fan mesmerized by the World Cup. I loved how all of the nations came together for this great event. I loved the suspense. I loved the pageantry. But like many Americans, I hated the flopping and the diving. It's a cliché take at this point, but there's something maddening about watching an athlete writhing around in phony pain, begging for a ref's holy intervention.

It's fair to say that this kind of pleading happens in every sport, but in soccer it happens too much for my taste. Back in 2014, I wasn't content just to complain about the begging in soccer. I needed to obsess about it. I needed to analyze it. I needed to write about it.

On June 29, 2014, Mexico was on the verge of making history. They were up 1–0 late in their round-of-16 match against the Netherlands, and they looked certain to advance to the quarterfinals. But after giving up a late equalizer in the 88th minute, the Mexicans were now trying to stave off heartbreak in extra time. They couldn't do it. Four minutes into extra time, Arjen Robben, the cagey Dutch forward, was wreaking havoc in the Mexican box when his foot met the cleat of a Mexican defender. Robben felt the contact and went to work. He knew just what to do. He dramatically flew groundward. His arms flailed, his head shot back, and his apoplectic face cried out in the form of a sweaty Greek tragedy mask.

As his body hit the turf, the referee blew his whistle and awarded the Dutch side the most coveted opportunity in the sport, a penalty kick. They didn't miss. They won. Mexico went home.

I was rooting for Mexico that day. And even though it wasn't the first time a penalty kick had decided a match, for me this was a particularly cruel example of the massive importance of crime and punishment in soccer. Sure, Mexico had dozens of other chances that day, but it was clear to me that the refs and that sudden interpretation of FIFA code represented the main inflection point in Mexico's World Cup run and the way it ended that afternoon.

Penalty kicks are the most valuable event types in soccer, whether fans want to admit it or not (but they all know it). I wanted to quantify this value with data. Fortunately, it being summer in America and a slow time on the sports calendar, my editors at *Grantland* were encouraging everyone at the site to produce loads of World Cup content; on the heels of the Mexican heartbreak, I proposed a quick piece about crime and punishment and the relative value of penalty kicks at the World Cup. So, like Robben, I went to work. I knew exactly what to do.

I wanted to verify one simple fact: penalty kicks are by far the best shots in the sport. So I mapped out thousands of shots and their probability of scoring and compared them to the probability of scoring from the penalty spot. The results were clear, and I wrote the following passage:

> Just as basketball coaches love to say that the best place to score on the court is at the free throw line, soccer exhibits a parallel trait: the best place to score in the World Cup is at the penalty spot. Consider this pair of facts:
>
> 1. During the group stage of the 2014 World Cup, players attempted 1,236 shots on goal; they converted 10 percent of them. Even within 5 yards of the goal, players still

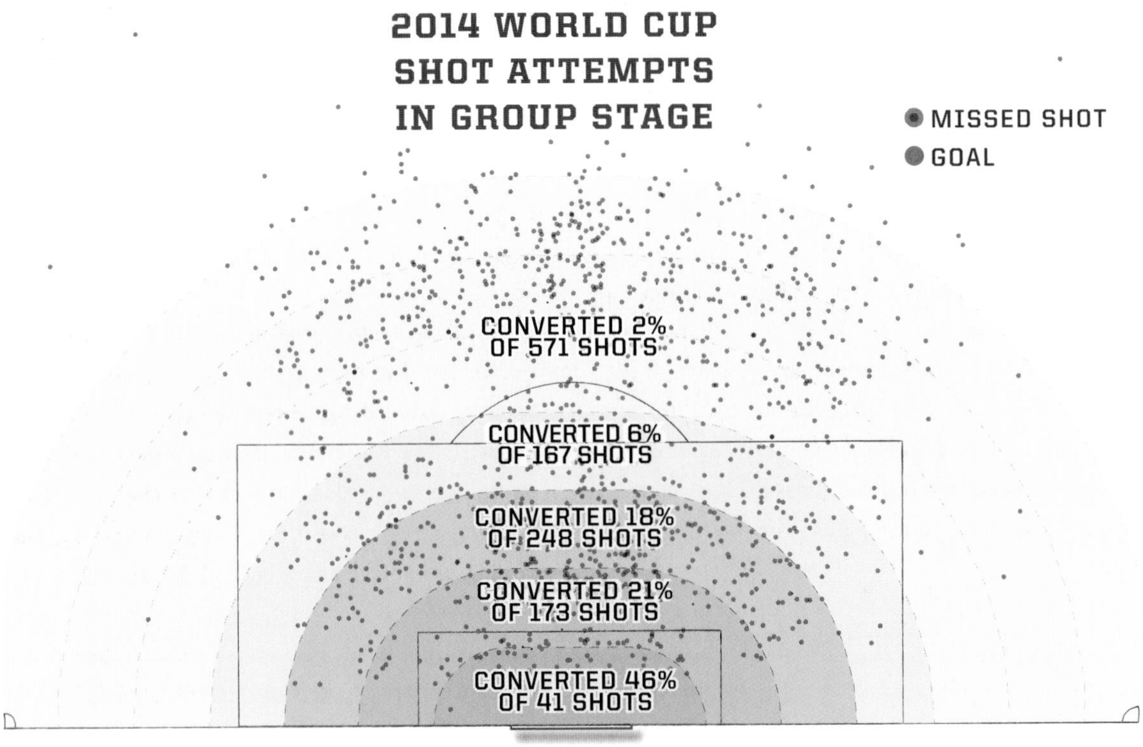

2014 WORLD CUP SHOT ATTEMPTS IN GROUP STAGE

● MISSED SHOT
● GOAL

CONVERTED 2%
OF 571 SHOTS

CONVERTED 6%
OF 167 SHOTS

CONVERTED 18%
OF 248 SHOTS

CONVERTED 21%
OF 173 SHOTS

CONVERTED 46%
OF 41 SHOTS

fail to convert even half of their shots (per Opta).

2. Since 1966, players have converted 81 percent of World Cup penalty kicks (also per Opta).

In other words, the best shots on goal at the World Cup almost always follow the sound of a whistle, something that savvy players like Arjen Robben are keenly aware of.

That the expected value of any penalty shot far exceeds that of almost any other "live play" scenario is not just some wonky sta-

tistical quirk. This is why Rafael Márquez's "trip" so easily "felled" Robben on Sunday. Although Robben was undeniably threatening the Mexico defense, even the slight opportunity to draw a whistle—and a subsequent PK—at the moment Márquez's boot disrupted his stride was too alluring to pass up. So Robben fell. And then the whistle blew. And, fair or not, Mexico went home.

While many hot takes today will surround the practice of diving, perhaps yesterday's events should also prompt a discussion about the underlying motivations for diving in the first place. Instead of putting the entire onus on the competitors to "do the right thing" in the heat of the biggest matches of their lives, why not examine the wild punitive imbalances that provide the root cause of the problem?

Penalty kicks are the most draconian and most influential penalties in any sport. This is compounded by a needlessly inflexible penal code, applied within an arbitrary box, that disables referees from exercising any sort of reasonable judgment. The problem isn't that Márquez may or may not have fouled Robben in the penalty area, nor is it that Robben may or may not have dove. The problem is the game's current system of on-field justice.

The fact that Márquez's incidental foul is punished the exact same way as exponentially more egregious acts, like Luis Suárez's intentional (game-saving) handball in 2010, is ludicrous. One is a misdemeanor, one is a felony, but in a world where no such distinctions exist, the sentences are identical, and the governing body errs on the side of punitive adjudication each and every time. In FIFA County, you go to the gallows for stealing a horse. You also go there for littering.

The point of the piece was simple: hate the game, not the player. Of course players like Robben should flop and flail like maniacs when they sense contact in the box: thanks to the rules of the game, if they draw a whistle and a penalty kick, they're awarded an almost certain goal. Penalty kicks result in situations that are much more likely to produce a goal than virtually any other in-game scenario. Drawing a foul like Robben did is a magnificent play.

The same holds true in the NBA. Fouls are a huge part of NBA basketball. It turns out that when you get 10 hyper-athletic, uber-competitive guys together on a basketball court, you also need to get at least three officials involved to regulate the action. But what started as a basic regulatory necessity has evolved, and today the league's refs and their whistles have become a huge part of strategy. Players are incentivized—arguably perversely—to manufacture these whistles.

Harden as Foul Magnet

Just ask James Harden, America's answer to Arjen Robben.

As a general rule, the average NBA possession is worth almost exactly one point. So one way to evaluate the value of players is to evaluate the value of the possessions they finish as individuals. Steph Curry is a two-time MVP not just because he can score a lot of points, but because on average virtually every shot he takes is a very efficient use of his team's possession. Rarely do you hear an announcer say, "Curry with a terrible shot!" No, it's quite the opposite: every time Curry even launches a shot for his team, you can sense the excitement from the fans and the hometown announcers. The fans may not know the specific math, but they know the simple fact that any Curry field goal attempt is good for the Warriors. Those oohs and ahhs that accompany the

hoopward flight of every Curry three-point attempt offer informal proof that he is a very valuable offensive threat.

But here's the contradiction: there are no oohs and ahhs when Harden draws yet another shooting foul. Despite the fact that our bearded free throw artisan is actually creating more points on average with each shooting foul drawn than Curry does with a wide-open three, and despite the fact that Harden, like Curry, has truly

mastered one of the most valuable acts in the game, Harden's signature trick fails to capture the hearts of NBA fans the same way Curry can.

The Rockets don't care. They care more about analytics than aesthetics. Their offense is like an MIT Sloan Sports Analytics Conference fever dream come true. More than any other team in league history, the Rockets obsess over numerical margins. They love "threes, frees, and layups" because on average these shots accrue points at higher rates than other attempts, particularly two-point jump shots, which are the Rockets' least favorite shot types.

Harden is a perfect leader for this approach.

In the 2014–15 season, he drew 542 fouls on opponents, by far the most in the league. That translates into almost seven calls per game. Think about that. A defensive player fouls out anytime he commits six fouls per game. Harden draws almost seven in an average game! This is remarkable, especially considering the fact that Harden is a guard, not a forward or a center. Most fouls in the NBA occur close to the basket. In fact, over 80 percent of the league's shooting fouls occur in the paint, and almost 60 percent of them occur in the tiny area right in front of the basket.

Therefore, any player who wants to lead the league in fouls drawn or free throws has to be active and physical

CONCENTRATION OF SHOOTING FOULS IN THE NBA 2013-14 TO 2016-17

BETWEEN THE 2013-14 AND 2016-17 SEASONS, NBA OFFICIALS CALLED 102,013 SHOOTING FOULS

ONLY 4% OF SHOOTING FOULS OCCURRED BEYOND THE 3-POINT LINE

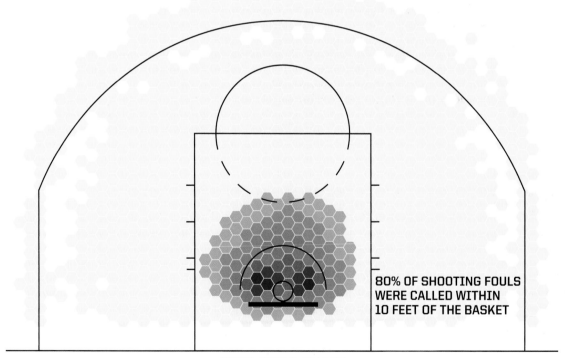

80% OF SHOOTING FOULS WERE CALLED WITHIN 10 FEET OF THE BASKET

TOTAL FOULS CALLED

5 200 400 600 800 1,000 1,200 1,400

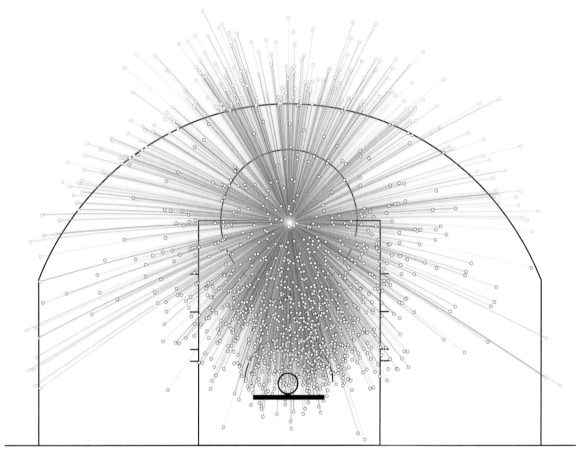

S
P
R
A
W
L
B
A
L
L

near the rim. With that in mind, it's no surprise that big ol' bruisers like DeMarcus Cousins and Joel Embiid are always at the top of these leaderboards. After all, they make their money by outmuscling opponents in the restricted area. But Harden isn't like those guys. He doesn't live and work in the paint; he just commutes there for meetings with important officials.

Perhaps more than any other player in league history, Harden has mastered the art of driving toward the bucket and drawing a shooting foul. A vast majority of his trips to the free throw line originate far away from the basket, but whereas normal attack guards are like basket-seeking missiles, Harden is a whistle-seeking missile. At times, he seems much more interested in drawing contact than in making a shot. Sure, he can make lefty layups all day given the chance, but unless he's getting a clean look at an easy layup, Harden's modus operandi is simple: convince a ref to call a foul and send the beard to his happy spot, the free throw line.

Hate the game, not the player. Just because the incentives are perverse doesn't mean the player is. Harden is brilliant. He combines equal parts athleticism, speed, intellect, and drama to architect sequences that get him to the line. It all starts with his patented Eurostep. Actually, he does not own the patent on the Eurostep—that belongs to Manu Ginobili, the greatest South American player in NBA history. Like any great player from a "soccer country," Ginobili knew the value of whistles a decade before the Rockets. Ginobili was Harden before Harden was Harden.

Ginobili is partially responsible for introducing the NBA to the Eurostep, a move so technically savvy that early in Ginobili's NBA career officials, struggling to determine its legality, often incorrectly called Ginobili for traveling in his rookie campaign.

What is the Eurostep? Well, it's an offensive maneuver that enables a driving player to more effectively attack the basket by introducing a change of direction right after the player gathers his dribble and approaches the basket. As the inimitable Jonathan Abrams described it in the *New York Times* in 2010, the Eurostep is "a move in which a player drives past a defender by stepping one way and then quickly taking a big lateral step in the other direction. The move is a crafty way to distribute the two steps allocated to a player after he stops drib-

bling, and it goes right to the edge of being a traveling violation."

The move maximizes the value of the driver's legally allowed two steps. A Eurostepping attacker essentially takes two big hops: one goes one way, the other goes a different way. It's a pain in the ass to defend. The first hop is what a defender often tries to guard, and then the hop back in the other direction creates either a clean look at the basket or enough contact with a flailing defender to produce a shooting foul.

Prior to the Eurostep, traveling was a pretty cut-and-

dry infraction. But when Ginobili and others started to figure out that you can become a much more effective rim-attacker if you perfectly time the gather of your dribble with your footwork, traveling became harder to correctly detect. And like Abrams said, these guys were flirting with the edge of a violation, making officiating more difficult.

A conventional driving shot in the NBA has three components: the dribble drive, the gather, and the actual shot attempt. If a player is fouled anytime after he gathers his dribble and attempts a shot, that qualifies as a shooting foul.

Morey + Harden

The brilliance of the Eurostep is that it greatly elongates the shooting foul "window" in both time and space. Eurostep maestros like Ginobili and Harden are more likely than other players to draw shooting fouls as they pivot and slither their way to the basket. Like snakes winding through a woodpile, they're able to change directions and find crevices or contact in ways that traditional drivers simply cannot. By optimizing the segue between their dribble-drive and their gather, they extend the act of shooting and interact with more potential foulers between their gather and their driving shot attempts.

On the one hand, this isn't rocket science; on the other, it's remarkable that more players aren't copying these guys. You can't throw a scatterplot at the Sloan Conference without hitting someone who'll tell you about the analytical genius of the corner three. Aside from dunks and layups, it's the best shot on the floor. That may be true, but even those corner threes, which are worth about 1.2 points per shot league-wide on average, can't hold a candle to the value of a pair of free throws.

Free throws are the real corner threes of the NBA. But even though they're the smartest shots on the floor, there's a curious silence about the charity stripe. More disciples of basketball analytics need to testify on the fact that a pair of Harden free throws are worth more than a wide-open Curry three-point attempt.

Simply put, the apostles of analytics can learn a lot by studying our bearded prophet down in Houston.

Aesthetically, Harden is the most influential player in the world right now. His game—a manifestation of the current trends in offensive basketball—is a prophecy.

The exact things that make him such an unusual superstar serve as a harbinger of what's to come.

And it's about more than just his free throws.

The Rockets' Offensive Philosophy

When Daryl Morey, Houston's general manager and the NBA's most powerful nerd, landed Harden in the most lopsided trade of the 21st century, he acquired not only the superstar he coveted but the perfect instrument for his numbers-driven basketball lab. The pairing quickly became the most harmonious player-GM combo in the NBA. Harden plays a brand of basketball that beautifully conforms to his GM's innovative visions.

Everyone who follows the NBA knows that the Rockets' offensive philosophy is built around threes and shots in the paint; they avoid the midrange the same way Charles Barkley avoids kale. The art of the midrange is dying across the NBA, but it's going extinct much faster down in Houston. The Rockets' offense is invested almost exclusively around the hoop, behind the three-point line, and, of course, at the free throw line.

In Morey's worldview, even a below-average three-pointer or paint shot is a better investment than a good shot in the midrange. As a result, in 2014–15 the team scored a minuscule 6.2 percent of its points in the midrange, and it's happy to sacrifice efficiency in its favorite spaces in favor of volume. While some stubborn old-timers turn a blind eye to the newfangled ways of the NBA, Morey and Harden bask in their glow.

An old-fashioned glance at Houston's shooting numbers suggests that the Rockets are an inefficient jump-shooting team. Though technically true, that impression is misleading. According to Morey's Law, being slightly "inefficient" within an efficient area is better than being efficient inside an inefficient area. Thanks to their lopsided shot distribution, by 2015 the Rockets remained among the NBA's top 10 most efficient jump-shooting outfits.

By 2018, Harden had become Morey's lawyer and ridden Morey's Law to the very top of the NBA. During the 2017–18 season, adhering to the "threes, frees, and layups" doctrine, Houston won more games and achieved a higher offensive efficiency rating than any other outfit in the NBA.

The Rockets are Harden's team: his individual shot chart is a microcosm of the team as a whole. At a glance, this does not look like the chart of one of the best scorers in the world. Harden is only an average shooter in almost all of his active shooting areas.

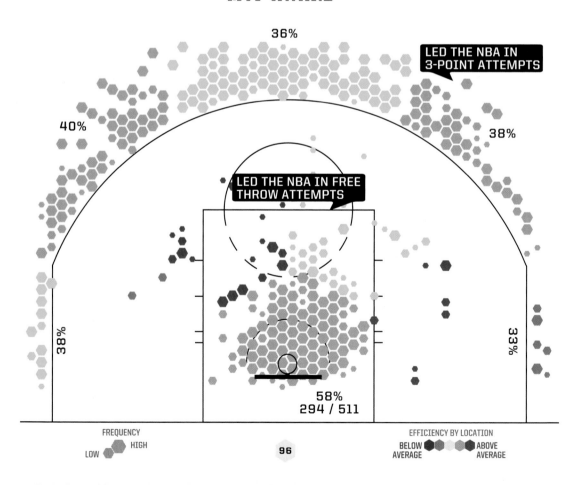

JAMES HARDEN
2017-18
MVP AWARD

36%

LED THE NBA IN 3-POINT ATTEMPTS

40%

38%

LED THE NBA IN FREE THROW ATTEMPTS

38%

33%

58%
294 / 511

S
P
R
A
W
L
B
A
L
L

FREQUENCY
HIGH
LOW

EFFICIENCY BY LOCATION
BELOW AVERAGE   ABOVE AVERAGE

Unlike players like Kevin Durant, Kawhi Leonard, or Steph Curry, Harden's jump-shooting efficiency doesn't jump off the page. There's very little dark red on that chart. Yet he still achieves wonderful offensive efficiency overall. How can a merely above-average shooter be one of the league's most ferocious offensive players? Easy. Morey's Law. Harden achieves world-class volume in the court's most efficient zones: near the rim, at the line, and beyond the arc. In his MVP campaign, he led the league in three-point shots and free throw attempts. He also forgoes almost any activity in the analytical no-no zones of the midrange. It's a simple plan and a clean road map to effectiveness. And a prophecy. Make no mistake: just because Harden is the first superstar to almost perfectly align his shot selection with analytics, he will not be the last.

To really appreciate Harden, you need to dive deeper than a basic shot chart; you need to recognize a couple of things he does as well as or better than anyone else playing the game right now.

Getting to the Line

We've already addressed this, but here's a stat that really puts Harden and his free throws into perspective: when he won the MVP in the summer of 2018, he became the first MVP in NBA history who had more made free throws than made field goals over his career at the time of his award. By the end of the 2017–18 season, Harden had converted 4,656 field goals, compared to 4,850 made free throws. Those shooting fouls are very valuable.

Although, it's not a common stat, Harden led the NBA in free throw attempts and made free throws four years in a row, culminating in that MVP campaign of 2017–18.

The Arc-hitect

Simply stated, in a league quickly realizing the ridiculous value associated with three-point shots, Harden is the NBA's best creator of these events. Guards create threes in two main ways: for themselves, and for their teammates. By 2018, Harden had become as good as Curry at creating unassisted triples and as good as LeBron James at creating threes for his teammates.

At some point in the middle of this decade, the unassisted three-point shot became one of the fastest-growing shot types in the NBA. In the 2013–14 season, NBA shooters tried 8,626 unassisted three-pointers, and by 2017–18 NBA shooters tried 14,483 of them.

In many ways, the unassisted three is the signature weapon of our era's biggest stars. Here's a list of NBA MVPs since 2011:

> 2011–12, LeBron James
> 2012–13, LeBron James
> 2013–14, Kevin Durant
> 2014–15, Steph Curry
> 2015–16, Steph Curry
> 2016–17, Russell Westbrook
> 2017–18, James Harden

All of these fellas love unassisted threes. Just as Steph Curry relied on unassisted threes to generate his record-setting three-point seasons, by 2018 Harden was relying on them as the centerpiece of his jump-shooting portfolio. And that's an understatement.

Watching the 2017–18 Rockets was really just an exercise in watching Harden in isolation sets. Generally speaking, three of his teammates would decorate the corners and wings beyond the arc, and Clint Capela would hang around the paint, which provided Harden with all the room he needed near the top of the floor to play his game.

Harden's game in a nutshell involves dribbling the ball, threatening the defense, keenly observing its reaction to said threat, then making a play. Typically, that play falls into one of a few categories: an unassisted three-point shot, a drive to the basket, or a potential assist to a spot-up shooter.

Nobody shot more unassisted threes than Harden did in 2017–18. During the regular season, he tried 564 of them, or 7.8 per game; Damian Lillard ranked second by trying 372. Harden's unassisted triples tend to cluster near the top of the arc. He's the quarterback of the Rockets, and that's his pocket. He triggers most of his half-court actions there, so it's no surprise that's where he shoots the most threes from. But that doesn't answer how he gets them.

Like Curry, Harden prefaces most of his unassisted triples with a lot of ball handling. In fact, of all the unassisted volume shooters in the NBA, nobody likes to dribble more before shooting than Harden. In 2017–18, 38 NBA players attempted at least 100 unassisted threes, but none of them dribbled as much as Harden before taking them. On average, Harden dribbled 8.2 times before launching one of his self-made three-point attempts.

To watch Harden is to watch a man pound the air out of the ball near the top of the arc, rocking back and forth, occasionally flinching like he's going to attack the paint, all the while reading every minuscule lean of his defender. More than any player in NBA history, Harden uses dribbling as a way to mess with the balance of his opponents. As soon as he sees a flaw in the defensive stance of his man, he pounces. If you lean one way, he'll shoot in your face; if you lean the other, he'll drive right past you. Harden also ranked third in 2017–18 in the NBA by logging 1,378 drives. Of the 69 players who logged at least 500 drives that year, only LeBron James was more efficient: Harden's drives yielded an average of 1.16 points, compared to James's 1.18.

During the 2017–18 season, nobody shot more than Harden at the top of the arc. Almost four times per game, Harden would take an off-the-dribble three near the top of the arc. Many of them came after he dribbled away the balance of an isolated defender; many came after he dribbled his way around a ball screen. Regardless, you can't grasp the art of Harden without grasping the basic notion that he creates much of his three-point productivity off his own dribbles.

But he is by no means selfish. Harden is the most prolific unassisted three-point creator on the planet, but he creates opportunities for others as well. In fact, Harden is also one of the most prolific creators of three-point offense for teammates. When you sum up his unassisted threes and the assisted threes he creates for teammates, you get one of the most definitive stats of the 2017–18 NBA season.

Between creating his own threes and creating threes for his buddies, Harden engineered a whopping 16.3 three-point attempts per game. His ability to create and manifest shooting opportunities for his fellow

Rockets is probably the most overlooked part of his game, which is crazy, because nobody in the world is better at it.

During the middle 2010s, Harden evolved into the perfect catalyst for Houston's three-happy strategies. Although he always ranks high in assists per game, that stat deceptively undersells him, as he ranks higher in points created via assists. Why the jump? Because 3 > 2. In short, Harden leads the NBA in assists that lead to three-point shots and is the best player in the league at creating tasty catch-and-shoot looks for his teammates.

Morey and Mike D'Antoni love their players to shoot threes, but there's more to shooting tons of threes than just deciding to take more long-range shots. Generating three-point offense has just as much to do with playmaking and assisting as it does with actually shooting and making those shots; over 80 percent of the league's triples (and 96 percent of its corner threes) are assisted.

In other words, any team hell-bent on shooting more threes needs to be looking to create more threes. For most of the decade, nobody was as prolific as LeBron James at generating those long-range buckets for teammates, but by 2019 Harden had become the king of this increasingly important skill.

What started with Morey's vision, fed through D'Antoni's brilliant offensive tactics, became fully realized in Harden's impeccable execution. The result is the most three-happy offensive machine in NBA history. The 2017–18 Rockets became the first team in the history of the league to shoot more threes than twos. That may sound like a trivial accomplishment, but given the cur-

TOTAL THREES CREATED 2017-18 SEASON

(Unassisted Threes Made + Assisted Threes Created for Teammates)

1. James Harden	1,177
2. LeBron James	1,153
3. Russell Westbrook	1,002
4. Chris Paul	907
5. Ben Simmons	801

rent trajectory of the NBA, it may also represent a seminal moment in league history.

Harden is Daryl Morey's dream come true, but not everyone fires up the flat screen hoping to see isolation sets, corner threes, and free throws all night. Any real discussion of Harden and the Morey-era Rockets has to include an important part of the story: many folks despise watching these geniuses.

Harden the Infuriator

Harden's astute understanding of the economics of basketball manifests in two ways. The first way is positive. When it comes to things like shot selection, playmaking for his teammates, and clock management, Harden's behavior on the court is as close to analytically optimal as anything we've ever seen. Unfortunately, the second way his brilliance manifests is negative.

On May 2, 2018, Harden and the Rockets were hosting Game 2 of the Western Conference Semifinals against the Utah Jazz. They'd torched the Jazz in Game 1, but Game 2 was a different story. Midway through the second quarter, Utah's rookie phenom, Donovan Mitchell, drained a three to put the Jazz up 19. None of the Rockets' high-powered offensive tactics were working. Their threes weren't falling. The lobs to Capela weren't connecting. Their defense was failing.

With one minute left in the half, Houston was down 16, and they desperately needed to end the quarter on a positive note. Harden had to find a plan B, and he found it in the person of Bennie Adams, the 51-year-old referee. More than any other player in the sprawlball

era, Harden views the refs as a stratagem. He knows how to leverage them. As the first half waned, he went to work. He scored seven points in the final minute, five of them on free throws. Infuriating free throws.

With exactly 60 seconds remaining in the half, Harden found himself dribbling on top of the Toyota Center decal just inside half-court. As he approached the right-wing area, he was guarded by Jae Crowder, who was in a classic defensive stance.

Harden is so observant. As he dribbled casually along the right wing, he slyly studied Crowder, waiting for any tiny mistake. With 57 seconds left, Crowder committed a blunder that would cost his team three points: he gently extended his right arm ever so slightly in front of himself. Harden knew what to do. While continuing to dribble with his right hand, Harden slithered his left arm beneath Crowder's extended right arm. Then he snapped up his dribble and attempted to shoot an awkward three, causing his and Crowder's arms to intertwine like ethernet cables behind a router. It looked awkward. It looked illegal. It looked like a three-point shooting foul, especially to Bennie Adams, who was conveniently standing eight feet away. Adams blew his whistle. Harden made three free throws. Thirteen-point game.

On the following possession, Joe Ingles, Utah's sharpshooting Australian wingman, missed a driving layup. It was a forgettable play that ended with Ingles's forward momentum from the drive carrying him across the baseline and nearly into the den of photographers camped out under the stanchion.

Ryan Anderson grabbed the board and handed the ball

to Harden right at the tip of the restricted area. But before Harden turned to dribble upcourt, he saw something he liked. He saw Ingles jogging back on defense. This is something that 99.9 percent of NBA players wouldn't think twice about, the time between a defensive rebound and the routine trot back to the other end being one of the most ho-hum sequences in basketball. But Harden seeks value and efficiency in places where most of his colleagues don't even think to look. With his team in the bonus, Harden saw another chance to score points 90 feet from his own goal.

As Ingles trotted back through the restricted area, Harden flung his own posterior into Ingles's path, creating a collision between a ball handler and a defender. Bennie Adams did not like it, and he again blew his whistle. And again he blew in favor of Harden. And again Harden "earned" two free throws. He made them both. With a little help from his pal Bennie Adams, Harden "scored" five quick points in 16 seconds, all at the line, all on savvy foul-drawing techniques.

Watching the NBA is great for many reasons. Many of us love to watch the game on TV while following along on a second screen, like a phone or an iPad, as we refresh Twitter or Reddit game threads. It's cool, because even if you're alone on your couch, you can read what other fans all over the planet are thinking as the drama unfolds. Well, that night, after those two whistles, the NBA internet caught fire.

Shortly after the Ingles collision, a Reddit user posted a clip of the play on the NBA subreddit and started a thread called "Harden backs into Jingles for the foul." The thread quickly gained popularity as thousands of us clicked, rewatched the clip, and browsed the comments.

Among the top comments, a few perfectly captured people's thoughts on the moment—and on Harden's game in general.

Thousands of upvotes went to u/ricklegend, who commented: "This is why I hate Harden and don't respect him as a player . . ."

A quick reply came from u/Coba2522, who supported this idea: "It's out of control. Selling fouls when shooting it attacking the basket is one thing, but Harden goes out of his way to run into people all over the court. It's incredibly unnatural and pathetic to watch."

Continuing the thread, u/AdamJensensCoat chimed in to say: "It's amazing to watch Harden double-down in crunch time. You know he's going to draw the foul . . . everybody knows it's coming . . . and but you don't know exactly how he'll manufacture the contact. Will it be a rip through? Will he do a flail jumper . . . will he achy-breaky eurostep and somehow tie up both your arms?"

But the most upvoted comment in the entire thread belonged to the great u/SDas_, who earned "Reddit gold" by writing, "This shit just isn't in the spirit of the game."

Jabroni

While all aspects of Harden's offensive game are undeniably effective, parts of it are straight-up maddening. The Ingles play was outrageous. The play before against Crowder was too, but for those of us who watched a lot of Rockets games during the 2016–17 season, the three-point shooting foul was nothing new. That season Harden drew 116 three-point shooting fouls, more than one per game.

That may seem like a random stat, but when you look at the top three NBA players in that category, Harden's 116 sure seems to jump out. It's more than twice as many shooting fouls as the second-place guy drew, and exactly four times as many as the third-place guy!

If three-point shooting fouls were like home runs in 1927, Harden would be Babe Ruth, and his teammates on the 2016–17 Rockets would be Murderers' Row. The second-place guy, Lou (Gehrig) Williams, was Harden's teammate that year. Besides those two fellas, nobody in the NBA drew more than 30 fouls on three-point shots. Harden had 116! If you look at those numbers and think something funny must be going on, you're wrong. It's not funny, it's douchey.

In 1987–88, Larry Bird, the greatest shooter of his era, made 98 threes. It was his career high for a season. Thirty years later, Harden drew 116 three-point shooting fouls.

Most shooting fouls occur near the basket. Just over 80 percent of NBA shooting fouls occur within 10 feet of the basket. But in 2016–17, only 43 percent of the ones Harden drew were in that range; 38 percent of the shooting fouls he drew came beyond the arc, which is astronomical considering that only 4 percent of NBA shooting fouls occur in three-point range. During the 2016–17 regular season, 1,119 three-point shooting fouls were called in the NBA, and Harden alone drew 10.4 percent of them. As a team, the Charlotte Hornets ranked second in the NBA with 73. The Milwaukee Bucks drew five.

MOST 3-POINT SHOOTING FOULS DRAWN, 2016-17

1. James Harden	116
2. Lou Williams	54
3. Kyle Lowry	29

The game is a lot more physical near the basket, and jump shooters enjoy a world largely free of contact. For Al Jefferson or LaMarcus Aldridge to even get a shot off in the post, they usually have to endure tons of pushing and grabbing from their defenders. When they score, it's usually in spite of a bunch of contact. Three-point shooters live in another world. If a perimeter defender so much as lays a finger on a perimeter shooter as he rises up for a three, a ref like Bennie Adams will blow his whistle.

We've already established that next to open dunks and layups, trips to the free throw line are easily among the most efficient outcomes for any offensive possession. Well, given the fact that three-point shooting fouls result in three free throws for the victim of the crime, they yield an even more cartoonish level of efficiency.

It's fair to say that drawing three-point shooting fouls is the most efficient play in basketball. It's also fair to say

JOURNEYS TO THE NAIL,
JAMES HARDEN,
3-POINT SHOOTING FOULS DRAWN, 2016–17

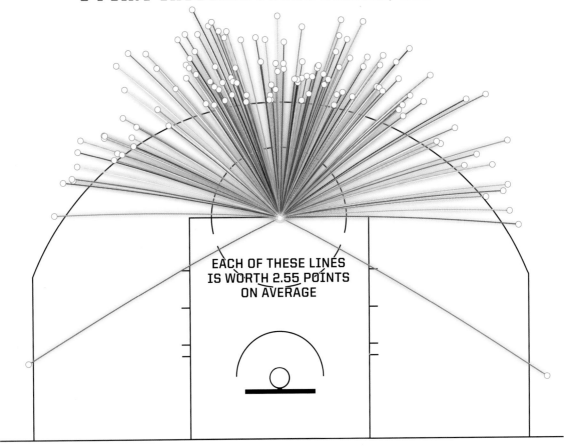

EACH OF THESE LINES
IS WORTH 2.55 POINTS
ON AVERAGE

that James Harden was the first player in the history of the game to understand this fact and exploit it over and over again, duping NBA refs over and over again and frustrating fans over and over again.

Harden is a career 85 percent free throw shooter, meaning that an average three-shot trip to the line yields 2.55 points for him. Harden is a career 36 percent three-

point shooter, which translates into an average three-point attempt yield of 1.08 points. The chasm between the value of the free throws and the value of the attempts—a difference of 1.47 expected points—tells you everything you need to know about how the NBA pampers its jump shooters these days. The only other place in sports where a similar chasm exists is in soccer, where drawing a foul in the box is so much more valuable than any other shot attempt would be. Remember Robben in 2014?

From a defensive standpoint, fouling a three-point shooter earns you the most punitive punishment in the game. It's the NBA's answer to football's 15-yard penalties for things like roughing the passer, or baseball's free bases for balks or hit batsmen. If it's fair to discern cultural values from modes of crime and punishment, the NBA cares more about fouling jump shooters than about anything else in the game. Hands off!

For years it wasn't a big deal. Calls for roughing the three-point shooter were exceedingly rare, occurring less than one time per game. Then Harden and Lou Williams got together on the 2016–17 Rockets. That season the two combined to draw 170 three-point shooting fouls. As a team, the Charlotte Hornets ranked second in the NBA with 73.

More than any other team in NBA history, the 2016–17 Rockets intentionally chased three-point shooting fouls. And it worked. As the Rockets battled the Thunder in the first round of the 2017 NBA playoffs, Harden and Williams drew 13 of these calls in just five games (Harden drew nine and Williams four), averaging more than seven points per game on the calls. And in a series where four of the games were decided by six points or less, those seven-plus points per game came in handy. For example, in Game 4, which Houston won by four, Harden and Williams generated eight points on these calls, including five points in the fourth quarter.

On average, NBA shooters draw a shooting foul on 1.7 percent of their 3-point attempts; that season, Harden drew them on 15.5 percent of his 3-point attempts. How'd he do it? Easy—by manipulating his defenders, the refs, and the rule base.

For most of us, the typical pick-and-roll event in basketball includes four characters: two offensive players and two defensive players. But for Harden, there is a fifth man to consider, and that man wears a gray shirt and black trousers and carries a magical whistling device.

During the 2016–17 campaign, many of Harden's three-point shooting fouls stemmed from forgettable pick-and-roll actions. Generally speaking, as Harden's defender fought his way over a ball screen, Harden would watch carefully. If the defender extended his arms in any way, Harden would "hook" them before rising up for what might be most kindly described as a "strange" or "unnatural" shot attempt. In reality, the "shots" looked awkward for multiple reasons. First, they often happened even before Harden got around the screen. In other words, he would begin to shoot a three well before he had any open space to do so, which just looks weird. Second, these "shots" would happen only after he'd hooked his nondribbling arm onto the arm of the screened defender. Harden would dribble with one hand and use his other hand to snake under the outstretched arm of the defender fighting over the ball screen. When he got a good hook, he'd immediately rise up, creating a chaotic choreography in the process. As he'd rise, what might be best described as sloppy arm spaghetti would occur. Harden would flail his head back and his arms wide, only to be impaired by the arm of the screened defender. It looked terrible. It looked physical. It looked illegal. And then the man in the gray shirt would act. First came the whistle.

And then the foul call. And then the three free throw attempts. And then the 2.55 points for the Rockets. Not to mention another foul on the poor defender trying to defend Harden all night.

It was genius. It was efficient. But was it fun to watch? Was it fair? Not really, but Harden is probably the smartest player in the NBA when it comes to understanding the interactions between league rules, referees' interpretations of those rules, and offensive efficiency. By 2016–17, he was doing things nobody in league history had ever done before.

By 2017–18, he'd become the Most Valuable Player in the NBA, quarterbacking the league's best offense to an impressive 65-win season. The Houston Rockets, as one of the league's stronger franchises, had never won more than 58 games before that season. But that 2017–18 group won 65, proving that the combined fever-dream offensive strategies of Morey, D'Antoni, and Harden weren't just good ideas in concept but were effective in real life too. These strategies were the future of basketball.

Future, We Have a Problem

The future was on full display as the Rockets blasted their way to the 2018 Western Conference playoffs. On May 28, 2018, James Harden and the Rockets laced them up and played the biggest game of their season. After blazing to the best record in the regular season and cruising through the first two rounds of the 2018 playoffs, the Rockets found themselves embroiled in a crazy Western Conference Finals matchup against the Warriors. The teams split the first six games, and neither arrived at Game 7 unscathed. Chris Paul, the

Rockets' second-best player, hurt his hamstring late in Game 5, while Andre Iguodala, the MVP of the 2015 NBA Finals, was out for the Dubs.

Regardless, the stage was set for the game of the year. Harden and the Rockets versus Curry, Durant, and the rest of the defending champs. The entire season for both groups had come down to one game. The winner would go to the Finals to play LeBron, and the loser would go to Cancún.

By May 2018, both the Rockets and Warriors had built parallel successes around three-point shooting, and it was no surprise that the outcome of Game 7 would hinge on which team could hit their 3s.

But Houston, well, it had a problem: in their biggest game in years, Harden and the Rockets went out and had the worst night for three-point shooting in NBA history. They made seven threes. They missed 37. Leading up to that night, in the history of the league, an NBA team had attempted at least 40 threes 380 times. Of those teams, no team had ever made fewer than nine—until Houston made only seven. Houston died as they lived. Beyond the arc.

As Game 7 unfolded, Houston meticulously built its own mausoleum, brick by brick by brick . . .

The 2017–18 Rockets were the first team in league history to take over half of their shots from three-point range, but they sure picked a bad time to have their worst shooting night of the year. A definitive Game 7, at home, against the team of the decade. They lost by nine. If they'd made three more threes—or four or five or six or seven more threes—maybe the outcome would have been different. But they didn't. Golden

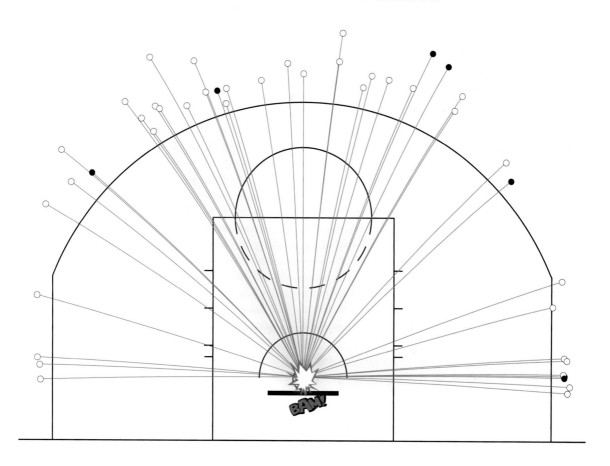

State, on the other hand, had a fine night from beyond the arc, hitting 16 of 39 attempts (41 percent), and won this game in a familiar way. Even though Houston outscored them in the paint and at the line, that didn't matter—the Warriors won. Just as we learned in 2016 when Klay Thompson went wild from downtown to beat the Thunder, the Warriors don't need to win the battles in the paint. They know they can win just by shooting threes. Or, with all due respect to Houston, I should say, making threes.

The biggest basketball game of 2018 was determined by three-point percentage. Nothing else mattered as much. Houston outscored Golden State in the two-point area

Team	Overall FGA	3P	2P	FTA
Houston	36/90 (40%), 92 points	7/44 (16%), 21 points	29/46 (63%), 58 points	13/22 (59%), 13 points
Golden State	39/80 (49%), 101 points	16/39 (41%), 48 points	23/41 (56%) 46 points	7/14 (50%), 7 points
Total	**75/170 (44%) 193 points**	**23/83 (27%), 69 points**	**52/87 (60%) 104 points**	**20/36 (56%), 20 points**

The new aesthetic: 60 missed threes, 35 missed twos, 23 made threes, 52 made twos.

and at the free throw line but couldn't overcome the 27-point deficit from downtown. Folks love to say "It's a make or miss league," and while that's true, it's really true about threes, which are increasingly determining the outcomes of the biggest games in the best basketball league in the world.

Game 7 of the 2018 Western Conference Finals included 83 three-point shots—one per every 34.7 seconds of game play. Think about that. To watch these games these days is to watch 24-foot jump shots over and over and over again. Moreover, to watch these games these days is to watch most of those shots miss. There's no question that Houston had a horrid shooting night in Game 7, but missing threes is not exactly rare. NBA shooters miss 64 percent of their three-point attempts. During the 2017–18 regular season, an average Rockets game included 45 missed threes: 27 by Houston, and 18 by their opponents. Almost one per minute.

Missed threes are now a key aesthetic of NBA basketball.

Just ask those of us who watched Game 7: we saw 60 of them. We saw one every 48 seconds of game play. Sixty times we endured the brief optimism of the rising arc of another three-point shot. Sixty times we fleetingly basked in the potential joy of a swish only to be shown the harsh reality of the ball's clank with the wrong part of the metal ring. Then the ricochet and the chaotic physics. Then the scramble for the ball. That's what we're increasingly watching now. Over and over and over again. With each year comes more missed threes. How many is too many?

All of us who watched Game 7 might describe it as intense or even as suspenseful, but none of us would characterize it as magnificent or beautiful. This was not Heat-Spurs 2013. It's not that every basketball game has to check those boxes, but at the same time, it's very important that the NBA's best games be at least occasionally gorgeous, right? Furthermore, all of these new threes are coming at the expense of other, more diverse styles of scoring. As the three rises, post play and mid-range jumpers decline and the game becomes more monocultural.

The Golden State–Houston series was really predictable to watch from a tactical standpoint too. Nearly every time down, Houston would set a ball screen that ended up getting Steph Curry defending James Harden. On the other end, Golden State would do the same, only trying to get Harden defending Durant or Curry. The Finals were more of the same. Golden State would get Kevin Love on Curry; Cleveland would find a screen that got Curry on LeBron James. A growing contingent of NBA observers started using terms like "monotonous" to describe the biggest games of the year.

It's worth asking: is this good for basketball? There's little doubt that analytics, in changing shot selection and strategy in the NBA, has modified the very aesthetic of pro hoops as well. But are these changes actually good for the spectacle of the sport? More and more baseball observers point to rising strikeout rates and more pitching changes per game and argue that the aesthetic of that sport is damaged. Many of them suggest that we have analytics to blame. Optimal strategies do not necessarily align with optimal aesthetics. Is this happening in hoops too?

Is the arc of the three, in aggregate, poetically analogous to most three-point attempts? Are we likely destined for a clank?

The Moneyball Aesthetic

More than any other team, the Houston Rockets of the 2010s have organizational values driven by the quest for efficiency. They're obsessed with futureball. You can see it everywhere from their roster construction to their shot selection. They love free throws, threes, dunks, and layups. They despise everything else. But as they chase the efficiency dragon, they're also playing an exaggerated version of sprawlball that, let's be honest, sometimes sucks to watch.

Not everyone loves the on-court aesthetics of Harden and Morey's group, and it's not hard to find many observers dismissing Rocketball as ugly or gimmicky. To watch the Rockets these days is to see a team spreading the floor with above-average shooters who try to stockpile more three-point attempts than everyone else. As a result, by 2017–18 an average Rockets game included almost 1 missed 3 per minute of play.

The critics say that watching the Rockets these days is for those who enjoy dozens of missed jumpers and a bearded weirdo running iso-sets, hunting for whistles first and buckets second. However, if you find yourself groaning at Rocketball, who do you have to blame? Morey? D'Antoni? Harden? While it's true that those fellas have designed approaches to maximize success within the framework of the league rules, they didn't make the rules.

The NBA legislated this brave new hoops world into existence; by elevating the worth of the three-point shot and shooting fouls over other forms of scoring, they have tempted this outcome for years. It's here now. Morey, D'Antoni, and Harden are just the ones most willing to exploit the silly mathematical margins that the league and its rulebook brought to pass.

And you know what? It's brilliant and it's effective. Let's be clear: few organizations have navigated the analytics era as well as the Houston Rockets, and few superstars deserve more credit for understanding the efficiency landscape molded by the NBA than James Harden. Hate the game, not the player.

Since taking over in Houston, Morey has built a sturdy NBA program. He's a stud between the spreadsheets, and it's not hard to argue that Morey is one of the most successful GMs in the league right now. Morey and

Harden have ridden the efficiency dragon all the way to the Western Conference Finals, which many of the game's brightest stars have never reached.

Still, for those of us who grew up watching Bird, Magic, and Jordan, the dissonance between what we perceive to be great basketball and what actually is great basketball is getting louder. The Rockets may be the team most emblematic of that dissonance: every Rockets game is another 48 minutes of evidence that the league's rapidly growing three-point economy has downgraded some of the sport's most aesthetically beautiful skill sets while upgrading some relatively ugly or monocultural behaviors. Rockets games have very little post-up action. They don't have many elbow jumpers or fadeaways.

Anyone watching the Rockets these days can be forgiven for finding it hard to believe that they're playing the same game that Hakeem Olajuwon or Kenny Smith played. It's hard to even trace the DNA back to Jordan, who by any measure is the seminal figure in contemporary hoops in America. When the Rockets are running offense, you won't see bobbing and weaving into space on the elbow or along the baseline anymore. There won't be any dream shakes. Instead, you'll see four dudes decorating the far edges of the scoring area while an off-the-bounce savant hunts and pecks and dribbles his isolated way through the middle of the court.

Who cares what it looks like? It works.

The Morey-Harden Rockets thrive on the perceptual gap separating traditionally great basketball from contemporarily smart basketball. While the rest of the league meanders over from the old way to the new way, the Rockets are blasting ahead of them all, becoming the first movers in a hoops era that will be remembered more for its obsession with efficiency than for its aesthetic.

Within the moneyball discourse, we lionize folks who use savvy numerical loopholes to find unblazed trails to efficiency. Hell, isn't that the entire meaning of the book? Isn't that why we even know who Billy Beane is?

But pro sports are about more than efficiency. They are a celebration of human athleticism and competition. Nobody has a poster of Daryl Morey on their wall. Nobody has a poster of James Harden shooting another free throw on their wall. Nobody has a poster of Corey Brewer or Eric Gordon missing another corner three on their wall. While it's true that the Rockets deserve credit for playing savvy basketball, I think it's also true that they provide us with a glimpse of the future and a chance to evaluate the direction of the best sport in the world.

Daryl Morey's vision is simple. It has less to do with threes and frees and more to do with simply winning basketball games by playing the game the right way. But as basketball's answer to Billy Beane, Morey is just the first NBA exec to realize that the "right way" entails a fervent quest for numerical margins. Morey studied business at MIT. He learned about "market inefficiencies" and how to exploit them. He learned to trust in numbers. He has successfully brought the business ideology of Wall Street to NBA courts, but did he bring the callous soullessness of Wall Street along with it? Is it possible to import one without the other?

You can read *Moneyball* as a testament to the analytical awakening in American sports, but you can also read it as a celebration of the irreversible integration of finance ideals and sports strategies. You can read it as a manual for integrating the ideological insights of finance capitalism into a front office, but you can also read it as evidence that our culture's outrageous mania for computation, quantification, and efficiency is now striding alongside our favorite athletes on the playing surfaces of Fenway Park and Madison Square Garden. Make no mistake, this mania has always been there, but in post-*Moneyball* America, computation, quantification, and efficiency have achieved a superstar status like we've never seen before.

If it's fair to say that the first decade of this century was marked by a cultural love affair with rapidly emerging technologies, it's also fair to say that the second half of the second decade has been marked by a society reevaluating that love affair. Maybe Facebook isn't as great as we thought. Maybe Alexa listens too much. Maybe Instagram isn't very good for our mental health. This Wikileaks thing might not be so cool after all.

Well, then, what about *Moneyball*, that seminal document from 2003 that charted the way forward for pro sports in our new century? What about that holy scripture that inspired a generation of disciples looking to spread the gospel of the spreadsheet across the wide world of sports? Did we exhibit a similar blind faith in the *Moneyball* ideals as we did in the Zuckerberg ones?

If the last 20 years have taught us anything, it's that the integration of computing, data, and strategy is incredibly powerful. But within the first half of that period, many of us were a little too optimistic and perhaps a little naive about how this integration would affect

things like privacy and democracy. Not to mention the midrange jumper and the center position.

It's not that the integration of computing, data, and strategy is responsible for ruining things like privacy and democracy (or the midrange jumper). It's that, left unchecked, it leads to significant changes. And just as some governments have been a little slow to understand and regulate the new corporate giants that guide our new economy, the NBA has seemed slow to adopt the same analytical reasoning that is propelling all of its franchises and their strategies. Just as some governments seem ill equipped in this era to effectively monitor corporations and protect citizens and institutions from them, the NBA seems ill equipped to navigate and legislate its way through the current climate.

For many of us who love hoops, free throws and catch-and-shoot threes are not the main reasons we watch the game. But as teams and players chase efficiency, these types of shots will become more and more common. Hell, the Rockets already shoot more threes than twos, and Harden has mastered the art of drawing three-point shooting fouls.

But while it's true that these shot types are the holiest for those who worship at the altar of efficiency, and while it's also true that analytical reasoning has enabled us to understand and enhance basketball strategy in savvy new ways, the inconvenient truth for the league right now is that it may also be making our beloved sport less appealing.

Moneyball might be smart, but is it fun to watch? Ask baseball fans. After all, baseball is the native habitat of moneyball. In October 2017, over 14 years after *Money-*

ball's publication, the *Wall Street Journal* published a fascinating article by Brian Costa and Jared Diamond called "The Downside of Baseball's Data Revolution—Long Games, Less Action."

The authors lay out a few ideas, mainly that the woke era of baseball analytics has manifested some shitty trends in entertainment, which, by the way, remains the backbone of the sports industry. It's kind of important. By 2017, from a strategic perspective, baseball teams were more efficient than ever, but baseball games were more boring than ever, featuring more strikeouts, more pitching changes, and fewer batted balls in play. Costa and Diamond argue convincingly that the emergent strategies associated with the Michael Lewis awakening are one big reason why. Here's a key passage:

> Baseball has never been more beset by inaction. Games this season saw an average gap of 3 minutes, 48 seconds between balls in play, an all-time high. There were more pitcher substitutions than ever, the most time between pitches on record and longer games than ever.

> A confluence of hitting, pitching and defensive strategies spawned by the league's "Moneyball" revolution have all played a role. That makes baseball, whose early use of big-data strategies was embraced by the business world in general, a case study in its unintended consequences.

> "The sport is going down a path that is a byproduct of very smart people figuring out the best strategies to win," says San Francisco Giants Chief Executive Larry Baer. "It's up to the owners to say, 'What's the impact on the consumers that are watching?'"

Is the same thing happening to basketball? Have similar unintended consequences occurred in our game?

While basketball's age of enlightenment has undoubtedly produced a more efficient set of habits, has it done so at the cost of something else? To apply Baer's question to the NBA, what's the impact on the consumers who are watching basketball?

Millions of Americans fell in love with the NBA because the league reliably features incredible athletes making awesome and acrobatic basketball plays. But two side effects of the league's growing obsession with efficiency threaten to make those magnificent outbursts less common. The first side effect is that as more and more of the league's possessions end with catch-and-shoot three-point attempts, fewer of the league's possessions end with more acrobatic tries in the two-point area. And for those of us who go to arenas to watch some of the best athletes in the world performing basketball actions we can achieve ourselves only in our dreams or via our game consoles, some of the trends associated with the Rockets' aesthetic are a little troubling.

On November 12, 2016, a little less than two years after Harden's free throw sonata in Memphis, I watched the Spurs play the Rockets in Houston. The Spurs won, 106–100. But it was an ugly game, and not just because neither team played well. The Rockets tried 47 threes. They made 15 and missed 32. They tried only 42 twos. Think about that for a moment. In a 48-minute game, the Rockets essentially shot a three-pointer every minute, and an average Rockets possession in that game was more likely to end with a three than with a two.

By the 2017–18 season, this was happening regularly: that year the Rockets averaged 42 three-point tries per game. And given the fact that those shots go in only about a third of the time, as we see more and more threes we're also going to see more and more bricks from downtown. Nobody talks about that. Nobody talks about the fact that the rise of the three can also be framed as the rise of the missed catch-and-shoot jumper, or the rise of the long rebound. FAN-tastic.

If I wanted to go to a gym and watch dudes miss 64 percent of their jumpers, I could go watch any church game in America.

Look at it another way. Threes are still very exciting, but how long will that be the case? As threes become more and more central to the game, at some point fans will find them less and less riveting. They will just be jump shots. Thirty years ago, threes were special because they were the rare diamonds of the offensive end, but with some teams launching them once per minute, it's hard to imagine that three-pointers will maintain their novelty or excitement.

Maybe the folks who watched that Spurs-Rockets game will bounce their grandchildren on their knee and gleefully tell them about the night they saw Trevor Ariza, Ryan Anderson, Eric Gordon, and James Harden combine to shoot 39 three-pointers. Maybe the folks who went to that Houston-Memphis game back in 2014 will tell their grandkids about the time they saw James Harden score 27 points on two made field goals and 22

made free throws. But I doubt it; those would be terribly bored grandkids.

Harden is a magnificent player, but he is also a hard superstar to love, which brings us to the second side effect.

As the league increasingly looks for more and more threes, the relative value of players who can sink catch-and-shoot threes and players who can create catch-and-shoot threes for teammates continues to rise, while the relative value of players with other kinds of skills continues to plummet. In addition, the relative value of tactics that beget three-pointers will continue to rise at the cost of those tactics that do not. Spread the floor and run a pick-and roll. No need to post up.

What do we want our superstars to look like? What exactly should make them super? What do we want our NBA games to look like? What is truly FAN-tastic?

As our rosters and tactics evolve to chase triples, so will the entire aesthetic of pro hoops. The Houston Rockets—exhibit A—already reflect a fully realized moneyball aesthetic. In this sense, we should be thankful. They are leading the way, but they are also providing a key case study. If you like watching the Rockets, chances are that you will like the way the league looks in a few years. If you don't, you won't.

Any team that wants to shoot over half of its shots from three-point range needs to have a roster full of three-point shooters and a playbook full of actions designed to get those guys catch-and-shoot chances. In other words, more Korvers and Arizas, fewer Rodmans and Al Jeffersons.

To their credit, the Rockets have built that exact team. And they've done it very well. They have the right general manager, the right head coach, and the right superstar for the brave new awakening. The result has been successful, but it can be ugly, and it begs the larger question: is winning ugly games within a beautiful sport really winning?

The good news is that there is an opportunity to examine this from a higher plateau. Since the publication of *Moneyball*, its prescriptions have almost exclusively been applied to optimizing one organization's chances of beating others. *Moneyball* framed analytics as a team-level activity; while that frame is completely valid, it's not singular. The good news is that the same set of ideas can be applied at the league level to optimize what we love most about NBA action, while minimizing what we don't like so much.

Analytics can help us build a better game.

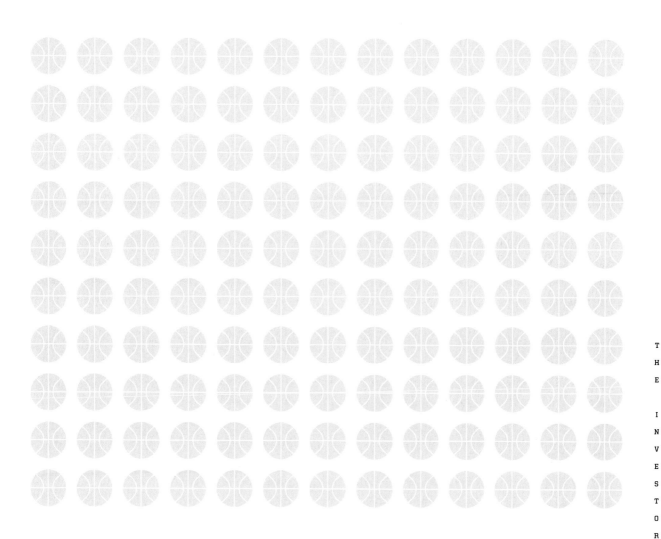

THE INTERIOR MINISTER

LEBRON JAMES

The 2016 Finals

ON JUNE 2, 2016, the Cleveland Cavaliers were in Oakland playing Stephen Curry and the Warriors in Game 1 of the 2016 NBA Finals. It was a familiar matchup; the two teams had squared off in the 2015 Finals, when Golden State beat a depleted Cavs team in six games. But those 2015 Cavs were broken: Kevin Love missed the whole 2015 Finals, and after getting hurt in Game 1, so did Kyrie Irving. The 2016 Cavs showed up in Oakland in much healthier condition. They were also a better team this time around. But so were the Warriors, who won more games (73!) than any other team in regular-season history. Even though the Cavs were healthy, the Warriors entered the series as the clear favorites. They had home-court advantage, the top-rated offense in basketball, and one of the best defenses too. Not only that, but they had a point guard who was the first-ever unanimous MVP.

But there's a reason teams have to "play the games," and if the 2016 NBA Finals demonstrated anything, it's that sports are unpredictable. This would be a series for the ages.

Game 1

Game 1 was close. Well, at least most of Game 1 was close. After LeBron made a driving layup with 2:12 remaining in the third quarter, Cleveland held a fragile 68–67 lead before Golden State smashed it. In signature Warriors fashion, they blew the game open with a torrential run, outscoring the Cavs 29–8 during a key stretch spanning the end of the third quarter and the first half of the fourth. Still, there was no shining star for the Warriors in their Game 1 win. They were led in scoring by Shaun Livingston, who scored 20, and Draymond Green, who had 16, while the Cavs were able to hold Steph Curry and Klay Thompson to a mere 20 points combined. But the Cavs were unable to capitalize on the quiet night from the Splash Brothers: the Warriors prevailed, 104–89.

Game 2

Game 2 was not close. Although Cleveland was able to take an early lead, Kevin Love left the game with a concussion early in the second half, and Golden State pummeled the Cavs, winning 110–77. The Cavs scored only 33 points in the second half. Ooof. Draymond Green led the Warriors with 28 points, seven rebounds, and five assists.

As the Associated Press recap hinted, the Cavs were in over their heads.

> OAKLAND, Calif.—Draymond Green emphatically flexed his bulging biceps with big plays on both ends of the floor, and these Golden State Warriors might just be far too strong for the Cleveland Cavaliers.
>
> That repeat title Golden State has spoken of since the very start more than eight months ago is suddenly two wins from reality.
>
> It will be the only way the Warriors' record-setting season ends right. For now, they sure seem unstoppable.

If the first two final scores were any indication, this was not going to be a competitive series. The Warriors hadn't just beaten the Cavs in the first two games in Oakland—they had set a new record for margin of victory. At lunchtime two days after Game 2, Andrew Lynch published an article on *Fox Sports* called "The Warriors Are Setting NBA Finals Records by Crushing the Cavs." Lynch opened the piece with a few ominous factoids:

> With Sunday night's epic 33-point beatdown in Game 2, the Warriors set a new mark for the largest cumulative margin of victory through two games of the NBA Finals at 48 points.
>
> It's been a while since we've seen such a lopsided Finals. The 1961 Boston Celtics and 1951 Rochester Royals are tied for the second-largest margin of victory through two games at 42 points.

These were not good indicators for LeBron and the Cavs, who had to find a way to regroup as they headed home for some must-win games back in Cleveland.

Game 3

Cleveland needed to win Game 3, and they needed to do it without Love, whose concussion kept him out of the game. They came out with urgency, blasting the Warriors throughout the first quarter, and helped redefine the narrative of the series by taking a 33–16 lead after one period.

Still, early leads against this potent Warriors team guaranteed nothing. The Cavs needed James and Irving to both be brilliant to finish this game and get back in the series. They were. James had 32 points, 11 rebounds, and six assists. Irving added 30 points and eight assists, and the Cavs stopped the bleeding from the Oakland games. They took Game 3 by the score of 120–90. It was a statement win. After the game, Steve Kerr told reporters, "Obviously, they just punched us right in the mouth right in the beginning."

If they could land another blow in Game 4, Cleveland would be right back in the series. If they couldn't, they'd be in deep trouble.

Game 4

Hello, deep trouble. On June 10, 2016, Curry finally got hot, scoring 38 points (21 from three-point range), and his Warriors beat LeBron James and the Cavs in the fourth game of the NBA Finals. If the Cavs had won, they would have tied the series and had momentum on their side as the teams headed back to Oakland for Game 5. But they lost 108–97 in front of their home crowd and were down 3–1 going back to Oakland; no team had ever come back from a 3–1 series deficit in the NBA Finals. The best team in regular-season history now had three chances to close out LeBron and the Cavs.

The Game 4 triumph in Cleveland had a lot in common with the Warriors' massive Game 6 victory in the Western Conference Finals that had gone down less than two weeks before. In the Game 4 win against the Cavs, the Dubs drained 17 threes against only 16 twos. They made 47 percent of their shots beyond the arc, while converting only a ghastly 36 percent of their shots inside of it. In that pivotal win of the 2016 Finals, they racked up 51 points on three-point field goals and 32 points on two-pointers. Cleveland kicked their ass in the paint, but lost the game anyhow.

The most successful team in regular-season history

GAME 4 POINT DISTRIBUTION

Shot Type	Warriors	Cavs
Two-point range	32	64
Free throws	25	15
Three-point range	51	18
Total	**108**	**97**

was out there winning huge playoff games while playing like shit in the two-point areas. In both Game 6 in Oklahoma City and Game 4 in Cleveland, the Warriors got more than doubled up inside the arc. Didn't matter. In both games, the Splash Brothers dominated the perimeter. It was the reality of the new NBA: any time you can hit 47 percent of 36 looks from long range (1.42 points per shot), you can afford to get torched in two-point range.

This isn't astrophysics, but Joe Lacob, Golden State's venture capitalist majority owner, told the *New York Times Magazine* that his team's approach was "light years ahead" of every other team in the league. These outsiders from Silicon Valley hacked their way to a hyper-efficient offense that inverted the basic tenets of the bygone eras of Bill Russell and Michael Jordan. And

GAME 4 MINUTES BY POSITION

Golden State

Position	Minutes
Point guard (Curry, Livingston)	59
Shooting guard (Thompson)	39
Small forward (Barnes, Iguodala, McAdoo)	84
Power forward (Green)	42
Center (Bogut, Ezeli, Varaejao)	15

Cleveland

Position	Minutes
Point guard (Irving, Dellavedova)	48
Shooting guard (Smith, Shumpert)	58
Small forward (James, Jefferson)	71
Power forward (Love, Frye)	35
Center (Thompson, who is really a power forward)	29

they were raining down triples on Russell Westbrook, LeBron James, and the rest of the fools still trying to slash and muscle their way to buckets inside the beltway. Consider yourself "disrupted."

It's not hyperbole to say that centers are less valuable than ever—it's a massive understatement.

Not only has the three-point line devalued "traditional" centers, but it has made it increasingly difficult for them to even get on the floor. In that big Game 4 Finals win at Cleveland, traditional centers logged a total of 15 of 240 possible minutes for the Warriors and 29 minutes for the Cavs, although the man playing center for Cleveland, Tristan Thompson, is arguably more of a power forward than a true center.

In the same way that the beltways of the 1960s and 1970s spurred suburban development and secondary economic centers like office parks and box stores on the edges of American cities, the NBA constructed its own beltway in 1979. And while it took a generation, the NBA beltway produced a similar effect: more and more economic activity started sprawling out to the suburbs, while many of the urban cores started to lose economic relevance. Main Street died and Walmart thrived.

Curry and the Warriors dominated the league with a Best Buy offense that the rest of America had already adopted. The best bargains are on the edge of town, in those big-box stores out past the splash park. You get more bang for your buck out there. What's more American than finding and exploiting economic margins?

Coming off the Game 4 win at Cleveland, Stephen Curry and the Warriors clearly represented a new model for NBA success. They'd won 73 games in the regular season. They had a two-time MVP and scoring champ running their offense. They had a fiery and versatile defense, led by Draymond Green. They were up 3–1 and headed home to the great Oracle crowd to clinch their second straight championship. No NBA team had ever blown a 3–1 lead in the Finals. Finishing off LeBron and the Cavs seemed to be a mere formality on the way to glory.

However, while shooting their way past the Cavs in Game 4, the Warriors lost a key player for Game 5. Late in the Game 4 win, Draymond Green hit LeBron James in the testicles. Draymond was light-years ahead of everyone else in the NBA when it came to testicle attacks. The hit on James was his second testicle attack in a two-week span. In the Western Conference Finals, Green had kicked Steven Adams right in his kiwis.

After Game 4 ended, the NBA reviewed the James incident and judged Green's offensive contact to be worthy of a flagrant foul. It was Green's fourth such foul of the playoffs. By rule, he was suspended for Game 5, and his absence would crack the door open for LeBron and the Cavs to extend the series.

Game 5

As the series shifted back to Oakland, it was hard to envision the Cavs winning Game 5. After all, Games 1 and 2 were blowouts, and the Cavs had just lost a huge Game 4 in front of their home crowd. But with their defensive leader sidelined, the Warriors had trouble slowing down James and Irving. Both guys scored 41 points. LeBron added 16 rebounds and seven assists

and led the Cavs to a huge road win to keep the series going and set up a sixth game back in Cleveland.

It's impossible to know, but Green's absence in Game 5 could have cost Golden State the game, and arguably a lot more. Regardless, Cleveland got the series back to their home floor. If they could win Game 6, they'd have a chance.

Game 6

In another must-win situation, LeBron and the Cavs came out and blasted the Warriors in the first quarter. They built a 20-point lead in the game's first 12 minutes. But one iconic moment would ensure that the game goes down in Cleveland sports history. As the Warriors tried to mount a last-ditch effort to get back in the game, Curry found himself racing down the lane for a layup. James had other ideas. James elevated above Curry from behind and swatted the holy hell out of Curry's layup, emphatically reminding the unanimous 2016 NBA MVP—and the entire basketball universe for that matter—that while the Warriors might be the best team in the world, James was still the planet's most dominant individual player.

The swat ignited the Cleveland crowd, and the intensity of the moment wasn't lost on either James or Curry, who barked at one another in the immediate aftermath.

Curry and the Warriors were rattled and frustrated. After taking a 3–1 lead, the series was about to be tied. Curry fouled out late in the game and in disgust threw his signature mouthpiece, striking a fan. Regardless, James logged another 41-point performance and swatted the series back to Oakland for an era-defining Game 7 showdown.

Game 7

June 19, 2016, was the most important pro basketball game in years. Although the teams had split the previous six games in the series, none of them were particularly close. All had been decided by at least 10 points. But Game 7 would be different. It would be a slow-paced brawl with a tight score and tons of lead changes. Midway through the second quarter, James once again announced his defensive presence with another rejection of another Curry layup attempt. It was another intense moment as the MVPs talked a bit of trash, but it wouldn't be James's most important block of the game.

The game came down to the final quarter and featured several huge moments down the stretch.

The Warriors collapsed at the exact wrong time. They failed to score in the game's final 4:39. With the game tied at 89 with 1:54 remaining, Andre Iguodala, one of the league's best open-court players and the same player who'd won the Finals MVP the previous year for defending James so well, grabbed a long rebound and raced down the court, alongside Curry, for what looked like a golden fast-break opportunity that could give the Warriors a late-game lead. But James once again flashed his all-world defensive prowess, this time coming out of nowhere and denying Iguodala's layup attempt before it had a chance to hit the backboard. That block may go down as the single best play in James's entire career.

The next day, on *ESPN.com*, Dave McMenamin captured the moment perfectly:

Iguodala grabbed the defensive rebound and streaked up the floor with the clock showing 1:54 remaining. Curry sprinted ahead on the left wing. When Iguodala passed half court, he found Curry with a chest pass and continued to run toward the hoop. Curry received the pass and immediately fed it right back, bouncing it off the floor in front of Iguodala so the swingman could catch it in stride.

Freeze the video from this moment and you'll see Iguodala at the right side of the foul line, J. R. Smith with two feet planted in the left side of the lane—albeit with his body facing Curry—and James standing on the 3-point line on the left wing.

What happened in the next two seconds defined the game. As Iguodala took two steps as he powered toward the hoop before going airborne, James sized him up and sprung at Iguodala's shot attempt from behind, blocking the potential layup off the glass with 1:50 remaining.

Had James not made the chase-down block, Golden State would have had the lead—and a raucous home crowd—on its side in the game's final moments.

Reflecting later on the play, James told *Cleveland. com*: "I was like, just don't give up on the play. Just don't give up on the play. Kyrie made a move into the lane, missed it, it shot long, and Iguodala, one of the best guys we have in the open court, gets the rebound, pushes it

to Steph, and I was just like, do not give up on the play. If you got an opportunity, just try to make this play."

He made the play. On the television broadcast, Mike Breen called the play: "Iguodala to Curry, back to Iguodala, up for the layup! Oh! Blocked by James! LeBron James with the rejection!"

Thanks to the block of the century, the game was still tied at 89. The 2016 NBA championship, a grueling sev-

en-game heavyweight bout, came down to its final four possessions.

POSSESSION 1: After J. R. Smith secured the blocked layup, the Cavs had the first chance to break the 89–89 tie. But with 1:27 left, following an isolation set that pitted James against Iguodala, James missed an awkward half-hook in the paint, and Golden State grabbed the rebound.

POSSESSION 2: As Curry dribbled the ball across half-court, 79 seconds remained in regulation. Harrison Barnes attempted to set a high ball screen for Curry, but Kyrie Irving was able to get over it and stay with Curry as he aggressively dribbled toward the three-point line. Still, we all knew what was coming. Curry had shattered three-point shooting records all season, and now he had a chance to win the game if he could drain one here. But he couldn't. Curry rushed into a step-back from the top of the arc and missed badly, not even drawing iron but only hitting the backboard. Kevin Love gathered the rebound and outletted the ball to Irving, who dribbled across half-court. Cavs head coach Tyronn Lue called time-out.

POSSESSION 3: With just over one minute remaining, LeBron inbounded the ball to Kyrie Irving, who was guarded by Klay Thompson, one of the league's most competent perimeter defenders. Thompson is tall, long, athletic, and smart. He was not an easy guy for Irving to beat off the dribble. No coach in the league would draw up a play to isolate Thompson in a big moment.

But here's the thing: in the sprawlball era, most teams switch defensive assignments every time the opponent sets a ball screen. So the offense can essentially choose which defender it wants to attack in isolation sets. In one of the most pivotal moments of the biggest game of the year, J. R. Smith came to the top of the arc to set a screen for Irving. As Irving dribbled to the right wing, Smith impeded Thompson, prompting a defensive switch that resulted in Curry defending Irving.

Despite the fact that Golden State possessed one of the best defenses in the NBA in 2015–16 and Curry had greatly improved his defensive chops throughout his career, Curry was still no Klay Thompson. Generally, Curry didn't guard his own position, and often the Warriors "hid" Curry on defense, matching him up with the opponents' less dangerous players, like J. R. Smith.

Regardless, in the most important offensive possession in franchise history, the Cavs drew up a play to attack Curry. After he set the screen, forcing Curry to switch onto Irving, J. R. Smith receded to the far left side of the floor, bringing Thompson with him and leaving Curry alone on Irving Island, defending one of the most dangerous isolation players in the NBA.

With 1:03 showing on the clock, the Warriors' former head coach, Mark Jackson, who was analyzing the game for ABC, described the Cavs' play design: "They're putting Curry in the pick-and-roll, trying to get him on Irving."

There was less than a minute remaining as Irving dribbled on the Oracle Arena decal 35 feet from the basket. He dribbled between his legs as he approached the three-point arc, eyeing Curry's defensive stance every step of the way. If there was anybody on the planet with a better handle than Curry, it was Irving; both guys had developed countless ball-handling tricks that

SPRAWLBALL

could create offensive opportunities by destroying their defenders' balance. Great defenders like Thompson or Kawhi Leonard are great in part because they can keep their balance in the face of these wild dribbling exhibitions, which usually cause less adept defenders to fail.

From the moment he received the inbounds pass from LeBron until he released the biggest shot of his life, Kyrie Irving dribbled 14 times. It was the 14th dribble that set him free. As he arrived at the right side of the three-point line, Irving had hypnotized Curry with a series of three hand-switching dribbles. For the fourth and last dribble in the sequence, Irving stuttered his feet, faked a between-the-legs dribble, and then lurched to his right side instead, catching Curry leaning just enough to create space to get off a step-back three-pointer. Curry extended his arm, but it was too late.

With 55 seconds remaining in Game 7 of the 2016 NBA Finals, Irving let go of the shot of the decade. Fittingly, it was a three-pointer that greatly increased Cleveland's win probability in the biggest game in franchise history. With 53 seconds remaining, the ball went through the net, giving Cleveland a three-point lead. 92–89.

POSSESSION 4: By the summer of 2016, Curry was a major superstar. He had become the league's most valuable player by harnessing the power of the three-point shot better than anyone ever had. His signature move was the unassisted triple. He'd dance and dribble his way into shooting space, while often mak-

ing his defender look silly. Late in Game 7, Curry had a chance to tie the game with that signature move.

After a screen, Curry found himself matched up on Kevin Love. It was the exact kind of matchup that Kerr and the Warriors loved to create. Curry was dangerous no matter who was guarding him, but pitted against a slower, less agile big man like Love, he became virtually unstoppable. With his gorgeous handles and nimble footwork, Curry could float like a butterfly. With his illuminati jumper, he could sting like a bee.

With just over 30 seconds left in the biggest game of their lives, Curry and Love squared off at the top of the arc. Curry jabbed and jabbed and tried to get that little crevasse of shooting space he needed to tie the game. But Love did the dance of his life and matched Curry stride for stride. As Curry rose up to take a shot—the Warriors' best chance to get back in the game—Love was right there, getting a hand up enough to affect Curry's attempt. The shot missed. Curry's heroic attempt ricocheted off the left rim before falling down toward the left block. With the score 92–89, the Warriors had one more chance if they could grab the rebound.

LeBron James grabbed the rebound. The Warriors fouled him. James sank one of two free throws, scoring the last point of the 2016 Finals and securing the win for the Cavs. 93–89.

Not counting the free throw at the end, the definitive possessions of the definitive game of the decade each ended with an unassisted three-point attempt for both teams. Even though James hit that free throw to secure the win, the three-point shot was the weapon of choice for both teams. And the one that went in determined the championship. It was a fitting end to a season in

which the Warriors had dominated the league by dominating the perimeter. But in Game 7, they were bitten by their own snake on their home floor.

James and his teammates had done the unfathomable. After getting blown out in the first two games, and trailing three games to one, they had come back against the most successful regular-season team in league history. It was a phenomenal performance by James, who gave the people of Cleveland not only a championship but one of the most memorable victories in hoops history.

But was this series his swan song? Was the 2016 masterpiece the end of his incredible run of championship dominance? Was the NBA moving away from interior dominators like James and moving toward perimeter dominators like Curry's Warriors and Harden's Rockets? There's no question that James was the quintessential superstar of the early 2000s, but he achieved that status almost defiantly. His game was not built for the sprawlball era.

The NBA Mural

In 2015, the NBA reached out to me about commissioning a new mural for the NBA offices in New York. They had a big blank wall, and they wanted to collaborate to put something nerdy and cool on it. I was thrilled and leapt at the chance; however, I didn't have a great idea for what to build for them. We agreed that the mural needed to be analytical but interesting. We could do shot charts for Curry, LeBron, and Durant, but that seemed too narrowly focused. We wanted something that also paid tribute to the league's overall dedication to analytics and data. After all, this would be on the wall in the league office for years to come.

WHO ARE THE BEST SHOOTERS FROM EACH OF THESE ZONES?

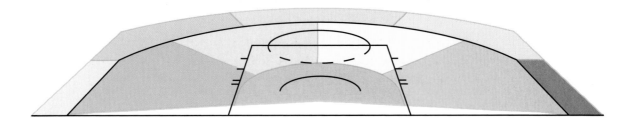

After a few back-and-forths, we landed on one of my favorite kinds of charts. Back in 2012, when I was still experimenting with shot data sets, I played with analyzing which NBA shooters were the most proficient shooters from different spots on the floor. For example, with a few lines of code we could easily calculate—over the course of a full season—which NBA player had the most buckets or the best field goal percentage from the elbows or from the corner three areas. We could find out who had the most points in the paint or in the restricted area. As I did these kinds of analyses, I couldn't wait to see the results.

But first, some folks at the league asked: Instead of doing this for just one NBA season, why not apply the analysis to the entirety of the NBA's shot location database? In other words, why not figure out which NBA player was the best shooter from the left elbow between 2002 and 2015? Why not figure out which guy was the best from the left corner over that 14-season span?

I loved the idea. So I dove into the data set, which included detailed records of nearly 3 million NBA shot attempts, and I went to work. We carved up the NBA shooting area into 10 zones and looked at which players were the most efficient shooters in each zone. The top shooter in those zones would get drawn on the mural.

The data set had millions of shots from thousands of different players. It had MVPs like Shaquille O'Neal, Steve Nash, Kobe Bryant, Stephen Curry, LeBron James, Kevin Durant, Dirk Nowitzki, and Tim Duncan—all of the 21st-century greats vying for inclusion on the mural. But only 10 guys could make the cut.

Even in the three-point era, basketball is a pretty simple game. The goal of the sport is to put the ball in the basket, and this task is generally easier the closer you get to the hoop. As a result, one primary objective of every defense is to fiercely defend the paint and ensure that the opponent doesn't get easy shots close to the rim. The zone near the basket is still the most hotly contested zone on the court. Offenses try to power their way down there to get close-range looks, and defenses do their darnedest to stop them. It's simple, but it's also

CONCENTRATION OF SHOOTING FOULS
IN THE NBA
2013-14 TO 2016-17

BETWEEN THE 2013-14 AND 2016-17
SEASONS, NBA OFFICIALS CALLED
102,013 SHOOTING FOULS

ONLY 4% OF SHOOTING FOULS
OCCURRED BEYOND THE 3-POINT LINE

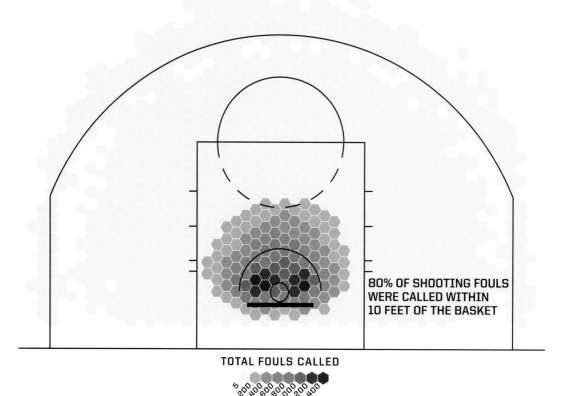

80% OF SHOOTING FOULS
WERE CALLED WITHIN
10 FEET OF THE BASKET

TOTAL FOULS CALLED

5 200 400 600 800 1,000 1,200 1,400

the reason that a whopping 60 percent of shooting fouls in the NBA occur in the areas within five feet of the rim.

For decades, the best players in the league were the guys who could overcome interior defenses on a regular basis. Players like Bill Russell, Wilt Chamberlain, and Kareem Abdul-Jabbar became the league's first real superstars by outplaying everyone else in the paint.

Kareem remains the leading scorer in NBA history: he converted an incredible 15,837 field goals in his 20-year career, and 15,836 of them were two-point buckets. He made one three in 1987.

The path that guys like Russell, Chamberlain, and Abdul-Jabbar blazed to NBA dominance started and ended in the paint. And while the emergence of the three-pointer has diminished its importance a bit, the area immediately within 7.5 feet of the hoop—which makes up just a tiny fraction of the NBA playing surface—remains hands-down the most tactically vital area on the floor. NBA scorers still rack up a whopping 40 percent of their shots in these interior spots.

As I did the analysis for the mural, I was most excited to see which player would emerge as the best interior scorer of the study period. Which contemporary stud would follow in the steps of Abdul-Jabbar and Chamberlain? Would it be Shaq? Would it be Tim Duncan? Would it be Dwight Howard?

Nope. Between 2002 and 2015, no NBA player blended frequency and efficiency close to the basket as well as LeBron James, who, by the way, is not a center at all.

James converted 67 percent of 7,648 attempts in the close-range area. NBA scorers as a whole converted 55 percent of their shots from this area. Poetically, James ended up being the centerpiece of the mural we built to examine scoring dominance in the early analytics era.

Writers have spilled millions of words to describe James over the years. Some argue that he's unlike any player to ever come along, and they're right. No player has ever combined size, athleticism, strength, speed, and smarts as well as James. In this sense, he's unprecedented. However, while James is unquestionably the best player of his generation, his key scoring trait—the ability to convert a ton of shots at a high rate near the basket—has been the key trait of the best players of virtually ev-

WHO ARE THE BEST SHOOTERS FROM EACH OF THESE ZONES? 2002-2015

ery generation. From Mikan through Chamberlain to Abdul-Jabbar to Shaq, the ability to reign near the rim is anything but an unprecedented route to NBA Most Valuable Player status.

As another era begins—an era of MVP Awards for Stephen Curry and James Harden—it's worth asking: Does James represent the end of his own era? Will he be the last MVP to control the game from the two-point area?

Do Curry and Harden represent the first of a new kind of perimeter-oriented player poised to dominate the NBA?

Although James has won the NBA MVP Award an incredible four times, if present trends continue, he may never do it again. James last won the award in 2012–13 as a member of the Miami Heat. Of the five MVP winners since then, three have led the NBA in made threes in their MVP campaign. Steph Curry did it twice, and James Harden did it once. Before Curry's first MVP Award, in 2014–15, MVPs never led the league in three-point volume.

Three-point proficiency was by no means a prerequisite for superstardom in the NBA that James entered in 2003, but it sure as hell will be in the NBA he exits in the coming years.

LeBron, the Hype

LeBron James was the number-one pick of the 2003 NBA draft, but he was hyped for greatness long before that. By 2002, James was already one of the most dis-

cussed high school basketball players of all time. He played prep ball in northeast Ohio, but thanks to ESPN and *Sports Illustrated*, millions of Americans knew his name before he was even a senior.

The American media isn't afraid to hype impressionable young athletes. No sir, we love to scour the fruited plains, identify adolescent super-talents, burden them with unreasonable expectations, then label them "failures" or "disappointments" if their careers land anywhere short of the greatness we preordained. Just ask Freddy Adu, Kwame Brown, Ron Powlus, or countless other young Americans who, despite reasonably successful careers, became "disappointments" in the eyes of the very journalists who constructed those expectations in the first place. It's a brutal and moronic pattern that's also a fertile trope irresistible to the hot takers.

Still, every once in a while an athlete matches the ridiculous hype and the failure police have to leave their handcuffs in their holsters. Tiger Woods did it. Both Williams sisters did it. Peyton Manning did it. And maybe once in a generation an athlete comes along who somehow makes our hype machine look too subtle.

By draft night in 2003, the hoops world knew that James was a fabulous talent. But the NBA is full of fabulous talents. What we didn't know was that James was a generational alpha dog who would be the face of the league for over a decade.

When players are 18 years old, scouts can readily identify physical traits like athleticism, height, length, and leaping ability; they can also easily evaluate basketball skills like jump shooting, ball handling, rebounding, defending, and passing. College hoops and the NBA are full of guys who check all of those boxes. But it's the less visible things that the scouts can't see that often differentiate NBA superstars from role players and rank-and-file millionaires.

LeBron James entered the league not only with an unmatched array of physical and basketball talent but also with two other qualities that propelled him to greatness: an excellent basketball IQ and a freakish dedication to improving his own game. The same kind of stuff that made Bird Bird, made Jordan Jordan, and made Kobe Kobe. These guys aren't just smart: they're smart and hyper-competitive, and one of the smartest things they do is channel that hyper-competitiveness inward when they're by themselves in a gym in July. Those traits don't conveniently fit into spreadsheets, but they are often the variables that determine the "ceiling" that a player will reach after making it to the NBA.

The long list of "lottery busts" in the NBA includes countless guys who weren't dedicated enough or smart enough to live their best basketball lives.

That's the thing about LeBron: not only did he enter the league with an unfair set of expectations, but he grinded his way to surpassing them. Despite the fact that NBA superstars seem to always be in our faces, the truth is that the truly great ones engineer their greatness when nobody's looking. They do the stuff that the others are unwilling to do.

With endless hours at the gym and an impeccable personal performance off the court—no arrests, no TMZ humiliations—LeBron James deflated the American media's cruelty boner waiting for him to "fail" or "disappoint" the basketball public. Regardless, millions of Americans still found ways to hate him.

By the time James was a senior in high school, two things made him the most hyped prospect in the country. First, his body: the kid looked like Karl Malone by the time was he was 17. He was 240 pounds, had very little body fat, and was chiseled from head to toe. Second, his hoops IQ: anybody who watched James destroy high school competition could easily see that he possessed incredible vision and a terrific feel for the sport. The McDonald's All-America game is full of kids who possess one of these two traits, but rarely does it feature a player with both.

By the time the NBA draft rolled around, the only player receiving even close to the same amount of hype was Carmelo Anthony, who'd just put his Syracuse squad on his back and won the NCAA Tournament as a freshman. It didn't matter. Anthony had a better jump shot and a proven ability to win big games, but the teenager from Akron was going number one. Justifiably so.

James's signature skill when he was a senior in high school may have been his passing game. He was simply a great passer. The predraft comparisons were rarely Michael Jordan or Kobe Bryant, but more often Magic Johnson. High school phenoms rarely develop great passing instincts. Why would they? Generally speaking, top-tier prospects are the most capable scorers on their squads by a wide margin. James was no exception: with that massive frame and explosive speed, high school defenders were helpless against him. In almost every possession, James could have simply attacked the paint or posted up to get easy looks near the basket. But that was never his approach.

In the early aughts, the aesthetic of the NBA was not great. During the first few seasons following Jordan's retirement, the league was full of wannabe Jordans try-ing to emulate the isolationist scoring dominance that had defined Jordan's iconic style. Throw Mike the ball, watch him work, watch him beat his defender, watch him score (and watch the other four offensive dudes just stand there). Make no mistake, watching Jordan do this was thrilling. But watching a league full of knock-offs try to do the same thing was not.

By the end of his career, the Jordan aesthetic had re-wired how America came to perceive basketball greatness. Jordan was truly the first player to dominate the league from the two-guard spot. It's not just that he won six NBA Championships and 10 scoring titles; it's that he did it in such a breathtakingly novel way, with ferocious rim attacks, beautiful fadeaways, and unstop-pable pull-up jumpers.

Air Jordan truly captured American hearts and eyeballs in ways that Russell, Chamberlain, Bird, and Magic never could. A generation of young American players all yearned to "be like Mike," which meant averaging 23 field goal attempts each game against only five assists. Playing like Mike meant a lot of isolation-style offense; it meant a lot of midrange jump shots; it meant scoring first, passing second.

By the time Jordan retired in 2003, the league was full of copycat teams and players trying and failing to repli-cate the heroball motif. But it could never be perfected again, and those who tried to do so ended up playing wildly inefficient, uncomfortably ugly basketball. There was only one Michael Jordan, and the teams that won titles immediately after Jordan's championship run ended were teams dominated by throwback big men like Shaquille O'Neal and Tim Duncan, who combined to win six of the seven Finals MVP Awards following Jordan's last championship in 1998.

By 2003, we were more than ready for the arrival of our next transformative player.

"Here Comes LeBron James"

James made his NBA debut October 29, 2003, in Sacramento. Despite the fact that the game featured two bad teams, ESPN put it on national TV. Every hoops fan in America was eager to get a first glimpse of the most hyped rookie in league history finally playing in the NBA.

It didn't take long for James to make his first highlight. Less than 90 seconds into the game, James was running the break. Brad Nessler was calling the game for ESPN, and as James grabbed a long rebound and began to lead the break upcourt, Nessler barked:

"Here comes LeBron James."

James took one full dribble as he crossed half-court and then in one smooth motion, while running at full speed—"on the run," said Nessler—James gathered his dribble just inside the three-point arc and quickly lofted a perfect lob pass toward the basket.

"This is his best part of his game," Nessler added just as Darius Miles received the perfect pass and slammed it home.

"And there's his first assist and it's a beauty!" Nessler had to raise his voice to be heard over the raucous reaction from the Kings fans.

Less than two minutes later, James curled off a baseline cut around a giant Zydrunas Ilgauskas screen. He caught a bounce pass from Darius Miles, took one dribble back toward the baseline, and rose up for his first career field goal attempt. It was a 17-foot jumper from the right baseline. He drained it.

By the end of the game, James put up crooked numbers in almost every column in the box score, something we would all learn to get used to. He scored 25, grabbed six boards, and dished out nine assists and had four steals and only two turnovers. Even as a rookie, James was almost always the best player on every court he ever stepped onto.

Through one lens, the kid from Akron had a tremendous year: James averaged 21 points, almost six rebounds, and nearly six assists per game, joining Oscar Robertson and Michael Jordan at that time as the only NBA rookies to average at least 20-5-5. Pretty good for a 19-year-old. He was playing very well, but the hype had him destined for greatness, and league history is chock-full of good young players who never became superstars. Even though he had a great rookie season, through another lens, James still had a long way to go to achieve greatness.

The 2003–04 Cleveland Cavaliers were not good. Even though they won 18 more games than the 2002–03 Cavs, they won just 35 games and lost 47. They did not make the playoffs. It's almost crazy to think about that now—the same guy who led his teams to the NBA Finals eight years in a row couldn't lead his squad to a .500 record as a first-year player. But it also speaks to just how much James improved between his rookie campaign and his prime. To study James is to understand an unsatisfied mind, a man who is his own harshest critic, and a player whose game has constantly evolved. The most hyped player in NBA history would drive himself to not only live up to the hype but exceed it by leaps and bounds.

On April 20, 2004, James became the youngest player to ever win the Rookie of the Year Award. The 2003 draft class was one of the best ever, and its best rookie was also one of the best ever. James easily beat fellow rookies Carmelo Anthony and Dwyane Wade in the voting. In a normal year, both of those guys would have easily won the award, but this was no normal batch of rookies.

As good as James was, his game was still raw, and flaws weren't hard to find. Sure, he ranked 15th in points per game his rookie year, but he took an ugly route to get there. A quick look at his rookie year shot chart reveals that James entered the league as a player who could create shots all over the court but struggled to convert those shots at even average rates—particularly outside of the paint, where he was simply terrible.

Later in his career, James would make the integration of volume and efficiency look almost effortless, but as a

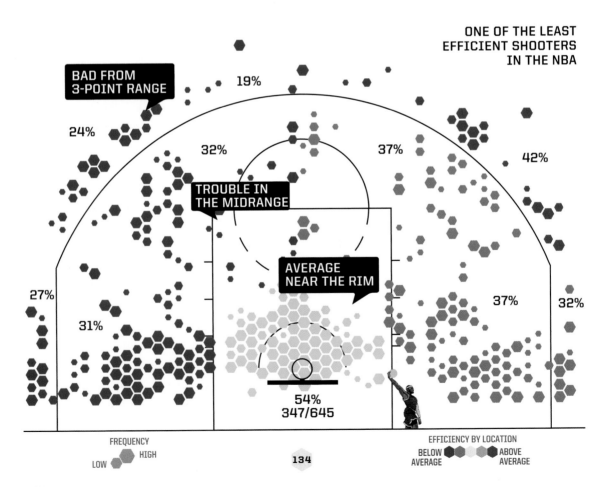

LEBRON JAMES
ROOKIE YEAR
2003-04 SEASON

ONE OF THE LEAST
EFFICIENT SHOOTERS
IN THE NBA

**BAD FROM
3-POINT RANGE**

19%

24%

32%   37%   42%

**TROUBLE IN
THE MIDRANGE**

**AVERAGE
NEAR THE RIM**

27%   37%   32%

31%

54%
347/645

FREQUENCY
LOW HIGH

EFFICIENCY BY LOCATION
BELOW AVERAGE   ABOVE AVERAGE

S
P
R
A
W
L
B
A
L
L

rookie he was one of the least efficient volume scorers in the NBA. In a league that converted 44 percent of its shots, he made only 42 percent of his. He wasn't a king yet.

He was okay near the bucket, but the kid couldn't shoot.

The nature of his rookie-year struggles revealed a key limitation that would pester James his entire career: his jump shot. Unlike Curry, who arrived with a phenomenal jumper and had to build his game around it, James had all the other stuff but needed to get a better jump shot.

During his rookie year, James struggled mightily to make his jumper. Out of 27 players who tried at least 500 two-point shots beyond 7.5 feet from the basket that season, James ranked dead last in field goal percentage. He made just 33.9 percent of his 614 midrangers in his rookie campaign. And if that wasn't bad enough, those types of shots made up a huge chunk of his shot diet, 41 percent, and he was hitting them at very low rates. That wasn't good.

His struggles extended beyond the three-point line. Three-pointers made up just 14 percent of his rookie-year field goal attempts, but James was also inaccurate beyond the arc. During the 2003–04 season, James was one of 74 NBA players who tried at least 200 three-point shots, but he ranked 72nd in percentage made. That wasn't good either.

Looking at three types of shots, we see that, as a rookie, James was average in the close-range areas and really bad in the midrange and three-point range areas. There's no other way to put it. It would take time and effort to change that.

In many ways, the phenom looked like the Greek God of Basketball: with elite athleticism, speed, strength, vision, and IQ, he could pass, attack the rim, defend, and rebound. But his jump-shooting numbers were his Achilles' heel.

Whether he knew it or not at the time, James was about to become the best player of his era; however, the jump shot was about to become the most important skill of his era, and it was the one skill he didn't possess.

To become the most dominant player in the early 21st century James would have to fix some things, especially that crooked jumper. Fortunately, one thing he did possess was a gritty work ethic. Every summer James would go home to Akron, then reemerge with some key improvements to his game.

He improved that wonky jump shot and everything else in his portfolio too. To look back at the ascendancy of this king is to study targeted metamorphoses that helped the 2004 NBA Rookie of the Year become one of the best ballers in the history of our beloved sport.

The kid from Akron assembled his game brick by brick, year by year, skill by skill. And through his first dozen years as an NBA player, he made changes that dotted his path to the top of the mountain.

By the time James met Curry in those epic 2016 Finals, the idea that James was an inefficient player would have been simply ludicrous. At that point, James was one of the most efficient players in the league, but it's also important to recall that this was not always the case. As a rookie, James was a below-average shooter, an average finisher, and a key member of a mediocre defense. But between that rookie season and those 2016 Finals, he morphed aspects of his game from bad to good to great.

The road from bad to good always passes through average on the way, and many of James's early strides as a player reflect the basic truth that you have to gain competency before you can gain excellence. Before he could be great at everything, he'd need to become average at some things.

The Atlas of Lebron: Mapping the Rise of the King

2004-05: Improving His Close-Range Efficiency

By the end of LeBron James's prime, his signature offensive skill was interior domination. Simply put, James dominated the paint for a decade. However, he didn't do so as a rookie, and the biggest early improvement of his game was as a finisher.

Looking at his second season shot chart, we see that James quickly improved his ability to score close to the goal, a trait that would continue to improve and eventually define his scoring excellence for years to come. As a rookie, he made just 54 percent of his shots in the close-range areas, which is actually below the league average in that zone (55 percent). As a second-year player, James learned how to attack the rim, draw fouls, and use his gargantuan frame to keep defenders at bay, and that close-range number surged to 64 percent.

The area near the basket is the only spot on the court where players make at least half of their shots. Not surprisingly, then, it's also the most heavily defended

zone in the game. So players who can regularly get close-range shots and make close-range shots quickly become some of the league's most prized assets. In his second year, James became exactly that.

James's improvements as a second-year scorer mimicked his team's improvements as a whole: both progressed incrementally. As James went from inefficient to average, so did the Cavs. The 2003–04 Cavs ended the season with an NET rating of −2.9, which ranked them 21st in the NBA and indicated that their opponents outscored them by 2.9 points per 100 possessions. NET rating is probably the single-best stat for looking at how well or badly a team is playing. After his rookie season, no LeBron team would ever post such a poor NET rating again. In James's second season, the Cavs improved marginally on both sides of the court, making it into the bottom part of the top half of the NBA in both offensive and defensive ratings. In short, they went from a bad team to an average one.

The 2004–05 Cavs won more games than they lost, but narrowly. James was the best player on his team, and it wasn't close. Aside from the All-Star center Zydrunas Ilgauskas, James was playing ball alongside a motley crew of NBA "talent"—that year the Cavs trotted out a starting lineup that included guys like Ira Newble, Jeff McInnis, and Drew Gooden. On the bench were guys like Eric Snow, Lucious Harris, and Robert Traylor. Not exactly Wade and Bosh or Kyrie and Love. As good as James was getting, he was only one man—a young man at that—and the story of his early career is at least partially a story of surrounding inevitable greatness with bands of mediocrity.

The Cavs of the early aughts didn't exactly provide James with a great incubator. Still, year after year,

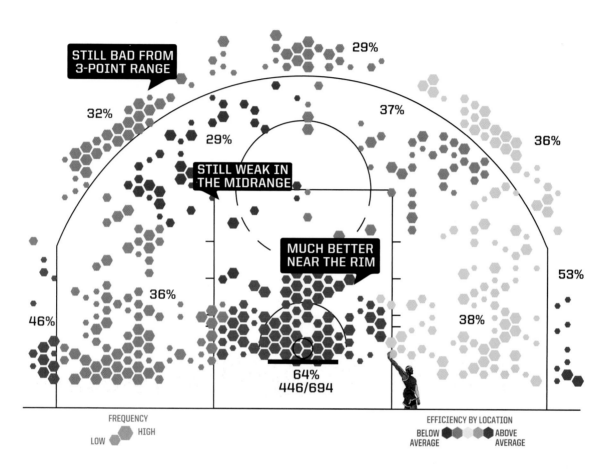

LEBRON JAMES
SECOND YEAR
2004-05 SEASON

STILL BAD FROM 3-POINT RANGE

29%

32%

37%

29%

36%

STILL WEAK IN THE MIDRANGE

MUCH BETTER NEAR THE RIM

53%

36%

46%

38%

64%
446/694

FREQUENCY
LOW — HIGH

EFFICIENCY BY LOCATION
BELOW AVERAGE — ABOVE AVERAGE

James would grow in spite of his surroundings, and starting in year two he began to lead his team to more wins than losses. But at 42-40, the 2004–05 Cavs finished fourth in their five-team division, and after a late-season slump, they again missed the playoffs. They fired head coach Paul Silas, with 18 games left to play in the season. It was a bad sign; after all, Silas had been brought in partly to mentor the league's next great superstar.

After two seasons in the NBA, James was clearly becoming a great player, but his team was missing the playoffs. That would never happen again.

Inventing Playoff LeBron

In the summer of 2005, the Cavs hired 35-year-old Mike Brown to coach the team. Before landing in Cleveland,

Brown was a top assistant for Rick Carlisle in Indiana, and prior to that Brown served as an assistant in San Antonio. Brown had championship coaching experience with the Spurs, but in San Antonio he also was part of the Gregg Popovich Player Development Industrial Complex. The hope was that Brown would not only help the Cavs play better on the court but also inject some developmental support into the organization. It worked.

On November 2, 2005, the team opened that season at home against New Orleans/Oklahoma City. James put up 31 points on just 16 shots, and the Cavs walked away with a 22-point victory. Both stats were harbingers of a new era in Cleveland—efficiency for James, and wins for his team. James would go on to average 31.4 points per game that year, and for only the third time in franchise history the team would win 50 games.

The 2005–06 Cavs were the first good team that LeBron James played for in the NBA. They qualified for the playoffs as the fourth seed and faced the Washington Wizards in the first round. It didn't take long for James to announce his presence. He recorded a triple double, scoring 32 points, grabbing 11 rebounds, and dishing out 11 assists as the Cavs took Game 1 at home. That combination of stats is rare for any game, but it's particularly rare in the playoffs. Jordan commonly put up 30 points or more in big games, but he rarely had 11 boards or 11 dimes. Magic would commonly get triple doubles in big games, but rarely put up 30-plus points in the process. Playoff LeBron was a monster, and he was just getting warmed up.

After the Wizards stole Game 2 in Cleveland, the teams returned to Washington for Game 3. With 23.4 seconds remaining in the game, the Wizards were up 96–95. It was the first real high-leverage playoff moment in the young buck's career; how would he respond?

James received an inbounds pass and walked the ball up the court. He ended up isolated against Antonio Daniels near the left elbow. Compared to James, Daniels was tiny.

Mike Tirico was calling the game on ESPN: "James . . . , has Daniels, [and] can go up over him if he wants." But James wasn't about to settle for an elbow jumper. He maintained his dribble and pushed his way down toward the left block, where he'd use a series of nifty moves to make the biggest shot of his career from his favorite spot on the floor—the interior.

The Wizards center, Michael Ruffin, surged over to protect the basket as James had his way with Daniels. Tirico continued, "Fakes right, goes left, bends in . . ."

James muscled around Daniels, elevated toward the basket, and collided with the giant Ruffin, who provided perfectly timed help. James and Ruffin rose up at the same time, right at the edge of the restricted area, and Tirico's voice rose up too to meet the moment:

" . . . over Ruffin, he got it to go! Time-out Washington! 5.7 to go. LeBron James hit the big shot again! So with that hoop, LeBron James, 41 points, the most points scored in the first road playoff game by any player in NBA history."

It was an amazing way to punctuate an amazing game for the kid from Akron. Not only did he score 41 points in his first-ever road playoff game, but he won the game with a clutch, physical play in crunch time. And he wasn't done.

A few nights later, on May 3, 2006, LeBron and the Cavs were back home playing a huge Game 5. The Wizards won Game 4, so whoever could win Game 5 would emerge as the clear favorite to take the seven-game series. The game was tense. It ended up in overtime, and once again, the Wizards held a one-point lead in the final minute. It didn't look good for the Cavs: they were down 120–119 with just 3.6 seconds left. They had the ball inbounding from just inside half-court.

Coach Brown drew up a play for James, who would start at the top of the key, run through a screen, cut down toward the baseline, and catch the inbounds pass 21 feet from the basket in an awkward spot in the left corner. Three Wizards—Antawn Jamison, Michael Ruffin, and Brendan Haywood—surrounded James. No problem. James used a powerful left-handed dribble to burst his way past Jamison on the baseline. He dribbled a second time as he raced toward the basket before rising up underneath the hoop and dropping in a right-handed lay-in. 121–120 Cavs, with 0.9 seconds left. James had just won the game again. This was his first playoff series, and he won Games 3 and 5 with game-winning shots. Game 6 would also go to overtime, and James would score 32 points to propel the Cavs to the series win.

For those wondering how James would perform under playoff pressure, the answer was obvious. In just his third year, the 21-year-old had shown the basketball world that he was going to be a force to be reckoned with. In 2006, we got to see "Playoff LeBron" for the first time, but he wasn't the king just yet. Despite some great performances from James, the Cavs lost to the Pistons in round 2 in a tough seven-game series. Still, it was a great year for LeBron and the Cavs. His improvements as a leader, along with the new coach, had helped get them into round 2 of the playoffs.

Defense Wins Championships

If the 2006 playoffs gave James his first taste of winning multiple playoff games, the 2007 playoffs would give him his first taste of winning multiple series. Coming off their first playoff appearance, the 2006–07 Cavaliers had high expectations. Mike Brown had changed the culture around the team, and his Spurs bona fides began showing up in one very important place: on defense.

In his second year with the team, Brown was able to build a much better defense for the Cavs, who finished the season with the fourth-ranked defense in the league. In his first three seasons, James had never been a part of a top-10 defensive outfit. Suddenly, he was the best defender on a top-five defense, and the Cavs were more dangerous than ever.

There are three components to defensive success in the NBA: tactics, talent, and will. Coach Brown provided the tactics and the schemes. The roster had enough defensive talent and smart enough soldiers to implement Brown's tactics. But then there's will. Many NBA teams have decent tactics and talent but still fail to play great defense. Defense is really hard; it requires that players burn calories on that end of the floor. As the leader of the 2006–07 Cavs, James set the tone. He played hard on both ends, and his teammates followed suit. It's a trait that some superstars have and some don't. Jordan played incredible defense. So did Bird. But it's not hard to find superstars who don't bother. Those players and their teams rarely win in the playoffs.

James was born to play defense. His body allows him to guard almost any position on the floor: he's quick enough to keep up with guards, and strong and big enough to bang around with bigs. His basketball IQ fuels his ability to not only follow a game plan but freelance and be at the right place at the right time. As James began to realize his defensive potential, the 2006–07 Cavs suddenly had a higher ceiling—and so did his career.

They finished the season as the second seed in the Eastern Conference. Just one year after barely beating Washington in round 1, they swept the Wizards in the first round, holding them to 92 points or less in three of the four games. That defense also helped in round 2 as the Cavs took out the New Jersey Nets in six games thanks in large part to the fact that the Nets scored more than 92 in only one game while scoring 85 or less in four. On May 18, 2007, James and the Cavs advanced to the Conference Finals by beating New Jersey 88–72. James closed out the series on a high note, leading his team in points, rebounds, and assists in the closeout game.

But a familiar foe stood between the Cavs and the 2007 NBA Finals—the Detroit Pistons, who eliminated the Cavs from the 2006 playoffs and seemed likely to repeat the feat in 2007. The Pistons owned the East for the first few years of the James era. Between 2003 and 2008, they made six consecutive Eastern Conference Finals and won an unlikely NBA championship by beating

Shaq, Kobe, and the Lakers in the 2004 NBA Finals. If James was to get to his first NBA Finals, he and his teammates would have to upend the lords of the Eastern Conference.

It would take one of the greatest individual performances in NBA history to get the Cavs over the hump. Once again, LeBron James, lifted to a higher stage, performed at a higher level. After the teams split the first four games of the series, they squared off in a massive Game 5 at the Palace of Auburn Hills. The winner of the game would be in the driver's seat to take the series and earn a Finals berth, as this Pistons team had already done multiple times.

On May 31, 2007, in one of his finest performances, James put a symbolic end to the Pistons' run of dominance. The Cavs won the game 109–107 in double overtime—or more aptly, LeBron James won the game. James scored 29 of the team's final 30 points, including the game-winning layup. He ended with 48 points. In the biggest game of his career, James played the best game of his career. He was unstoppable. Forty-eight points, nine rebounds, and seven assists. He played over 50 minutes that night. It was the greatest playoff performance in years, and it deflated the Pistons. The Cavs won the series in Game 6 on their home floor, but lost to the Spurs in the 2007 Finals.

A quick aside: In LeBron's rookie year, the Pistons won the title, while playing the sport in a vastly different manner than James's later foes. The 2003–04 Pistons made 333 three-point shots. In 2015–16, Stephen Curry made 402 by himself. Those championship Pistons took just 15 percent of their shots from three-point range; the 2017–18 Houston Rockets took over half of their shots from three-point range. As James matured and became the most famous face of the league, the league he played in mutated and the three-point shot became increasingly central to its game play.

Learning to Score at Will

By averaging exactly 30 points per game, James won the NBA scoring championship in 2007–08, despite still struggling to become a truly efficient jump shooter. A quick look at his shot chart suggests that James was "inefficient" that season. There sure is a lot of blue on his chart, but on closer inspection, we can see that, while he remained a mediocre jump shooter, he was an absolute beast near the hoop. He converted 472 field goals inside within 7.5 feet of the bucket. He was also hyper-efficient near the basket: he converted 68 percent of his 699 shots in that zone, flashing the dominant blend of interior volume and efficiency that would come to be his calling card as he entered his prime.

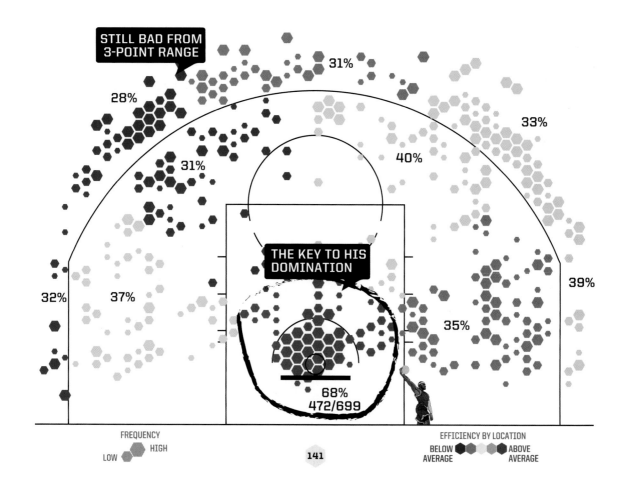

LEBRON JAMES
SCORING CHAMP
2007-08 SEASON

STILL BAD FROM 3-POINT RANGE

28%   31%   33%

31%   40%

THE KEY TO HIS DOMINATION

32%   37%   39%

35%

68%
472/699

FREQUENCY
LOW   HIGH

EFFICIENCY BY LOCATION
BELOW AVERAGE   ABOVE AVERAGE

Swiss-Army-Knife LeBron

By 2008–09, LeBron James was clearly the best player in the NBA, in part because he was so freaking versatile. That year he led his team in points, rebounds, assists, steals, and blocks. Think about that. That's nuts. Curry could never do that. Jordan could never do that. Shaq could never do that. In addition, James finished second in the NBA Defensive Player of the Year voting. As if that weren't enough, he was leading his team to new heights. The 2008–09 Cavs won 66 games and lost just 16 times. Everything was clicking—or was it?

Maybe James led his team in all those statistical categories because he was the most complete player in the NBA. Or maybe that accomplishment revealed a lack of talent around him. The Cavs didn't make the Finals that year; they lost to Orlando in the Eastern Conference Finals. Two years after making his first Finals, LeBron hadn't gotten back. The team seemed to be going backwards despite James's increasing dominance. There was a growing narrative that James couldn't win a ring.

Taking Ownership of His Surroundings

After the disappointing end to the 2008–09 campaign, James and his colleagues rebounded and once again dominated the regular season. But as they had learned the previous year, regular-season dominance guarantees nothing in the playoffs. Once again, the Cavs faltered, losing an ugly series to the Celtics in the second round. The Celtics had nobody as good as James, but they did have three surefire Hall of Famers in Kevin Garnett, Paul Pierce, and Ray Allen. If one of them had

a bad game, the others could pick up the slack. James never had that luxury. If he had a bad game, his team was doomed. As he exited the 2010 playoffs, he also entered free agency.

Seven years into his career, he could finally choose not only where he wanted to play, but whom he wanted to play with. He wanted to win. He wanted a better environment. He wanted out of Cleveland.

Just before 9:30 p.m. on July 8, 2010, LeBron announced that he was leaving Cleveland and "taking my talents to South Beach." He was joining Dwyane Wade, Chris Bosh, and Pat Riley in Miami. The decision stunned the NBA and devastated Cleveland. Many questioned his loyalty, but from a basketball perspective, nobody could question that the decision put James in a better place. In Miami, he wouldn't have to carry his team every night. Like his foes in Boston, he would be part of a Big Three and a more complete roster.

The summer of 2010 was the first time James leveraged free agency to put himself in a different situation. It wouldn't be the last. James is the leading figure in a generation of NBA players who are a lot more likely to leverage free agency and migrate between teams. Whereas previous superstars like Magic, Bird, and Jordan rarely, if ever, switched jerseys, James took a different approach to his surroundings. He chose to play for multiple teams in different cities.

In 2010, James challenged the pro basketball community to reject the foolish notion that NBA players have to be "loyal" to a city or a franchise or an ownership group despite the obvious fact that that kind of loyalty is a one-way street. Those same entities never have to be "loyal" to the players. James took the steering wheel of his career in 2010 by making the smartest free agency choice available to him. Naturally, he got killed for it by an outrageous American sports discourse happy to foam at its mouth and spew ridiculous judgments about his loyalty, while simultaneously unable to digest the fact that a young man might want to move from Cleveland, Ohio, to Miami, Florida, and from a poorly run NBA franchise with an uneven roster to an expertly run franchise with great teammates. What a dick, amirite?

In retrospect, James's move to Miami exposed an embarrassing belligerence in American sports media toward players who dare to change teams for personal or professional gain. The idea that big-time pro athletes should be beholden to the situations and organizations into which they were drafted is not just ludicrous; it also violates the free market capitalism that's supposed to be the centerpiece of America itself.

The way pro athletes are forced to begin their career is unlike any other professional situation most of us experience. NBA rookies are told where to live, who to work for, and who to work with. They don't choose their own path. The NBA owners have designed this system intentionally. Moreover, the league rewards its worst-performing teams with the highest picks in its draft system. So players like James who toil for years to become the most elite amateur prospects in their sport are rewarded by getting marooned in the least successful professional franchises each and every year.

NBA franchises like the Kings and the Cavaliers perennially suck and perennially get to pick at the top of the draft. The best franchises always pick at the bottom. This system often thrusts the world's best basketball prospects into shoddy basketball environments, forcing one of two things to happen: either the prospects thrive and drive the bad team to improve, or the negative environment wins out, the prospect becomes "a bust," and the organization is rewarded with more top picks. James was an example of the prior outcome: he succeeded in spite of the questionable ecosystem in Cleveland. His greatness was too great to be dampened by the mediocrity around him. In his first seven years in the NBA, James turned one of the NBA's least successful teams into a contender. Still, he was only one player, and the team couldn't win a title.

Each spring James and his teammates would lose to another team that might not have had anyone as good as James but had more depth on its roster. The teams that sent his early teams home from the playoffs, like the Pistons, Celtics, and Spurs, had talent everywhere. The organization in Cleveland failed to surround James with championship-caliber colleagues. So naturally the media would criticize James relentlessly for failing to "win a ring" and question whether he was truly great, despite the fact that he was obviously the best young player the NBA had seen in a very long time. The narrative was as moronic as it was brutal.

James needed a change. He deserved a change. LeBron James walked away from Cleveland in 2010, wisely turning the page on the first chapter of his career and entering a championship-caliber environment in Miami, complete with competent ownership and a front office willing and able to build a great roster. Of course, this highly rational choice by the young motivated star caused the hot-takers to lose their shit. James was a sellout. He was taking a shortcut to his championships. He was an asshole. People took to the streets to burn his jerseys in downtown Cleveland.

The team's owner, Dan Gilbert, published an instantly regrettable hate letter that featured incredibly petty personal attacks that unintentionally revealed that the Cavs organization lacked grace and good leadership traits at the very highest levels. For many of us, the letter inadvertently helped immediately justify James's decision to split from the Cavs. It's hard to pick out the worst excerpt from Gilbert's infamous message to his fan base, but here are three solid candidates:

1. "You simply don't deserve this kind of cowardly betrayal."

2. "I PERSONALLY GUARANTEE THAT THE CLEVELAND CAVALIERS WILL WIN AN NBA CHAMPIONSHIP BEFORE THE SELF-TITLED FORMER 'KING' WINS ONE."

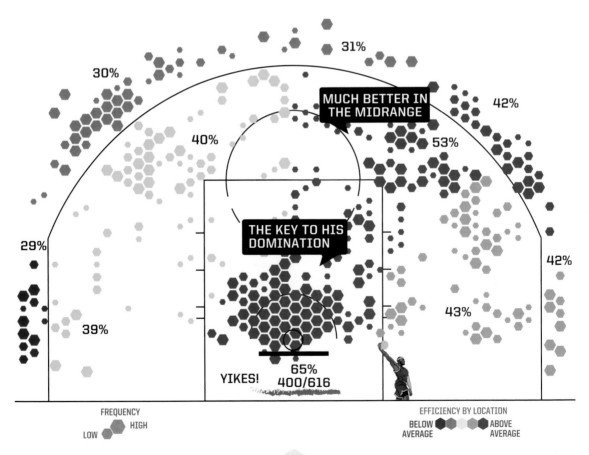

LEBRON JAMES
FIRST YEAR IN MIAMI
2010-11 SEASON

S
P
R
A
W
L
B
A
L
L

31%

30%

42%

MUCH BETTER IN THE MIDRANGE

40%

53%

29%

THE KEY TO HIS DOMINATION

42%

39%

43%

YIKES! 65% 400/616

FREQUENCY
LOW ⬡ ⬡ HIGH

EFFICIENCY BY LOCATION
BELOW AVERAGE ⬡⬡⬡ ABOVE AVERAGE

Looking back, it's still shocking to see how prevalent these kinds of sentiments were. James wasn't just the most hated athlete in Cleveland—he began this decade as the most hated athlete in America. And all because he had the nerve to leave Dan Gilbert's basketball team.

Building a Better Jumper

One of the benefits of joining a more talented team is that you get better shots. After James migrated to Miami, his on-ball burden lessened. Suddenly he could rely on Dwyane Wade and Chris Bosh to create offense too. Suddenly opponents couldn't focus all their defensive attention on him. Naturally, as James's usage dwindled, his efficiency increased. He was getting cleaner looks, and his numbers as a jump shooter surged.

Looking at his 2010–11 shot chart, we see James showing signs, for the first time in his career, of becoming an above-average jump shooter. Although he still struggled from three-point range, his numbers near the elbows were very strong.

Unfortunately, the legacy of LeBron's 2010–11 season would have little to do with his improved midrange jumper. Despite winning 58 games and earning a trip to the Finals, the 2010–11 Miami Heat were a disappointment. Following LeBron's decision to join up with Wade and Bosh, the expectations were clear: championship or bust. So in that sense the campaign was a

bust. Although they cruised through the Eastern Conference bracket, beating Philly, Boston, and Chicago in five games each, their momentum ended in the Finals.

The Dallas Mavericks entered the playoffs as the third seed in the West, but led by the incredible shooting of Dirk Nowitzki, they had upended the Blazers, Lakers, and Thunder on their way to the Finals. The 2011 Finals were a rematch of the controversial 2006 NBA Finals, which had featured Wade and the Heat beating the Mavs in six games, thanks to what many consider to have been some questionable officiating that favored Miami. Well, in 2011, the Mavs exacted revenge by upsetting the most hyped—and most hated—NBA team in years, beating Miami in six games and preventing James from winning his first championship.

The haters rejoiced. LeBron still didn't have his title.

Summer 2011: Hakeem Postgame

The summer of 2011 was one of the biggest off-seasons in James's career. How would he respond to the loss? How would he respond to being the most hated superstar in the league and all the critics saying he couldn't win a title no matter what city he played in?

Following the bitter loss to Dallas in the 2011 Finals, LeBron came into 2011–12 a different player. He came in on a mission. It wasn't necessarily apparent on a game-by-game basis, but some very interesting changes emerge from a look at his shot chart.

LeBron officially became an efficiency monster in 2011–12. He made 53 percent of his shots, a new career high. The uptick had a lot to do with his decreased activity

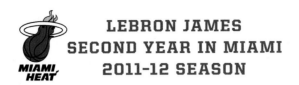

LEBRON JAMES
SECOND YEAR IN MIAMI
2011-12 SEASON

FIRST NBA CHAMPIONSHIP

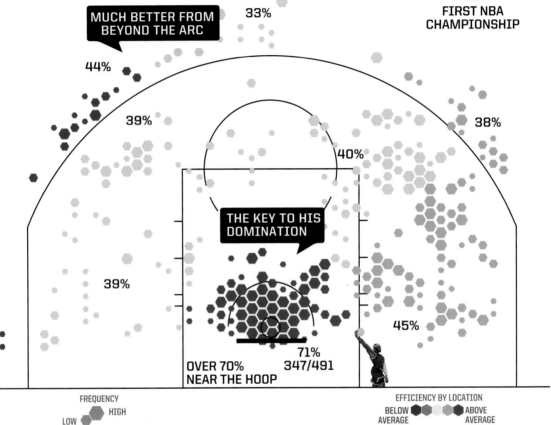

MUCH BETTER FROM BEYOND THE ARC

33%

44%

39%

40%

38%

THE KEY TO HIS DOMINATION

39%

45%

71%
347/491

OVER 70% NEAR THE HOOP

FREQUENCY
LOW — HIGH

EFFICIENCY BY LOCATION
BELOW AVERAGE — ABOVE AVERAGE

S
P
R
A
W
L
B
A
L
L

as a jump shooter and increased activity closer to the hoop. He was trading in those "average" jumpers in favor of more of his monstrous rim attacks, where he hovered around 70 percent in field goal percentage.

He stopped shooting threes as much. After setting his career high by launching 387 threes in 2009–10, James shot only 279 during his first year in Miami. But in his second year on South Beach, that number plummeted all the way down to 149! At the exact same time the NBA and all its superstars were increasing their three-point activity, James was cutting his in half. From an efficiency standpoint, it was addition by subtraction; by removing less efficient parts of his shot portfolio, he gave more energy to his best skills and increased his overall efficiency.

After the loss to the Mavericks, James enlisted the off-season tutelage of Hakeem Olajuwon, one of the greatest post players in the history of the league. Some obscure YouTube footage shows the pair working out in a gym like Luke and Yoda on the left block. James worked on his footwork and his balance. He worked on his midrange fadeaway. He came back with some new tricks and a new approach to scoring—less jump shooting, more post-ups.

He got a lot better in the midrange. Looking at the history of LeBron's shot charts, there are a lot of blue hexagons in the jump-shooting zones. But by being more selective with his shots and improving his accuracy, LeBron elevated his jump-shooting efficiency in 2011–12, proving that he might just be a good shooter after all. That skill would come in handy for years to come.

2012-13: Peak LeBron

Forget the three-point line. The most important place on the court is still the little area right next to the

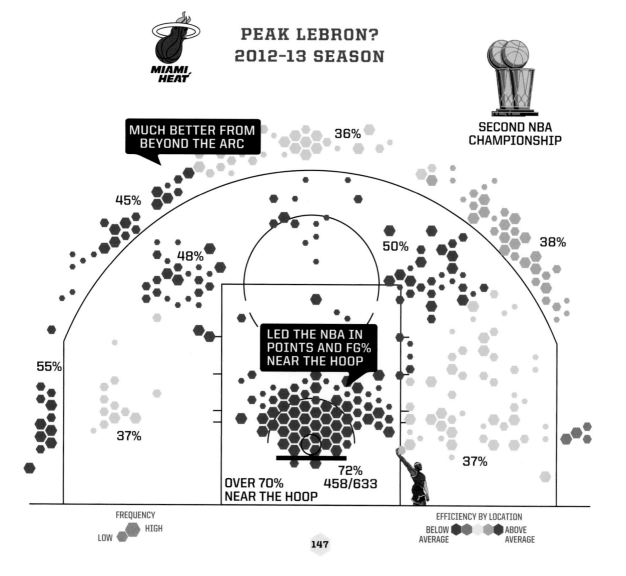

PEAK LEBRON?
2012-13 SEASON

MIAMI HEAT

SECOND NBA CHAMPIONSHIP

MUCH BETTER FROM BEYOND THE ARC

36%

45%

48%

50%

38%

55%

LED THE NBA IN POINTS AND FG% NEAR THE HOOP

37%

37%

72%
458/633

OVER 70% NEAR THE HOOP

FREQUENCY
LOW — HIGH

EFFICIENCY BY LOCATION
BELOW AVERAGE — ABOVE AVERAGE

hoop. Anyone who has studied shot efficiency around the court quickly realizes that the best place to score on the court is near the rim. There's a misconception that analytically woke hoops nerds want everybody to shoot more threes. While that's kind of true, what we also know is that dunks and layups are way better than any other option, including threes. The best return on your investment is close to the basket. In his prime, LeBron James owned this area. It's hard to pick out any single year as the best of his overall career, but for scoring, it's hard to argue that 2012–13 was the best of his best.

And the craziest stat of all from that year: James led the league in both volume and efficiency around the basket.

That season the Heat would defend their championship by beating the Spurs in an incredible seven-game series that everyone will rightly remember for Ray Allen's three-point shot. However, that shot won Game 6; the Heat still had to win Game 7 against Popovich, Duncan, Parker, and Ginobili. And it wasn't Ray Allen who won that game.

It wasn't Ray Allen who scored 37 points and grabbed 12 rebounds with history on the line.

No no, Ray had zero points in Game 7. James made five threes, was eight-for-eight from the line, and, with 27.9 seconds left, made one of the biggest shots of his life, a pull-up jumper from 19 feet to put his team up by four. If he'd missed, the Spurs would've had a chance to tie or win in the game's final seconds. But he didn't miss, and seven years after his big-time game-winners against Washington in the first round, LeBron was now winning huge games with jump shots instead of rim

attacks. That Game 7 was a fitting end to what might go down as James's best season ever. He was clearly the best player all year, and clearly the best player in Game 7 against an all-time great opponent.

Still, one stat from that campaign stands out.

During the 2012–13 regular season, 168 NBA players tried at least 200 shots inside of eight feet—that's over a third of the league's population—but only one player converted over 70 percent of those shots. James made 72 percent of over 640 close-range shots and was easily the most efficient interior scorer in the whole league. Better than Durant. Better than DeAndre Jordan. Better than Blake Griffin. It wasn't close, but efficiency is only part of the story.

Here's where it gets crazy: the same fella who was that interior efficiency monster was also the league's leading scorer in this area too!

Basketball is a pretty simple game when you can score at will near the rim. We learned that from Mikan, Russell, Chamberlain, Adbul-Jabbar, and Shaq. And in a league with 450 guys, when one of them is both the leading scorer and the most efficient scorer in the league's most important area, it's pretty obvious who that league's most valuable player is.

For those who doubted James's place in NBA history, the NBA's official press release announcing his 2013 MVP Award, should've erased that:

NEW YORK—LeBron James of the Miami Heat is the winner of the Maurice Podoloff Trophy as the 2012–13 Kia NBA Most Valuable Player, the NBA announced today. James earns the honor for the second consecutive year and the fourth time in five seasons. The only other player to win the award in four of five seasons is Bill Russell (1961, '62, '63, '65), and the only other players to win at least four regular-season MVPs are Kareem Abdul-Jabbar (six), Michael Jordan (five), Russell (five) and Wilt Chamberlain (four).

Russell. Adbul-Jabbar. Jordan. Chamberlain. James. Is that good company for a 28-year-old or what?

While James's interior dominance steered his game to new heights, it wasn't the only thing he ramped up in 2012–13. His jump shot also came around. He made 40 percent of his threes. He made almost half of his shots around the elbows. Those are Dirk numbers. Those are Chris Paul numbers. And it was that skill, the elbow jumper, that helped him ice Game 7 in Miami. To look at his shot chart from that year is to glance at Peak LeBron—one of the best players in league history at his absolute apex. This was a guy who could beat you everywhere on the floor. Yes, he was an absolute beast in the paint, but his jumper was dangerous too.

A decade after entering the league, James had the most dangerous offensive arsenal the league had seen since Jordan. By 2013, the kid who was one of the least efficient volume scorers in the entire league in 2004 wasn't just one of the most efficient scorers in the league—at 28, he'd become one of the most efficient and versatile offensive players the NBA had ever seen. And he had won two straight NBA championships. Moreover, the 2012–13 Spurs may go down as one of the best teams ever to not win a championship. That group had it all: offense, defense, coaching, champions decorating their roster. Before 2013, Popovich and

Duncan were undefeated in four previous trips to the NBA Finals.

And James was the best player on the team that beat them. One of the defining elements of James's long career is consistency. He's been so good for so long that it's hard to pinpoint exactly when he was at his best. But you could argue that 2012–13 was when he put it all together and became "King James." Between the individual accomplishments and his team's Finals victory over the great San Antonio Spurs, that arguably may have been his crowning moment.

At the same time, that year was definitely peak Heat. After winning two consecutive championships, the Heat couldn't threepeat. They lost the 2014 NBA Finals to a familiar foe: those pesky Spurs, who, just as LeBron did after the 2011 Finals, used the 2013 Finals loss to come back better, stronger, and more determined than ever. The 2014–15 Spurs would not be denied, and they exposed the Heat in a Finals rematch. The Spurs played nearly perfect egalitarian basketball, moving the ball at breakneck speed, trading in good shots for great shots, and playing impeccable defense. They were a juggernaut. They were determined. They were champions. James and his teammates were tired.

To make matters worse, they didn't have home-court advantage in the 2014 Finals, which marked Miami's fourth straight trip to June basketball. Game 1 of the 2014 Finals would take place in the sweltering heat of San Antonio. Oh, and the air conditioning didn't work. In one of the most bizarre Finals games in NBA history, Game 1 of the 2014 Finals was played in a virtual sauna. Temperatures were as high as 90 degrees on the floor. James and his teammates came to fight, but didn't expect the fight to happen in a pizza oven. James cramped up at the worst time and had to leave the closely contested game at a crucial moment in the fourth quarter. The Heat could not recover, and the Spurs took the first game of the series.

It was a cruelly ironic way for an exhausted team called the Heat to lose. Even though Miami came back and valiantly stole Game 2 in San Antonio, that was the only game they would win in the series. The Spurs were too good. The Heat weren't good enough. Duncan and Popovich would not be denied two years in a row. They won the 2014 NBA championship, and LeBron had another decision to make.

Following four straight trips to the NBA Finals with the Heat and two championships, James once again entered free agency in the summer of 2014. Maybe all the "loyalty" stuff got to him, or maybe he just wanted to go home, but he left Miami and took his talents back to Cleveland, Ohio.

Now squarely in his prime, with championships under his belt, LeBron went home to settle some unfinished business: he wanted to give his hometown team its first-ever NBA championship. Simply put, the Cavs were always a forgettable NBA franchise. Sometimes they were good, oftentimes they were bad, but they had never been great. James wanted to change that. He wanted to bring greatness to Ohio.

On July 11, 2014, LeBron James announced via a carefully written statement in *Sports Illustrated* that he was "coming home." Despite all the burned jerseys and the hate letter from Gilbert, James was determined to make it right, determined to go back to Cleveland and win a title for his hometown team.

The Second Cleveland Administration

In James's four-year absence, the Cavs sucked. There's no other way to put it. While James was winning rings in Miami, Cleveland was winning NBA lotteries. Following LeBron's departure in 2010, it didn't take long for Cleveland to fall off of a cliff. The 2010–11 Cavs won just 19 games. They lost 63. They had one of the worst offenses in the NBA, and they had one of the worst defenses too. Their leading scorer was Antawn Jamison. It was ugly, but remember the NBA loves to lavish its ugliest ducklings with some of its most prized resources: top draft picks. In the spring of 2011, as LeBron and the Heat were marching to the NBA Finals, the Cavs got the fourth pick in the draft, setting up their ability to draft Tristan Thompson, the strong rebounding big man from the University of Texas. But that wasn't all. In a midseason stroke of genius by then-GM Chris Grant, the Cavs shipped out Mo Williams and Jamario Moon to the Clippers in exchange for Baron Davis and the Clippers' 2011 unprotected first-round pick. Well, in May 2011, that particular pick came up as the number-one pick in the draft lottery, giving the Cavs their first top pick since 2003, when they chose LeBron James.

Thanks to Grant's savvy transaction, the Cavs selected Kyrie Irving, the one-and-done phenom point guard from Duke. And although it might not have been clear back in 2011, grabbing Irving and Thompson in that draft help set them up to lure James back to Cleveland three years later.

Irving was sensational. He was better than any player James played with in his first stint in Cleveland. But unlike James, Irving wasn't good enough to propel his early teams into the playoffs, so the Cavs continued to lose for the following few seasons and the NBA continued to lavish them with lottery picks. While the Cavs didn't win much while LeBron was in Miami, they did win a few NBA lotteries. After the 2011 trade, they got the number-one pick from the Clippers, and incredibly, they also yielded the top picks in both the 2013 and 2014 drafts. In the four years James was in Miami, Cleveland snagged the top pick three times.

Although they drafted Anthony Bennett in a draft day mistake in 2013, by selecting Andrew Wiggins in June 2014 the Cavs were suddenly a legitimate option again for James. With Wiggins, the Cavs front office now had another enticing asset they could use in a trade to make their roster even better. In the summer of 2014, they turned Wiggins into Kevin Love in a blockbuster deal setting up the NBA's newest Big Three in Cleveland. As ESPN reported on August 23, 2014:

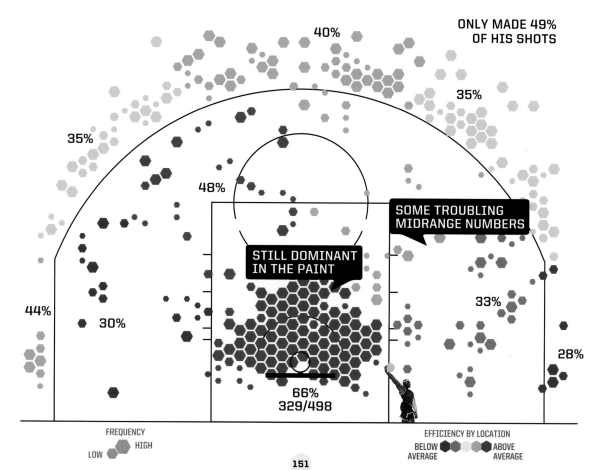

LEBRON JAMES
BACK IN CLEVELAND
2014-15 SEASON

ONLY MADE 49% OF HIS SHOTS

40%

35%

35%

48%

SOME TROUBLING MIDRANGE NUMBERS

STILL DOMINANT IN THE PAINT

44%

30%

33%

28%

66%
329/498

FREQUENCY
LOW — HIGH

EFFICIENCY BY LOCATION
BELOW AVERAGE — ABOVE AVERAGE

With LeBron back in the fold and Irving and Love on board, the 2014–15 Cavs were suddenly the favorites to win the Eastern Conference. As a testament to James, the Cavs had missed the playoffs each year he was in Miami, but with him back, suddenly they were title contenders again. LeBron was squarely in his prime, and the supporting cast was championship-worthy. Unfortunately, that supporting cast was fragile too.

As an individual scorer, James had exhibited a few troubling trends that reflected the stresses of changing teams and offensive environments. One of the defining stats of his ascendancy is that his field goal percentage increased every season between 2006–07, when it was 48 percent, and 2013–14, when it was 57 percent. But after returning to Cleveland, James struggled to be the efficiency monster he'd become in Miami. In his first year back in a Cavs uniform, he converted just 49 percent of his field goals, his lowest mark since 2007–08.

What happened? It was simple. He was taking harder shots. He was relying on more unassisted, off-the-dribble shots. Back in Miami, the Heat had coalesced into a very good offensive group greater than the sum of its individual parts. LeBron's last Miami team ranked fifth in the NBA in offensive efficiency and first in true shooting percentage. They were an offensive machine. They had learned how to play very well as a group, share the ball, and create good shots for each other. That wasn't the case back in Cleveland. The 2014–15 Cavs were new to one another, and it would take time for them to truly coalesce. James had to create more of his own shots. In his last year in Miami, 39.5 percent of his two-point buckets were assisted. In Cleveland, just 31.5 percent were. In his last year in Miami, 39.9 percent of his shots came from three feet inside of the basket; that first year back in Cleveland, just 33.2 percent of his shots did. His increased reliance on unassisted tries and jumpers was dampening the King's overall efficiency numbers.

The 2014–15 Cavaliers were a good team, but not a great team. They won 53 games and featured the third-best offense in the league, but complemented it with an average defense, which ended up ranking 18th in the league. They swept the Celtics in the first round of the 2015 playoffs but ended up losing Kevin Love to a shoulder injury in the process. They still managed to burn through the Bulls and the Hawks in rounds 2 and 3, then found themselves in the Finals against the league's hottest new team, the Golden State Warriors.

On June 4, 2015, the teams hooked up in Oakland for Game 1. It was an awesome game that ended up in overtime. James led all scorers with 44 points, but it wasn't enough. The Warriors were too talented and too deep for the Cavs, who struggled without Love. The Warriors' bench was the biggest difference, outscoring the Cavs bench 34–9. Once again, the supporting cast around James in Cleveland couldn't pull their own weight, and to make matters worse, Irving hurt his knee in the overtime loss. The next day the Cavs received devastating news: Irving had a fractured knee cap and would miss the rest of the series. Suddenly the Cavs' Big Three was down to a familiar Big One. It was like the old Cavs again. LeBron and the Cavs put up a good fight but lost in six games.

His first year back in Cleveland had a similar end as his first year down in Miami—a Finals loss. But his second year in Cleveland would have a different ending.

When you have championship expectations, years that end without trophies are deemed failures. LeBron has never done well with failure. The loss to the Warriors stung him, and he wanted nothing more than to exact revenge and bring that championship back to Cleveland.

On January 18, 2016, Curry and the Warriors traveled to Cleveland for a highly anticipated Finals rematch. The Warriors entered the game with a ridiculous 37-4 record; the Cavs came in at 28-10. But the bout wasn't even close. The defending champs torched the Cavs on their home floor while the world watched and openly wondered if the Cavs could ever beat these dudes from Oakland. The Warriors were getting every shot they wanted. The Cavs' defense looked helpless. It was 70–44 at halftime. The Warriors put up another 34 in the third. It was a laughable 104–67 after three. If this game was any indication, these two teams were not equals, and the Cavs stood little chance of winning a title that year.

A few days later, the Cavs made a drastic move: they fired their head coach. Something needed to change, and as they say, you can't fire all the players. As *ESPN. com* reported:

David Blatt's second NBA season seemed to be going better than his first. Now, it's over.

Blatt was fired Friday by the title-chasing Cleveland Cavaliers and replaced by top assistant Tyronn Lue, according to general manager David Griffin.

Blatt had guided Cleveland to the NBA Finals last year, and the Cavs had the Eastern Conference's best record (30-11) midway through this season, but in discussing the coaching change during a news conference late Friday afternoon, Griffin cited "a lack of fit with our personnel and our vision."

In January 2016, after firing their head coach halfway through the 2015–16 season, when they had the best record in the Eastern Conference, and replacing him with assistant coach Tyronn Lue, there were legitimate concerns about the new head coach's ability to handle the pressure. A 38-year-old ex-player, Lue was suddenly thrust into one of the toughest seats in the NBA: besides the pressure to produce a championship, he had to take on the tactical and cultural responsibilities associated with leading James and the Cavs to the promised land.

It's not that changing your coach in the middle of the season in the NBA is unprecedented; it's that it's never a good sign for aspiring champions. Championship cultures in the NBA are generally aligned in leadership in three key places: on the roster, in the head coaching position, and in the front office. For example, the Spurs dynasty featured Tim Duncan leading the roster, Gregg Popovich leading the coaching endeavors, and R. C.

LEBRON JAMES
CHAMPIONSHIP IN CLEVELAND!
2015-16 SEASON

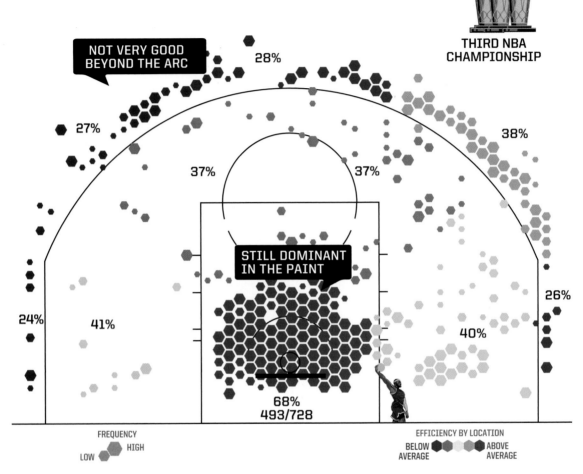

THIRD NBA CHAMPIONSHIP

NOT VERY GOOD BEYOND THE ARC

28%

27%

38%

37%   37%

STILL DOMINANT IN THE PAINT

24%   41%

26%

40%

68%
493/728

FREQUENCY
LOW   HIGH

EFFICIENCY BY LOCATION
BELOW AVERAGE   ABOVE AVERAGE

Buford pulling the strings in the front office. The Warriors championship teams had Curry and Draymond on the floor, Kerr as head coach, and Bob Myers as GM. In Miami, LeBron led the roster, Erik Spoelstra was a great head coach, and Pat Riley was as good as it gets in the front office.

The firing of Blatt in January 2016 indicated that this holy trinity was broken in Cleveland and the team was going to try to reinvent it on the fly, in the middle of a championship run. It would be up to Lue to make it happen, and while the legacy of the 2015–16 season is memorable for several reasons, what Lue was able to do that season remains generally unheralded. Between January and June 2016, Lue pulled off one of the great coaching runs of this century. When he took over the team in January, nobody believed that the Cavs could beat the Warriors; five months later they did it.

LeBron's third championship run was incredible for many reasons. On top of replacing their coach in the middle of the year, the Cavs beat the best regular-season team in the history of the NBA after trailing them 3–1 in a best-of-seven series. As for James himself, he was still the best player in the world. He was still the most dominant interior scoring force in the NBA. But his jumper was wonky again, especially from long range. In the 2015–16 season, James made just 30.9 per-cent of his three-point attempts. The elbow jumper that he had built up so well was no longer as good as it was in Miami.

But even with some diminishment of LeBron's jumper, his team's overall ability to make jumpers surged, in large part owing to his own ability to generate offense for his teammates.

LEBRON JAMES
ASSISTED 3S
2013-14 TO 2017-18

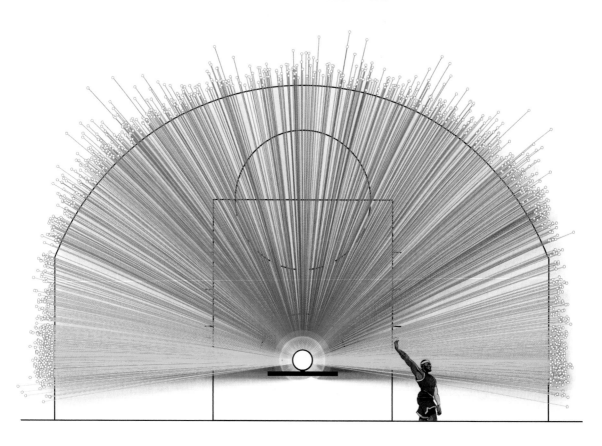

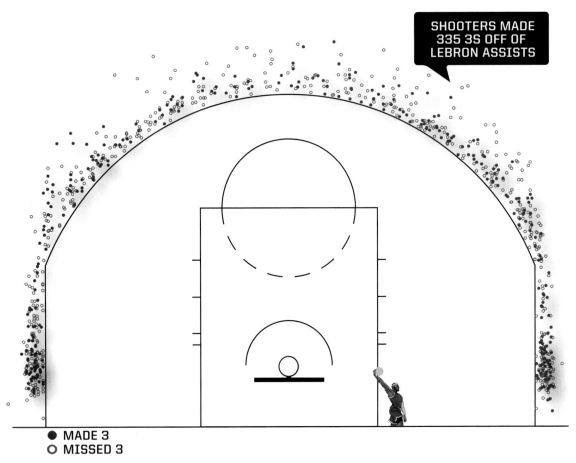

SHOOTERS MADE 335 3S OFF OF LEBRON ASSISTS

● MADE 3
○ MISSED 3

Three-Point Assists

When it comes down to legacies, the first two decades of pro basketball this century will always be associated with two things: LeBron James and the rise of the three-point shot. On one level, it's fair to say that LeBron and his unreliable jumper didn't really fit in with the dominant trend of his day. But climb to a higher plateau and you'll see things differently. In fact, a close look at LeBron's career shows that he's been one of the biggest producers of threes in the entire league—just not as a shooter, but as a passer.

Simply put, James creates more threes for his teammates via assists than any other player in the NBA. In the five-year span beginning in 2013–14 and ending in

SPRAWLBALL

2017–18, James led all NBA players by assisting on 1,289 regular-season made threes. In that same time period, only one NBA player made more threes as a shooter: Stephen Curry. What Steph has done for shooting threes this decade James has done for assisting them. So while it's fair to say that as a shooter James can't hold a candle to his rivals at Golden State, he leverages his incredible court vision and feel for the game to make his splash as a passer.

The thing about threes is that most of them require an assist. Generally speaking, over 80 percent of NBA three-point tries are assisted. So as teams strive to increase three-point productivity, players whose actions regularly create good looks for their teammates from beyond the arc are increasingly more valuable. Through this lens, in an era that will be remembered for a wild surge in three-point shooting, no other player has been more valuable as James.

So it turns out that James is a card-carrying member of the sprawlball club—just a different kind of member. While the most visible players driving the three-point era are shooters, most of these shooters are standing on the shoulders of creators. What's harder: draining a catch-and-shoot three or creating a good catch-and-shoot three for another player? Well, neither is easy, but it's telling that while the NBA is quickly filling up with guys who can knock down catch-and-shoot triples with relative ease, it's not exactly filling up with guys who can just as easily create them. That creator skill requires a rare blend of playmaking ability, court vision, ball handing, athleticism, and unselfishness.

James requires opponents to pay so much attention to him as a scoring threat that shots are opened up for his teammates. He's a tractor beam that sucks in defenders every time he holds the ball, and then, on top of that, he's got elite vision and world-class passing skills. It's that combination that has made his three-point assisting so prolific. And however subtly, that assistance actually proves that the defining player of his era is deeply intertwined with its dominant trend. In the prime of his career, James channeled his elite playmaking ability to create more triples than anyone else ever had.

It's perhaps the least heralded component of his ridiculous basketball portfolio, but LeBron's ability to create open catch-and-shoot threes for his teammates is one of the cornerstones of his teams' successes in the sprawlball era. Just ask Mike Miller, Ray Allen, Shane Battier, J. R. Smith, or Kyle Korver, who all benefited from the King's perimeter generosity. Make no mistake, Curry has been the emergent three-point scorer of the current era; however, James is its defining three-point creator. Both players have excelled at a time when three-pointers are increasingly deciding games, and both players have helped their teams get more of them. They've just done it in different ways.

Hollywood Calling

By the summer of 2018, James had completed another stint in Cleveland. He'd brought home a title and once again lifted the Cavaliers franchise to contender status, bringing the Cavs to four straight NBA Finals. That summer, James was once again a free agent and looking at his options: (1) he could team up with a few other superstars in a place like Houston or Boston to build a super-team somewhere to beat his Golden State rivals; (2) he could stay in Cleveland; or (3) he could go to the

Lakers to resuscitate the most famous franchise in the NBA.

On July 1, 2018, via a tweeted press release from his agency, Klutch Sports, James let the basketball world know that he was going to the Lakers. He would pull up his tent and change teams for the third time in his career. In 2018, at age 33, James left Cleveland for a second time and moved to Los Angeles to join a young, uneven roster light-years away from being a great team. But hey, this was the Lakers, and if anyone could quickly wake up the NBA's greatest sleeping bear, it would be LeBron.

For those who thought James would stay in the Eastern Conference or join another team already near championship form, the move was surprising. For those who believed James wanted to be in L.A. near the bright lights, it was a no-brainer.

Regardless, for the first time in almost a decade James found himself playing for a team unlikely to get to the Finals. At the dawn of the 2018–19 season, James was playing in the Western Conference for the first time in his career. To get out of the West, not only would his team have to beat the Warriors, who had bested James three of the previous four seasons in the Finals, but they'd also have to beat Harden and the Rockets, who took Golden State to seven games in the 2018 Western Conference Finals.

Both Golden State and Houston built their paths to glory from downtown. Both teams achieved greatness with long-range jumpers. As the dominant player of his era, James built his scoring reputation in the paint, in the same place as his superstar ancestors from Mikan to Shaq. But as James moved westward, very few top teams had a superstar even trying to do that anymore. The Warriors had Steph, Klay, and Durant. The Rockets were breaking records by shooting more threes than twos. Greatness in the NBA was now a perimeter attribute. In this sense, James was the last of the Mohicans, the last in a long line of the great players dominating the game in the crowded two-point areas.

The three-point line has rewired the entire way the NBA works. It has changed the fundamental relationship between shot difficulty and shot value, as many of the league's players can now easily drain catch-and-shoot threes. The entire league, including James, has reacted to that change and chases those shots more and more. Meanwhile, tough two-point shots and the athletes who can make them are less popular than ever.

As James winds down his incredible career, it's worth asking a few questions. First, has the three-point line changed the way we value not only shot greatness in the NBA but also player greatness? There's little question that James is the greatest basketball player to set foot on an NBA court since 2003, but in a world that continues to increasingly value perimeter shooting at the direct expense of every other basketball skill, will we ever see James's brand of Swiss-army-knife greatness ever again? Will the game's most ferocious interior scorers continue to be its biggest superstars, or are those days numbered? In the next generation, will our idea of greatness resemble the monocultural three-point shooting obsessions driving the NBA right now? If the Warriors and Rockets are any indication, the answer is pretty obvious.

THE MAN LOVE LEFT BEHIND

ON AN AVERAGE NIGHT in the NBA, players of all shapes and sizes fly around the court in continuous action featuring frequent bursts of breathtaking athleticism. From raining down threes to finishing alley oops or protecting the rim, there are many ways to excel in the best basketball league in the world.

At its best, the NBA provides a diversified economy that supports several means of production; big players like DeAndre Jordan reign near the rim, smaller shooters like Steph Curry excel on the perimeter, and wing players like Kawhi Leonard thrive in the midrange. On any given possession, a good team can threaten to score from almost any spot on the offensive part of the floor.

But it hasn't always been this way. And it's not hard to argue that among the most constant and definitive shifts in the overall NBA aesthetic is the gradual and ongoing expansion of shooting spaces. Thanks to the continued obsession with threes, the ways to score are increasingly sprawling outward. The league has slowly migrated away from the restricted area and out toward the beltways, and that sprawl is affecting everything, including the basics, like how big the league's most valuable players are. Spoiler: they're shrinking. We used to have MVPs like Chamberlain and Russell, and then we had Jordan and Malone. Now we have Nash and Curry. Soon it will be Kevin Hart and Ryan Seacrest.

Back in the day, a vast majority of points were scored near the basket, and the three-point line didn't even exist. Longer jump shots were rare then because they were riskier and offered no extra reward. Naturally, the league valued large powerful players who could score in the paint and tactics that would enable them to do so. Dump it into Chamberlain and let him go to work.

Then, in arguably the biggest rule change in American sports history, the NBA added the three-point line in 1979. It was the same season the league added Magic Johnson, one of the defining players of his era, and certainly the best point guard of his time. The NBA was about to change.

The new arc was a concept borrowed from the ABA, whose commissioner at the time, the prophetic George Mikan, suggested that the new line "would give smaller players a chance to score and open up the defense to make the game more enjoyable for the fans."

He didn't say what might happen to certain kinds of bigger players or certain forms of two-point offense.

Although Mikan's prophecy was accurate, it took some time to get there. In Magic's rookie season, the average team took only 2.8 three-pointers per game, and only five players made 50 or more shots from beyond the arc. Back then, three-pointers accounted for only 3 percent of field goal attempts in the NBA; by the 2017–18 season, that number had ballooned to 34 percent.

Through the simple lens of points per game, the three-pointer had gone from a forgettable role player that scored just 2.4 points per team per game in 1979 to a dazzling superstar that poured in 31.5 per game in 2017–18—more than the game average for that season's scoring champ, James Harden. And like any generational superstar, it began to occasionally account for 60 or more points per game in big playoff moments, like that epic night in the 2016 Western Conference Finals when the Warriors scored 63 from beyond the arc to stave off elimination against the more physical, more interior-minded Oklahoma City Thunder.

Although a snapshot of the league right now reveals a seemingly diversified scoring economy, snapshots can be misleading. A time-lapse image of the league would expose an evolving organism in the middle of a drastic metamorphosis, even if year to year the changes have been slight. The trajectory has been consistent and unrelenting, and the league is now wildly different than it was a few decades ago.

As we give more and more of the game to the triple, as well as the players and tactics that produce them, we give less and less to the powerful frontcourt players who used to dominate the game in the two-point areas. As a result, the value of the traditional power forward and his skill set is at an all-time low, and it's still diminishing. Is this a change that we want?

It was June 26, 2008, and an ESPN camera slowly zoomed in on the most famous podium in hoops. The unmistakable voice of Stuart Scott briefly narrated, "The pick is in, the commissioner is at the podium. What you got, Commish?"

David Stern slithered to the lectern, rested his hands on the edge, and in that monotonously beleaguered speech pattern proclaimed: "With the fifth pick . . . of the 2008 NBA draft . . . the Memphis Grizzlies select . . . Kevin Love . . . from UCLA."

The broadcast cut to a shot of the 19-year-old power forward, who stood up from his chair and hugged his dad, Stan, another power forward who 37 years prior was the ninth overall pick in the 1971 NBA draft. This apple didn't fall far from the tree. What a moment. Father and son power forwards enjoying a remarkable experience.

But young Love was entering a league that Pops wouldn't recognize, a league where power forwards with skill sets like Stan's were an endangered species. Stan Love stood 6'9" and weighed 215 pounds, and his job on the court was clear: protect the paint, set good screens, and grab more missed shots than the guy next to you. Stan's job description never included "spread the floor" or "knock down triples." Hell, triples didn't even exist in the NBA that Stan was drafted into.

Make no mistake, the contemporary definition of a power forward still sounds a lot like Stan, at least according to the internet. If you Google "what is a power forward," it returns the following:

pow·er for·ward

Noun. *Basketball.* a large forward who plays in the low post and typically has good rebounding skills.

Okay, Google, wake up. That definition is behind the times. By 2008, the way guys like Stan played the power forward position was already on the way out, both literally and figuratively. In the pace and space era, the game was changing, and perhaps no position would be more deformed than the power forward, and perhaps no player would come to emblemize the changes more than Stan's son, Kevin.

A few minutes after Stern announced Love's selection, America's Hot Take Laureate Stephen A. Smith, was interviewing the young Love about his prospects

in the NBA. "Kevin, last year, watching you in college, you were buff and bigger. Now you're slim, you lost some weight, you got some muscles, I mean, what's going on here? What can we expect from the new Kevin Love?"

Kevin—who, at 6'8" and 255 pounds, wasn't quite "slim" yet—paused before responding, "Well, I feel like, you always know what you're going to get from me. I feel like I can be a double-double guy."

It was an understatement. Even at 19, Love possessed an extraordinary blend of scoring skills and rebounding ability that would make him a box score juggernaut. He didn't just become a "double-double guy"; before long he became *the* double-double guy in the NBA.

After the draft, the Grizzlies ended up trading the rights to Love to Minnesota, a team run by General Manager Kevin McHale, who just happened to be one of the best power forwards to ever play the game and a guy who logged 243 double-doubles during his own playing career. McHale obviously saw something in Love, and the young power forward from UCLA would begin his pro career as the youngest player on the 2008–09 Timberwolves.

Love made his NBA debut on October 29, 2008, coming off the bench in a home game against Sacramento. He turned heads right away with his first bucket, a layup late in the first quarter. He almost logged a double-double despite playing only 19 minutes. The Associated Press recap headline from that game reads: "Minnesota rookie Kevin Love made an impressive debut with 12 points and nine rebounds in 19 minutes . . ."

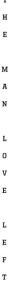

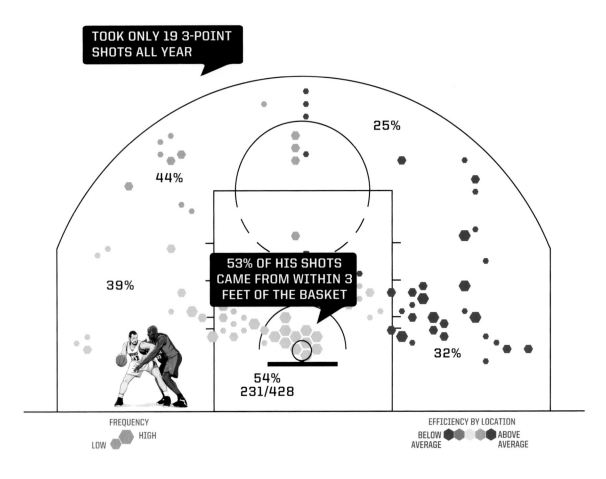

KEVIN LOVE
2008-09
ROOKIE YEAR

TOOK ONLY 19 3-POINT
SHOTS ALL YEAR

25%

44%

53% OF HIS SHOTS
CAME FROM WITHIN 3
FEET OF THE BASKET

39%

32%

54%
231/428

FREQUENCY

LOW   HIGH

EFFICIENCY BY LOCATION

BELOW   ABOVE
AVERAGE   AVERAGE

That debut performance was a harbinger of things to come. In his rookie campaign, Love appeared in 81 of 82 games and started 37 of them. But Love's seminal contributions in the NBA took the form of a very traditional power forward. Over half of Love's shots came within three feet of the hoop, and just like the collective NBA back in 1979, 97 percent of his shots came in the two-point areas. Most games he didn't take even one three-pointer. This kid was out there playing power forward more like McHale than Nowitzki.

Looking at Love's shot chart from his rookie year, a few things stand out. First of all, you can see that the vast majority of his shots came in the paint. That's normal for a power forward who loves to post up. Same with the high volume near the left block. All that activity just outside of the paint on the baselines is an obvious fingerprint of a frequent post-up player.

Over the course of a season, nearly every active NBA shooter ends up getting a bunch of shots in the paint as guards get transition buckets and floaters and wings slash their way into that area. But those areas just off the blocks also represent the signature fall-aways and little hooks that belong to old-school post players. Nobody else really shoots there, but "back-to-the-basket"

guys like Abdul-Jabbar, Duncan, and McHale feasted on those shots. And so did the young Love, who loved the left block.

If it's true that double-doubles are the signature statistical hallmark of NBA power forwards, then few can argue that Love rapidly became one of the most successful in his generation. During his third year in the league, the 2010–11 season, Love logged at least 10 points and 10 rebounds in an incredible 53 consecutive games. Barkley never did that. Karl Malone never did that. McHale never did that. Neither did Garnett or Duncan. Love was 22 and already a historically great double-double guy. He had become only the second player in the 21st century to average over 15 rebounds per game.

However, looking at his shot chart from that breakout season, we also see slight hints of the metamorphosis that would come to define Love's career.

Remember, as a rookie, Love took just 3 percent of his shots from three-point range—the same share taken by NBA shooters back in Magic's rookie year of 1979–80. But in his second year, that number grew to 16 percent, and Love was suddenly taking nearly two triples per game. In his third year, he was taking almost three per contest. Each year his three-point volume was going up, and his weight was going down. When you see the numbers on his 2010–11 chart, you can start to see why.

That season Love made 41.7 percent of his three-point attempts. He made

KEVIN LOVE
2010-11

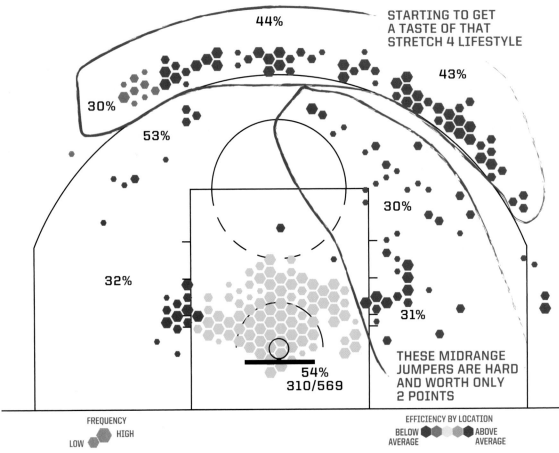

STARTING TO GET
A TASTE OF THAT
STRETCH 4 LIFESTYLE

44%

43%

30%

53%

30%

32%

31%

54%
310/569

THESE MIDRANGE
JUMPERS ARE HARD
AND WORTH ONLY
2 POINTS

FREQUENCY

LOW   HIGH

EFFICIENCY BY LOCATION

BELOW   ABOVE
AVERAGE   AVERAGE

31.3 percent of his two-point attempts between 10 and 16 feet. The math was simple, and his future was clear.

In October 2015, *Grantland* was on the verge of shutting down, but a new NBA season was still coming and our writers and editors were defiantly intent on rear-ranging chairs on the *Titanic* by pushing out tons of NBA preview content. At some point in mid-October, I was on the phone with Kevin Love for a preview piece. At that moment, Love was a fascinating study. Now 27, he was squarely in his prime, but in the summer of 2014 he'd been traded from Minnesota to Cleveland. With the Timberwolves, he'd spent years as the primary scoring option on a bad team, but in Cleveland he found himself suddenly playing third fiddle behind LeBron James and Kyrie Irving and chasing a title.

His first season in Cleveland was full of championship hype, but it ended with a thud. Love suffered a bad shoulder injury that sidelined him during the Cavs' run to the 2015 NBA Finals, where they hobbled and toiled but eventually lost to the Warriors in six games. Would they have won if Love had been healthy? Who knows, but Love was preparing for the 2015–16 campaign intent on finding out.

When we talked on the phone, Love didn't know it yet, but he was embarking on a season that would see him become an NBA champion. The Love who became a champ was barely recognizable compared to the double-double guy from Minnesota. The new Love was thin and spent almost all of his time on offense beyond

THE TRANSFORMATION OF KEVIN LOVE

Season	Age	Team	% Two-Pointers	% Three-Pointers
2008-09	20	MIN	97.2	2.8
2009-10	21	MIN	83.6	16.4
2010-11	22	MIN	79.4	20.6
2011-12	23	MIN	73.4	26.6
2012-13	24	MIN	69.1	30.9
2013-14	25	MIN	64.4	35.6
2014-15	26	CLE	58.9	41.1
2015-16	27	CLE	55.1	44.9

the three-point arc. What happened to the chunky post-up guy from UCLA?

Love's an easy guy to interview. He's engaged, positive, and quotable. I used my conversation with him to discuss his remarkable metamorphosis from power forward to stretch four—and if you think that is an exaggeration, consider the table on the previous page.

Love had not just become a stretch four; by some measures, he'd become the most prolific stretch four in the league. It was remarkable—in just seven seasons, he'd turned inside out. But like the collective NBA with its increasing infatuation with triples, Love didn't change overnight; each year, Love simply took a bigger share of his shots from three-point range and a smaller share from two-point range.

As a 20-year-old rookie, Love took 3 percent of his shots beyond the arc; now that number was up to nearly 45 percent for the 27-year-old vet. Recall that, during the 2015–16 season, NBA shooters broke a record by at-

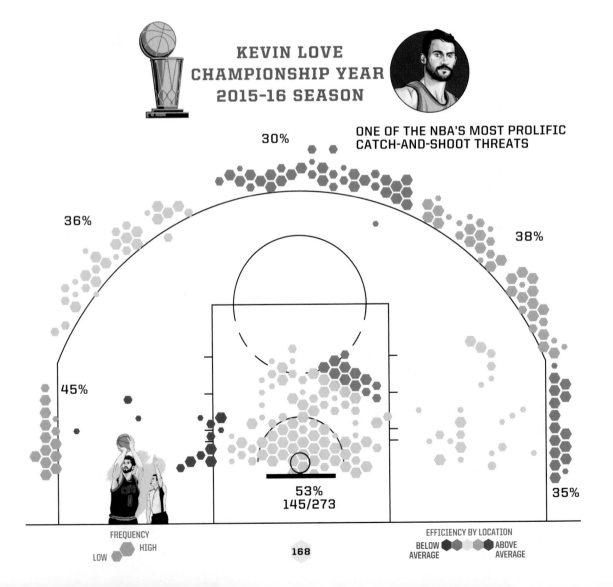

KEVIN LOVE
CHAMPIONSHIP YEAR
2015-16 SEASON

ONE OF THE NBA'S MOST PROLIFIC
CATCH-AND-SHOOT THREATS

30%

36%

38%

45%

53%
145/273

35%

FREQUENCY

LOW   HIGH

EFFICIENCY BY LOCATION
BELOW   ABOVE
AVERAGE   AVERAGE

S
P
R
A
W
L
B
A
L
L

tempting 29 percent of their shots from three-point range. In other words, the player whom many consider to be among the best power forwards in the league took 45 percent of his shots from three-point range—a much higher share than the league as a whole.

■■■■■

After we spoke that October, Love spent his season taking more catch-and-shoot three-pointers than many of

the league's most prominent sharpshooters. The same guy who just a few years earlier was banging his way to over 15 boards on a nightly basis was now taking more threes per game than guys like Kyle Korver, J. J. Redick, and Danny Green. That's nuts.

Love took 5.7 threes per game. To put that figure in historical context, consider that Reggie Miller in his remarkable 18-year only tried more than six threes per game in one season! And that was a season during the

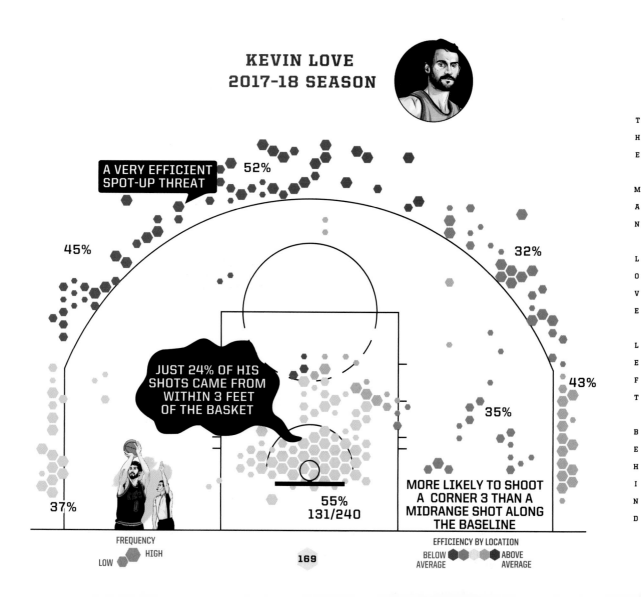

KEVIN LOVE
2017-18 SEASON

A VERY EFFICIENT
SPOT-UP THREAT

52%

45%

32%

43%

JUST 24% OF HIS
SHOTS CAME FROM
WITHIN 3 FEET
OF THE BASKET

35%

37%

55%
131/240

MORE LIKELY TO SHOOT
A CORNER 3 THAN A
MIDRANGE SHOT ALONG
THE BASELINE

FREQUENCY

HIGH

LOW

EFFICIENCY BY LOCATION

BELOW   ABOVE
AVERAGE   AVERAGE

THE MAN LOVE LEFT BEHIND

	Minutes per Game	3PM per Game	3PA per Game	3P%
Ray Allen, 2008 playoffs	38	2.1	5.3	39.6
Ray Allen, 2013 playoffs	25	1.7	4.2	40.6
Kevin Love, 2016 playoffs	31	2.3	5.6	41.4

three-year period when the NBA was experimenting with a shortened three-point arc. As a reminder, Reggie was not a power forward.

In addition, in both of Ray Allen's title runs (2008 Celtics and 2013 Heat), he shot and made fewer threes per playoff game than Love did during the Cavs' 2016 title run.

Power forwards used to spend all their time in the paint, or very close to it, but those days are gone. This trend is not unique to Kevin Love: the league is now chock-full of exemplar power forwards who spend more time away from the rim than close to it. Entering their prime, All-Star power forwards like Serge Ibaka, Carmelo Anthony, and Chris Bosh continued to "expand their range," and the league-wide numbers make it clear that power forwards almost all shoot threes now.

In the sprawlball era, these players help their offenses most by getting out of the way. The quest for offensive efficiency has revealed not only that post-up plays are much less efficient than other offensive actions, but that moving bigger players away from the basket is a simple way to reduce the defense's ability to prevent penetration actions. One result is that what used to be considered effective traditional post players have become tactically less valuable than a marginally efficient stretch four. Another is that the ability to shoot threes has become a key bullet point in the job description of the contemporary power forward.

And yet another result is that we're seeing a huge cohort of incoming bigs who never play with their back to the basket. Dragan Bender and Marquese Chriss, the two top power forwards taken in the 2016 NBA draft, came pre-equipped with the long-range jumper. It's a standard option on the "new model" four, while the ability to post up is akin to a tape deck in a 2019 BMW. You can't be Kevin McHale anymore.

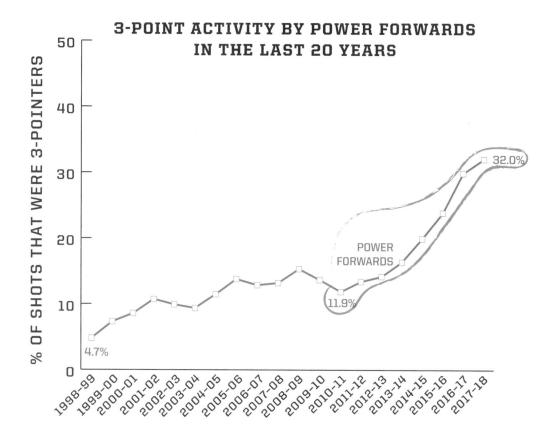

3-POINT ACTIVITY BY POWER FORWARDS IN THE LAST 20 YEARS

% OF SHOTS THAT WERE 3-POINTERS

4.7%

11.9%

POWER FORWARDS

32.0%

1998-99 1999-00 2000-01 2001-02 2002-03 2003-04 2004-05 2005-06 2006-07 2007-08 2008-09 2009-10 2010-11 2011-12 2012-13 2013-14 2014-15 2015-16 2016-17 2017-18

At its best, basketball promises positional egalitarianism. A 6'1" playmaker can be as valuable as a 6'9" rebounding specialist; a 6'4" sniper can be as important as a 7'1" rim protector. When George Mikan and the ABA introduced the world to the three-point line in the 1970s, Mikan waxed poetic about the line opening up the game and giving the little man a chance to score. Well, here we are a generation later, and while there's no question that the line has opened up the game and provided smaller players with a pathway to value, when we see Kevin Love shooting more threes than Reggie Miller and Dennis Scott ever did, it's also fair to ask: has this gone too far?

By 2018, Kevin Love, slimmer than ever, was the Cavaliers' starting center. His migration to the five spot echoed a trend happening around the league. Kevin Garnett and Tim Duncan both went from fours to fives as they aged. So did Chris Bosh, LaMarcus Aldridge, and Kevin Love in their primes, and who could forget Draymond Green, the iconic "big" at the center of Golden State's "lineup of death"? Green is 6'7".

Traditional centers have all but vanished from the game. And many of the guys who do excel at the position are actually power forwards like Love. With the soaring perimeter enthusiasm in the NBA this century, the positional egalitarianism that makes basketball so great has waned, and nobody has been more affected than the big man who posts up, who's all but gone.

We could crusade for making post-up players great again, but let's also realize that Kevin Love is not the problem here. One man's metamorphosis from power forward to stretch four to stretch five is no big deal. But here's the thing: the way the league and its rulebook tempts and incentivizes players like Love to make this transition is slowly killing traditional skill sets and aesthetics that were once at the very heart of basketball.

As a young player, Love was positioned to be one of the best power forwards of his generation as he racked up double-doubles on a nightly basis, dominated the glass, and was a monster on the left block. He could have been the next Kevin McHale, but he saw the game taking a different tack and so he changed his own game.

In McHale's time, power forwards scored, rebounded, and blocked shots. They still do, but more and more of them shoot threes too. And more and more of them are shooting more and more threes. In the sprawlball era, when "pace" and "space" are like wedding vows, traditional post-up players struggle to fit in; they clog the lane, slow down the game, and don't lure their big defenders out of the paint. On the other wide of the ball, these antiquated offenders enable defenses to stifle attacking guards while muddying up the drive and kick engines at the center of most of the contemporary NBA's typical offensive machines.

McHale grew up in the tiny hamlet of Hibbing, Minnesota. But it's Hibbing's other favorite son, not McHale, who has the best advice for young power forwards trying to find their way in today's NBA.

"Don't stand in the doorway, don't block up the hall . . . , for the times, they are a-changin'."

There's a Dylan quote for every occasion, and this one seems especially relevant for this conversation. The saddest thing about Kevin Love's transformation isn't that a kid poised to be the best power forward of a generation consciously morphed into a stretch big instead;

it's that his metamorphosis was the right decision. It was the smart move. It helped him win his first championship.

By the 2013–14 NBA season, there was really only one competitive NBA team that played two traditional bigs. That year's Memphis Grizzlies had arguably the best frontcourt in the NBA. They started Zach Randolph at the four and Marc Gasol at the five. As a hulking and cunning southpaw, Randolph loved backing defenders down on the right block before finishing with a limitless array of post-up moves that would make McHale proud. In contrast, Gasol loved the high post and offered the Grizzlies a great combination of screening, passing, and pick-and-pop shooting ability. Both of these guys were undeniably great, but both thrived exclusively in the two-point areas. Neither guy could or would stretch the floor or shoot threes.

Virtually any NBA team with both of these great players on its roster would start them both. But with Randolph on the block and Gasol patrolling the elbows, Memphis had trouble spacing the floor. Not only did their massive figures block up the basket area and the key corridors connecting it to the perimeter, but their tendency to hang near the paint kept their gigantic defenders around those zones too.

Even with Mike Conley, one of the league's fastest attacking point guards at the controls, the Grizzlies struggled to generate the key penetrate-and-pitch sequences that beget the holiest act of the sprawlball era: the catch-and-shoot three.

In a league that contained several teams intentionally trying to lose games, the 2013–14 Grizzlies ranked dead last in three-point production. Not only were the long-range inadequacies of Gasol and Randolph directly hindering the Grizzlies' ability to generate three-point production with their bigs, but their tendency to loiter in their favorite hangout spots on the offensive chessboard was also preventing smaller playmakers from generating three-point production.

Simply put, the two big men were killing the three in Memphis.

Love knows about this effect, and when we spoke just before the upcoming 2015–16 season, he even called it out. In response to a question about his offensive transformation, Love told me this about the overall increases in long-range-shooting bigs:

"You know I grew up in an era when it was just starting, and it's been a progression. Bigs were starting to shoot 18 feet out, then 20 feet out, then 22 feet. Guys like Dirk [Nowitzki] and Peja [Stojaković], guys that were six-foot-10 or seven feet, stepping out and taking that shot. Guys like KG [Kevin Garnett] and Chris Webber stepping out and hitting big shots. The Big Fundamental was hitting 18-foot glass shots. But I think the European game has had such an influence on this expansion."

According to Kevin, even though he played in a very different time, it was Stan who urged his son to wake up to the emerging realities of how bigs were trying to find their way in the sprawlball era.

"My dad was like, 'You need to watch these guys and do what they do, because they can really shoot the ball.'"

Love's outward migration was right in time, and right in tune with the direction of the NBA as a whole. And whether we like it or not, according to Kevin, this is no passing fad—we're just getting started with bigs shooting threes. The Randolph-Gasol Grizzlies will become a relic of the past:

"I think the trend will continue in that direction. We rarely see two 'true bigs' out there as block players."

By 2017–18, the Grizzlies had let Randolph walk away from the team to sign with Sacramento, and Gasol—a player who'd never tried more than 17 threes in a season before 2015—attempted 320.

At first glance, it doesn't make sense that a great young power forward like Love would migrate away from the paint and the offensive rebounding position on purpose. But it's addition by subtraction when it comes to population density in the core of today's drive-and-kick NBA offenses. Less is now more: by getting off the block and heading to the suburbs, Love opened up the floor for his playmaking teammates.

And by simply becoming just an average catch-and-shoot specialist from three-point range, he weakened the opponent's interior defense much more than he could by being one of the most prolific post-up players in the game. After all, basketball is a team game, and rim protection is the most important defensive role on the floor. Love didn't just take his game to the edge of the scoring area: he brought his defender with him, thereby weakening the opponent's paint defense in a way that Randolph or McHale could never have done.

The truth is that after the NBA curtailed hand-checking in 2004, the scoring area was opened up for the game's fastest ball handlers. Previously, when faced with a player like Steve Nash, defenders could simply grab him and hold him to slow him down, but once that strategy was prohibited under the new rules, guys like Nash turned into MVPs by running around making plays for their teammates. Teams responded by becoming more guard-oriented in their tactics. The reality was that, with dribble-drives now the centerpiece of the game because of the rule change, stretch fours helped their team by getting out of the way more than power forwards did by crashing the glass and posting up.

This revelation has gradually been accepted in virtually every practice facility in the NBA. In the sprawlball era, it's better to be Ryan Anderson than Zach Randolph. It's better to be Kevin Love than Kevin McHale. Who needs an up-and-under or a half-hook when you can have another catch-and-shoot three?

Unfortunately, with the three-point line and the rules where they are right now, even an average catch-and-shoot attempt is undeniably more efficient than any post-up opportunity. Three is greater than two every time.

During the 2013–14 season, Love was one of the most active post-up players in the league, logging 674 post-ups. Only 10 players had more. On average that year, a Love post-up chance yielded 0.89 points. That same season, Love started falling in love with the three-ball: he attempted 399 catch-and-shoot threes that season, and on average those attempts yielded 1.16 points. He posted up 8.75 times per game while he launched

KEVIN LOVE
POST-UPS PER GAME:

2013-14: 8.8
2014-15: 5.5
2015-16: 6.1
2016-17: 5.7
2017-18: 4.6

catch-and-shoot threes 5.1 times per game, but it's hard to justify those frequencies given their respective efficiencies. Why in the world would you invest more in a play worth 0.89 than one worth 1.16? That basic analytical question, ladies and gentlemen, has driven the NBA's massive aesthetic upheaval. It's driven power forwards to become stretch fours and changed the very nature of how big men are valued in professional basketball.

Those numbers just cited are stark enough by themselves, but add in the fact that low-post players clog up the tactically vital arteries that enable contemporary offenses to create the holy catch-and-shoot three and it's no wonder that old-school post-up players are a dying species in the NBA. They're inefficient, and they get in the way. Love and his teams took notice—and drastically scaled back their post-up behavior.

By 2017–18, Love was a lot of things. He was an NBA veteran. He was a champion. He was an All-Star. But was he still a power forward? Was anyone really? There was a time in the NBA when being a four meant being a power forward, and power forwards were valued for their post-ups, rebounds, and physicality on both ends. That time may not be over, but we're getting there, and Love is evidence of that. But Love has never been alone. As we'll see in the next chapter, the erosion of post-up activity and the drastic shifts in how NBA big men play the game has by no means been limited to Love and his teams.

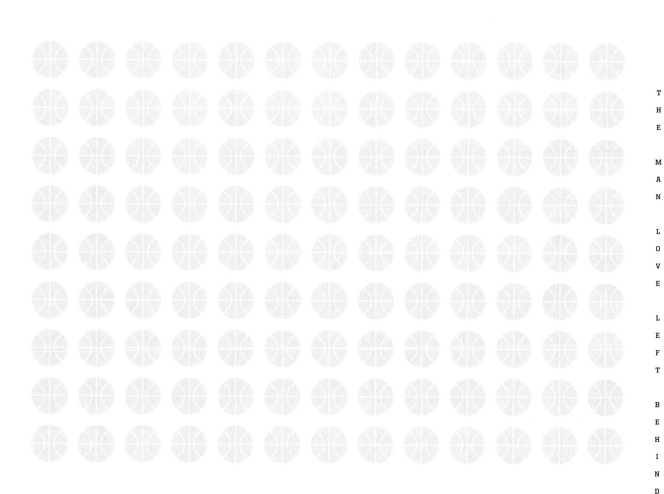

WHAT A TIME TO BE A FIVE

JUST AS MANY power forwards like Love evolved into stretch fours, the bigger ones who couldn't shoot threes evolved into "centers." Guys like Draymond Green, LaMarcus Aldridge, and Tristan Thompson all started this decade as forwards and ended it as centers. Guys like Greg Monroe and Al Jefferson, once lauded as the future of the position, are now having a tough time even getting contracts. In a related story, they can't shoot threes.

When the NBA curtailed hand-checking earlier this century, the league didn't just prohibit defenders from slowing down ball handlers on the perimeter; its rule change also greatly promoted the mobility of the game's fastest players and raised the value of such mobility. In a world with no physicality on the perimeter, suddenly guards had freedom like never before. Unsurprisingly, dribbling into jumpers, aggressive pick-and-roll sets, and dribble-drives toward the rim have now become the centerpieces of NBA strategy. The hand-check curtailment has also had the effect of greatly increasing the league's intolerance for immobility at any position. In a post-hand-check NBA, the pick-and-roll has become even more dangerous now that defenses have quickly realized that switching defensive assignments is the best strategy for slowing down the guards. Thus, centers who could guard multiple positions suddenly became disproportionately more valuable as offenses around the NBA swiftly honed in on the dominant strategy of the decade: isolating quick ball-handling guards against the opponent's slowest defenders.

In a world with no perimeter touching allowed, isolating a fast ball handler against a slow center provides a great advantage. In that world, Stephen Curry and James Harden become the most valuable players in the NBA.

Also, in that world the only bigs worth paying are the most mobile and athletic ones, who, relative to their peers, are increasingly valuable. Meanwhile, the NBA's biggest and least mobile bigs have become pariahs.

Plodding strength has never been less valuable in the NBA, and being slow has never been more unacceptable. This is bad news for the game's biggest players. On defense, speed and agility have become more important than physicality. Bigger small forwards have become power forwards, power forwards have become centers, and traditional centers, like Roy Hibbert, have become unemployed.

On July 17, 2018, TMZ posted one of its signature LAX ambush videos. You know the format. A weary celebrity is walking out of baggage claim and some paparazzi fella shoves a camera in his face and starts engaging in an unsolicited conversation. Well, this time the celebrity was two-time NBA All-Star Roy Hibbert.

At 7'2", Roy towered over the interviewer and politely answered a series of random questions about the Denver Nuggets, LeBron James, and the new-look Lakers. But then the conversation turned to Hibbert's own NBA career. Although he had last played for the Nuggets in 2016–17, Hibbert remains best known for his years in Indiana, where he was the centerpiece of one of the best defenses in the NBA.

In the 2013–14 season, Hibbert and his Pacers were dominant on the defensive end, finishing the year with the best defensive efficiency rating in the NBA. For his part, Hibbert had earned a reputation as an elite shot blocker and one of the most formidable defensive big men in the whole league. At 27 that year, he finished in second place in the league's Defensive Player of the Year vote and was already a key figure on one of the best teams in the Eastern Conference. Nobody would have guessed that he would be out of the league four years later.

The 2013–14 Pacers got about as far as you can get without going to the Finals. They lost a grueling six-game series to LeBron and the Heat in the Eastern Conference Finals. Hibbert would never get that close again. Following a disappointing campaign the next season, Hibbert was traded to the Lakers in exchange for a second-round pick. An insulting return for any All-Star, let alone a dominant interior force like Hib-

bert. But here's the thing: by 2015, dominant interior players were less valuable than ever, and certain types of centers—the biggest and slowest ones—were quickly becoming passé in a league increasingly obsessed with defensive versatility and perimeter play. Hibbert may have been the prototype of a great defensive center at the beginning of the decade, but by the summer of 2018, he was out of the league. When the TMZ fella asked Hibbert about returning to the league and maybe rejoining the Lakers, the 31-year-old simply said, "I'm good on it right now," adding, "It's time to move on."

A poetic quote from the exact type of player the NBA has moved on from, in favor of a new kind of great defensive center. Like Draymond Green, who is six or seven inches shorter than Hibbert but is still strong enough to block shots and grab rebounds while defending multiple positions and chasing smaller guys around the perimeter.

Brow-Draymond

On December 13, 2016, the Golden State Warriors were in New Orleans facing the Pelicans. Although the Warriors entered the game as big favorites, late in the game they found themselves in a dogfight. With 10 seconds left, the Pelicans had the ball and were down just two points; they could tie or even win with a bucket.

They tossed the ball to Anthony Davis, their superstar big man, who was posting up Draymond Green down on the left block. At 6'10" and 253 pounds, Davis had three inches and about 25 pounds on his defender, and if he scored, the Pelicans could send the game to overtime.

Davis had his back to the basket, about 15 feet away. Green, one of the most talented defenders in the league, was right behind him. There was no double team.

It was archetypal hoops: a post-up situation featuring two All-Stars would decide the game. Green had both hands squarely on Davis's body. His left hand was firmly squeezing the phenom's front side as his right claw grabbed and twisted Davis's jersey so much that it was impossible to see the "2 or the name "DAVIS" on its backside. Green was manhandling Davis the same way a TSA agent would manhandle someone he'd just caught with a gun at the security checkpoint.

The whole arena fixated on these two men. Davis was frozen. He couldn't get any closer to the rim, and with Green's kung fu grip on his jersey, he couldn't even get off a risky fadeaway. When Davis tried to spin his way out of the situation to face Green instead, Green quickly slapped at his arms, causing him to lose the ball. The Warriors recovered the loose ball, and after a frustrated Davis got a technical foul for yelling at the refs, Steph Curry missed a rare free throw, but the Warriors got the rebound and called time-out. The Pelicans were forced to foul. Green made a few free throws to ice the game.

For Warrior fans, this was just another instance of their defensive superstar—the smallball center of the future—rising up and playing great David defense against another Goliath in a pivotal moment.

For Pelican fans, it was horseshit. Green committed a blatant violation in plain sight in the most important sequence of the game, and all three refs simply ignored it. It wasn't hard to see: Green and Davis held their Russell-Chamberlain pose in the post for over two seconds while every eyeball in the entire arena stared at them, including the six eyeballs attached to the officials tasked with detecting and whistling these kinds of violations.

Green's two-handed approach to post defense should be an automatic foul. Per NBA rules, when guarding an offensive player with the ball in the post, a defender may use one hand, one forearm, and/or one leg to maintain his position. On this play, Green clearly used two hands, which is just as illegal as, say, grabbing the elbow of Klay Thompson as he shoots a three. According to the rulebook, "two hands by a defender is an automatic foul, whether or not the offensive player's speed, quickness, balance, or rhythm is affected."

This isn't some obscure NBA bylaw, but a regulation sitting at the core of the rulebook. How contact in the post is officiated is among the most important regulations in the history of the sport. It affected Shaq, Duncan, Hakeem, Wilt, McHale, Russell, Mikan, and virtually every game ever played in the game's history. In fact, the most common fouls in the history of the league are defensive players getting too handsy near the basket.

The day after the Warriors' victory in New Orleans, the league came out with a "Last Two Minutes Report" that indicated a foul should have been called on Green

for being too handsy with Davis. This was worthless consolation, however, for Davis and his teammates and for other observers who are sick and tired of the league seemingly ignoring its own rule base in the low post and denying big interior players the same rewards of mismatches that it bestows on perimeter players.

The Draymond Rules

Green's physicality in the post is what enables him to "hold his own" against much larger offensive players, thus allowing his team to play super-fast smallball lineups that are virtually impossible to defend on the other end of the court. But Green's ability to hold his own arguably rests in his ability to "hold" his defensive assignments. Regardless, along with the incredible jump shooting, these smallball lineups are among the defining traits of a Warriors juggernaut that proclaims itself to be "light-years ahead"* of everyone else in the NBA.

It's not that Green isn't a terrific defender—he most certainly is, and he's also one of the smartest players in the league right now. He's one of a precious few NBA players who can effectively guard every position. Most NBA centers couldn't dream of guarding guards or more athletic wings. Green's versatility enables the Dubs to seamlessly switch defensive assignments every time they encounter a ball screen. Although, at 6'7", Green is a tall man by any reasonable standards, he is the shortest guy to regularly play the center spot in the

---

* In an infamous April 2016 interview with the *New York Times Magazine,* Joe Lacob, the majority owner of the Golden State Warriors, claimed that Warriors management was "light-years ahead" of "every other team in structure, in planning, in how we're going to go about things." Three months later, the Warriors became the first team in NBA history to blow a 3–1 lead in the NBA Finals.

contemporary NBA because NBA big-man standards are wildly unreasonable. However, those standards may soon be changing, especially if the league allows smaller defensive players to freely manhandle mismatches in the low post, as Draymond did that night in New Orleans.

As a center, Green is clearly a David in a league full of Goliaths. And in the same way that a ref might let a guard awkwardly caught in a switch defend a big in the post, refs kind of let the smaller Green get away with bending the letter of the law. It's human nature to pull for the little guy, and in the low post, when there's "a mouse in the house," the refs get caught up in letting the mouse be a little more physical than he should be. When you're watching a player like Steven Adams, Anthony Davis, or Dwight Howard back down Draymond Green, it's hard to not identify Green as the feisty underdog.

The issue, however, is that officials allow Green to defend his matchups in the post in ways that his matchups are not allowed to defend him.

Imagine for a second that a massive center like Steven Adams grabbed and held Green the same way that Green grabbed and held Davis. Not only would it look ridiculous, but Adams would immediately be called for a violation. That's a double standard, and smallball becomes a more feasible strategy each time it happens. Fortunately for Golden State, that double standard manifests regularly as Green grabs, twists, and two-hands Goliaths on a nightly basis. Moreover, imagine if a larger defender like Adams resorted to this kind of physicality to combat his uncomfortable defensive mismatches with guards like Curry out on the perimeter. Something tells me that wouldn't go over very well.

Regardless, between the current rule base and current rule enforcement, the NBA has created a version of basketball that advantages fast versus slow mismatches on the perimeter a lot more than it advantages big versus small mismatches in the interior.

This isn't about Golden State, and it's not really even about Draymond Green. It's way bigger and way older than that. The NBA has consciously legislated against the center and his game for years. And letting the kind of post defense that Green plays slide is just the latest in a long line of slights that have slowly made life as an NBA big more difficult.

Make no mistake, the diminishing relevance of NBA centers has more to do with league laws and league law enforcement than with any kind of tactical awakening in Oakland or analytics revolution in Houston. Small-ball didn't start in Oakland—it started in the league office with a series of rule decisions that began light-years before Warriors owner Joe Lacob was even sentient, and it has been amplified by a fleet of refs who seem to constantly overlook illegal contact down low while being hyper-vigilant about contact on the perimeter.

By 2017–18, Draymond Green and his teammates were basking in a regulatory landscape designed to reduce the potency of big interior players. Decades before Green emerged as a new nut-kicking kind of NBA center, NBA rule-makers were doing their part to make old-school bigs like Mikan, Russell, Chamberlain, and Abdul-Jabbar a little more impotent each decade. They made goaltending illegal because Mikan was too dominant on defense. Then they widened the lane and pushed Mikan's and Russell's post-ups farther away from the basket on offense. Then they pushed Chamberlain even farther

DRAYMOND GREEN

The addition of the three-point line—on top of the "Mikan Rule," which doubled the width of the paint to make post-up plays harder and other rule changes— was a death sentence for the relevance of the game's most historically relevant position group. In the two decades leading up to the implementation of the three-point line, centers won the NBA's MVP Award 18 or 19 times, depending on how you classify Bob Mc-Adoo.* In the two decades leading up to the publication of this book, centers have won the award once (Shaq in 2000). The last time a center won the NBA MVP Award, Steph Curry was 12 years old and James Harden was 11.

By 2018, NBA centers were still dealing with a laughably antiquated set of Mikan-Russell-era rules designed to make interior domination impossible on both ends of the court. These rules have never been revisited in the face of some of the most drastic aesthetic changes the league has ever seen.

Four decades into the three-point era, centers are now more likely to shoot threes than to post up. They're just trying to survive amid a generation of players and coaches hyper-focused on exploiting the artificially inflated value of perimeter shooting introduced by the three-point line.

Central Inefficiency

Centers in the NBA are now akin to manufacturing plants in the Rust Belt trying to survive a post-NAFTA economic reality. The irony of it all is that George Mikan, the NBA's first real superstar big man, was the

out than they pushed Mikan. Then, in the middle of Shaq's prime, they introduced the defensive three-second rule to limit the amount of time that big men could spend in their native habitat in the restricted area.

But the biggest nut-kick of them all came in 1979. When the league added the three-point line, it forever devalued interior offense and interior defense. Whether by design or by accident, the league made ho-hum long jump shots worth 50 percent more than difficult seven-foot hook shots in traffic. And while we always frame the addition of this remarkable regulation as a way to "open up the game for smaller players," it could just as easily now be described as a way to forever cheapen the value of interior players.

---

* McAdoo is listed as both a power forward and a center.

one who in his post-playing days as commissioner of the ABA introduced the three-point line to big-time pro basketball, forever deforming how players would play his own position. The addition of the line forever cheapened the form of basketball that made Mikan famous to begin with.

Nowadays, in an analytically woke era, the biggest and strongest (and often slowest) players and their antiquated two-point toolbox are rapidly being dismissed as "inefficient." It's unclear how to even play "center" right now, since it's unclear what that means. It certainly doesn't mean spending time in the center of the playing surface like it used to mean. That's now illegal on both ends of the court.

The idea that post play is somehow now inefficient says more about all of the rule changes that brought us to the sprawlball era than it says about post play. In a league that treats point guards like princesses and post-up players like tackling dummies, it's no wonder that guards are suddenly winning the Most Valuable Player Award every year now. It's not that they're better at basketball—it's that basketball is much better for them. We've engineered a new value system that deems their skill sets more valuable than those of the big men. And that's an understatement.

When the NBA added the three-point line in 1979, it did not revisit the Mikan Rule, the widened lane, illegal defense, goaltending rules, or other previous changes. The league simply added the line. In doing so, it continued the inexorable devaluation of interior players that had begun with the Mikan Rule. The three-point line then combined with the perimeter-touch rules to finish what the Mikan Rule had started: making the post player increasingly obsolete.

Just take one look at the NBA playing surface. The two-point area is littered with lines, dashes, boxes, and a painted area associated with different rules and regulations. You can stand here, but only for less than three seconds; you can play defense there, but only if your man is nearby. There are no equivalent lines beyond the arc. Despite the fact that more and more of the game is played on the perimeter, there are no lines, dashes, or boxes dictating the behaviors of perimeter players. They have free rein.

The non-enforcement of the few rules still in place to protect old-school back-to-the-basket players—like, say, the one that says a defender like Green can place only one hand on the back of a post player—simply adds insult to injury. The outcome of all this is that the best centers in our game right now are forced to play a version of the position that would be unrecognizable to Mikan himself. They've been reduced to screeners, lob catchers, and rebounders—unless of course they can shoot the almighty three-ball.

Perhaps no player epitomizes this change in the position more than Anthony Davis, who, as of the publication of this book, is one of the two or three best young big men on planet earth. And he's still only in his midtwenties. Despite his youth, Davis has already shown remarkable improvements in his game. He's a better defender, a better passer, and a better scorer than he was as a rookie. Oh, and he's already shooting more than two threes per game. On the one hand, the story of Davis's development is an inspiring reminder that grit can transform a person's abilities. It's a narrative arc that hits many of the same beats as the ones about Steph Curry and LeBron James. That's not a coincidence: superstardom in the world's best basketball league is reserved for the players who combine the most amazing talents with the most relentless work ethics.

On the other hand, it's another indictment of the current jump-shooting obsession that's transforming the nature of pro hoops. It's another data point suggesting that today's NBA is compelling more and more of its athletes to spend more and more time 25 feet from the basket and less and less of it in the paint. Since Davis entered the league, centers like him have been affected the most. How dare you try to back down the 6'7" Draymond Green in a key end-of-game sequence?! You're better off facing him up in isolation, man.

Even as the best young center in the game right now, Davis can't leverage that physical prowess into efficiency in the post. In the entire 2017–18 season, despite being the focal point of his team's offense, Davis posted up only about eight times per 100 possessions. Why? These plays aren't very efficient; on average, they yielded less than one point per possession—below the average points per possession in the NBA that year.

Compare Davis's post-up numbers with James Harden's isolation numbers. First off, Harden, who is also the focal point of his team's offense, was in isolation plays over twice as often. Harden ISOs happened 18.5 times per 100 possessions. The big reason why? Efficiency of course. On average, those Harden ISOs yielded 1.11 points per possession. And in case you think I'm cherry-picking numbers here, Jrue Holiday, Davis's slashing teammate in New Orleans, averaged 1.03 points per possession on his ISO plays. Why post up with the best big man in the league when your point guard running an ISO set is much more efficient?

Player	Post-ups per 100, 2013-14	Post-ups per 100, 2017-18	% Change
Al Jefferson	28.9	13.8	-52
Dwight Howard	22.2	13.0	-41
Blake Griffin	15.7	9.4	-40
DeMarcus Cousins	16.3	10.0	-39
Kevin Love	11.6	8.6	-26

Consider this: In the 2013–14 season, 22 NBA players posted up at least 500 times. By 2017–18, only eight players did so. In 2013–14, five players posted up at least 1,000 times; by 2017–18, only one NBA player, LaMarcus Aldridge, checked that box. Looking at some of the most prominent post-up guys during this same span, a common thread quickly reveals itself: post play is dying across the league, and dying quickly.

You might notice something else those five guys have in common: they have all changed teams in the last five years. Maybe these drop-offs have more to do with changes of scenery than with the overall demise of post play. Fair point. Let's explore the same idea at the league level. Per the league's own tracking data, there were 32.9 post-ups per game in the 2013–14 season; there were 23.1 per game by 2017–18. That's a massive drop-off in just five years. And like the rise of the three, this trend is by no means complete, no matter how you slice it.

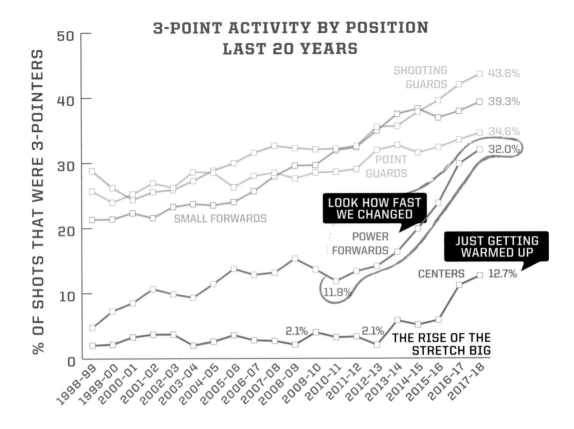

3-POINT ACTIVITY BY POSITION LAST 20 YEARS

% OF SHOTS THAT WERE 3-POINTERS

SHOOTING GUARDS — 43.6%

39.3%

34.6%

32.0%

POINT GUARDS

SMALL FORWARDS

LOOK HOW FAST WE CHANGED

POWER FORWARDS

JUST GETTING WARMED UP

CENTERS 12.7%

11.9%

2.1% 2.1%

THE RISE OF THE STRETCH BIG

1998-99 1999-00 2000-01 2001-02 2002-03 2003-04 2004-05 2005-06 2006-07 2007-08 2008-09 2009-10 2010-11 2011-12 2012-13 2013-14 2014-15 2015-16 2016-17 2017-18

But like my hippie sister always says, you never quit doing anything, you just start doing something else. Well, then, if these bigs are quitting the post game, what are they doing instead? You guessed it—they're shooting threes. Many of the most talented, most athletic young bigs in the NBA are focusing more on spot-up skills than post-up skills and forcing themselves to become better jump shooters.

The numbers are crazy. In the last decade, the three-point activity of NBA centers increased over 500 percent. During the 2008–09 season, NBA centers took just 2.1 percent of their shots from three-point range, and they hit an identical rate again in 2012–13. By 2017–18, however, that number had surged to 12.7 percent.

Make no mistake, this trend is just getting started. Consider that 32 percent of shots from every other position on the floor are currently coming from three-point range. If centers want to see their future, they can just look at their friends at the power forward spot: in the 1998–99 season, power forwards took just 4.8 percent of their shots from three-point range. That figure grew to 11.9 percent by 2010–11. By 2017–18, those fellas took 32.0 percent of their shots from beyond the arc.

One-Two-Three-Four-Five-Six

For generations, coaches, players, and fans have used a numerical shorthand to refer to the five traditional basketball positions. Ones are point guards, twos are shooting guards, threes are small forwards, fours are power forwards, and fives are centers. The graphic showing 20 years of three-point activity is pretty striking, especially for fours and fives this decade, who are experiencing rapid changes in three-point shooting norms. But how do we explain these changes?

Two things are happening. First, a lot of current fours and fives are beginning to shoot more threes. In fact, almost every prominent big man playing this decade has exhibited major upticks in three-point activity. We've already covered Kevin Love at length; it's also happening with centers like Pau Gasol and his brother Marc. Young bucks like Nikola Vucevic, Nikola Jokic, and DeMarcus Cousins are quickly changing their shot diet too. It's not hard to find examples. During the 2010–11 season, only three NBA centers averaged at least three three-point attempts per game; by 2017–18 season, 18 did that, and guys like Cousins were averaging over six three-point tries per game.

But second, and more alarming, there's something else hidden in those numbers: the entire nature of our positional shorthand is morphing. Suddenly, guys we thought of as bigger threes, like Rudy Gay, are getting a lot more minutes at the four. Similarly, guys we thought of as fours just a few years ago, like Kevin Love, LaMarcus Aldridge, and Dirk Nowitzki, are fives now. And as more and more traditional fours earn a lot more minutes as fives, what happens to the more traditional fives? Unfortunately, there are only so many minutes to go around, and the most traditional fives, especially the biggest and slowest ones who can neither "guard multiple positions" nor shoot triples very well, become "sixes." What's a six? Al Jefferson is a six. Roy Hibbert is a six. Andrew Bogut is a six. Sixes are casualties of the sprawlball era. Sixes either retire or go play in another country. Jefferson went to China. Bogut went to Australia. Hibbert retired at 31.

Aside from LeBron James, the most dominant player in the post-Jordan NBA has been Shaquille O'Neal, the

THE OUTWARD MIGRATION OF THE CENTER

SHAQUILLE O'NEAL
2001-02 SEASON

JUST ONE 3-POINT ATTEMPT ALL YEAR LONG

92% OF SHOTS
WITHIN 10 FEET
OF THE BASKET

FREQUENCY

LOW   HIGH

DEMARCUS COUSINS
2017-18 SEASON

6.1 3-POINT ATTEMPTS PER GAME

55% OF SHOTS
WITHIN 10 FEET
OF THE BASKET

EFFICIENCY BY LOCATION

BELOW
AVERAGE   ABOVE
AVERAGE

massive centerpiece of four championship teams in the decade immediately following Jordan's retirement. In some ways, Shaquille was a throwback player; dominating the game and winning championships from the center position was more like Kareem, Mikan, or Russell than like Mike. In other ways, it appears that Shaq was also the last of a breed. He was the last center to win the NBA MVP Award (in 1999–2000), and comparing his shot charts with those of the league's best center from the current era presents a striking difference. Shaq never attempted more than five threes in any season of his career. By 2017–18, Cousins was averaging more than that on a per-game basis.

You don't average over six threes per game by camping out in the paint like Shaq. No sir, the only way you can get to that number is by "spacing the floor" and stationing yourself beyond the three-point arc for large chunks of the game. Shaq never did that, but Cousins does that increasingly: 94 percent of Cousins's three-point attempts involve an assist, which means he's a catch-and-shoot specialist standing around and waiting for playmakers to find him open on the perimeter. To say that Cousins plays basketball slightly differently than Shaq is akin to saying that catchers play baseball slightly differently than center fielders.

Twenty-five years after the "Be Like Mike" campaign, many of the best players in the league are playing less like Jordan and more like Paxson, Kerr, or Hodges. Back in the '90s, it wasn't Jordan's fadeaways or rim attacks that represented the future of the league, but rather the spot-up shooting of his teammates. Be Like Paxson.

Bigs like Love, Cousins, and Davis would rather face up or spot up than post up. Of course they would— it's easier and it's more efficient! The same league that

makes every 24-footer magically worth 50 percent more than every tough fadeaway from the left block also turns a blind eye to the kinds of illegal defense that make post play the hardest it's ever been. While the refs are allowing as much contact as ever in back-to-the-basket situations, they're simultaneously emphasizing "freedom of movement" measures designed to reduce contact on guards and wings away from the basket.

It's no wonder the big fellas like Cousins and Davis stopped turning their backs to the basket and started turning them on their basketball ancestors.

I'll always remember watching a Pelicans game in 2015 with my friend Mason Ginsberg, who covered the Pelicans for *SB Nation*. I had just written a *Grantland* feature on how fast Davis's game was developing. At 23, he'd already become one of the most complete offensive bigs in the league. He could post up, he could handle the ball, he could set screens and roll to the rim for lobs, and he could pop out for what had quickly become one of the most reliable 20-foot jumpers in the whole league.

Mason and I talked a lot about that jumper and its tactical relevance to the Pelicans. We discussed that 21-foot pick-and-pop shot and how it's such a key asset for today's bigs despite the fact that the pick-and-pop jumper isn't easy and it takes years for even the most talented bigs in the league to get it down.

Garnett had it by the time he reached his prime. So did Bosh. David West had it. Blake Griffin couldn't hit it to save his life early in his career, but he worked like a dog to get it as he entered his prime. Davis was as good as any of these guys at this shot when he was 23.

So Mason and I were talking about this golden jumper when Mason took the conversation to its logical extension: "Just wait till next year, he's going to start shooting a lot of threes!"

He was right. Davis's form and ability to shoot would easily extend a few feet farther, and soon he could make that pick-and-pop even more dangerous. Soon he could stand outside the arc, make like Paxson, and wait for his teammates to kick it out to him for open triples.

But as Mason said that, I had another revelation: I don't want to see Anthony Davis shoot threes.

The kid is arguably the freakiest blend of skill and athleticism that's come into the league in my lifetime. He's a seven-footer with guard skills, a massive leap, length for days, and a silky jumper. By 2015, I'd already labeled him the most dangerous two-point scorer in the league.

But here's the thing: thanks to the current regulatory framework and the basic analytical realities associated with two- and three-point shots, we are incentivizing this player—the most athletically gifted big in the world—to live farther and farther from the basket and emphasize the least unique facet of his game.

We are inspiring him to post up less and spot up more. Given the current rule base and the obvious strategies it encourages, he's not "Crash Davis," he's more like "Standstill Davis."

I don't want to go to the arena to watch Anthony Davis or Boogie Cousins spot up from 24 feet. But that's exactly what going to a Pelicans game in 2018 had become. I want to see those guys maneuver, leap, dunk,

block, push, rebound, and just be an overall menace in the two-point area.

But here we are, watching a league that by design has essentially legislated out the back-to-the-basket game, which used to define the game. Instead, you can find all the best scoring bigs in the league facing the basket, where they're more likely to spot up than to post up. Just look to the perimeter outposts where Steve Kerr used to stand.

Between the current rule base and current rule enforcement, it's very difficult, even impossible, for the league's biggest players to take advantage of size mismatches down low. Just as we saw when Draymond Green pushed and grabbed Davis in that key sequence in 2016, bigger players simply can't dominate smaller players like they used to. The Warriors are the best team of this decade for many reasons, but one of them is their famous "smallball" approach, which uses Green at the center.

The Warriors' smallball lineup is a direct contrast to the 2017–18 New Orleans Pelicans, who attempted to pair Cousins and Davis to overpower opponents with two dominant bigs. It was a fascinating experiment that combined two of the NBA's best big men on one roster. But that experiment failed: the Pelicans were average on both ends of the floor, especially compared to the smaller lineups the Warriors use. Not only do the smallball lineups kill on offense, but the Warriors are arguably the best defense in the league when they go small as well. You can't beat 'em. And as they say, if you can't beat 'em, join 'em. That's exactly what Cousins did in the summer of 2018 as he left Davis and New Orleans and signed a below-market-value free agent contract with the Golden State Warriors.

THE FUTURE AESTHETIC OF THE GAME

THERE'S NO DENYING that the addition of the three-point line to the NBA's playing surface completely changed basketball. It's been 40 years, however, since that addition; the NBA has now had the three-point shot for a longer time than it has not. With the exception of a brief three-year window in the 1990s when the league moved it in, the line has remained in the exact same position. In fact, the current configuration of the NBA court has been in place longer than any previous configuration. So for many us, threes are losing their luster. The shooters are too good and too comfortable, and the shots are too common.

Consider this crazy stat: during a single season, 2017–2018, NBA shooters made 25,807 three-point shots. That's more than they made during the entire 1980s. Between 1979 and the conclusion of the 1989–90 season, NBA shooters converted 23,871 three-pointers.

Historically, the league has demonstrated an impressive willingness to change its rulebook and its playing surface to keep game play diverse and interesting. In 1947, when the league outlawed the zone defenses that were

stagnating game flow, one of the main defensive tactics in the sport disappeared. In 1950, to reduce roughness and deliberate fouling, the league added jump balls after every made free throw that occurred in the last three minutes—as opposed to simply giving possession to the fouling team after the free throw.

In 1951, the so-called Mikan Rule drastically changed the appearance of NBA courts by doubling the width of the lane from six feet to 12 feet, primarily to reduce the unprecedented post-up dominance of George Mikan. Thirteen years later, in 1964, the league widened the lane again, to 16 feet, this time to reduce the post-up dominance of Wilt Chamberlain Now, 55 years later, it's still the exact same size.

These two "widenings" are fascinating to revisit for a few reasons.

First, they demonstrate that the league has always messed with the lines on the court to make it more difficult for one type of play or aesthetic to dominate a game. NBA basketball is constantly evolving, and while some of these evolutions have been organic, others have been engineered by generations of rule-makers at the NBA office. Like the Sagrada Família in Barcelona, the architecture thus far is already incredible, but pro basketball is a masterpiece in progress—it's never a finished product.

Second, the two lane widenings reveal that many of the league's boldest rule changes were designed to make life harder for big men—and easier for small men. It's hard to even fathom that now as we sit and watch fewer and fewer true centers and power forwards even lace up sneakers in the NBA, but in the time before the arc, big men were the prime attractions; they dominated the show, and smaller players were much less relevant.

Between 1946 and 2018, NBA rule changes fit a simple pattern of discouraging big physical game play in favor of smaller, more perimeter-oriented action. And while it's tempting for Michael Lewis to come along in 2017 and label "smallball" as some kind of 21st-century stroke of computational genius, the truth is that the current aesthetic and trends in pro hoops have less to do with clever data hacks and everything to do with the culmination of 70 years of big-man bias. This long series of rule changes have made the game much easier for guards and wings, and much more difficult for bigs. The three-point line is just one example.

Rule Changes and George Mikan the Player

When George Mikan championed the addition of the three-point line as a commissioner of the ABA, he was quoted as saying that the new line would give "smaller players a chance." Mikan's role in the three-point saga is poetic; no player in the history of the NBA affected the aesthetic of the game or its rulebook more than George Mikan. Not Russell. Not Chamberlain. Not Jordan. Not Magic. Not LeBron. Not Curry.

Mikan's absolute dominance on both ends of the court led to three of the biggest rule changes in the history of the sport: goaltending, the 24-second shot clock, and the Mikan Rule.

In the time before Mikan, very few players were big enough and athletic enough to play above the rim. Mikan was, and naturally he used those abilities to block the shit out of tons of shots. Some were on the way up, but most were on the way down. Many times he didn't even block these downward attempts—he just caught them and threw an outlet pass to a teammate. It was all legal. He became so dominant that both the NCAA and pro basketball added goaltending to their rulebooks, outlawing Mikan's signature defensive tactic and reducing the potency of his game, while simultaneously massively increasing the potency of jump shots. In a world without goaltending, big men could turn a huge share of jumpers into turnovers. But when the NBA outlawed goaltending, the way was paved for jumpers to become a lot more prevalent and for defensive bigs to become a lot less potent.

Mikan dominated on the offensive side as well. In 1950, in one of the most infamous games in early NBA history, the Fort Wayne Pistons decided that the only chance they had against Mikan and his Minneapolis Lakers was to not even give them offensive chances. So they held the ball. For a long time. It worked. The final score was 19–18. It was super-boring but effective, kind of like Ryan Anderson's three-point shots today. A few seasons later, the NBA implemented a 24-second shot clock.

But that's not all. As the seminal dominant big in NBA history, Mikan also caused one of the biggest changes to the league's playing surface. Since he was so big, so skilled, and so athletic, he naturally became the league's first dominant low-post presence. His teammates would simply dump the ball down to him in the post, and Mikan would go to work and get great looks against much smaller, much less skilled defenders. In the early stage of his career, he led the league in scoring every year for one simple reason: he would catch the ball about one yard from the rim, pivot once, and get a clean look right at the basket. He could finish with his left or right hand. He had a reliable little hook shot that nobody in the league could defend. Basic basketball. Mikan and his teams won the title every year.

He was so good, it wasn't fair. Lakers games were boring. Mikan owned the low post. He controlled every game by camping out in the low block area, which back then was just three feet away from the basket.

Six feet was a magical distance in the original architecture of the NBA's playing surface. The backboard was six feet wide. The midcourt circle and free throw circles each had a six-foot radius. But arguably the most important lines on the floor back then delineated the edges of "the key," which actually looked like a keyhole (or other things depending on your level of Freudian infatuations).

Mikan owned the game in this configuration. So much so that the NBA expanded the key—doubling the width of that tactically critical zone from just six feet wide to 12 feet wide. By 1951, Mikan's campground was twice as

THE ORIGINAL NBA COURT

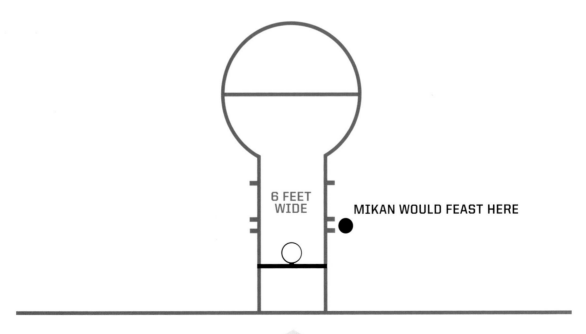

6 FEET
WIDE

MIKAN WOULD FEAST HERE

far away from the rim. His dominance immediately diminished, and both his field goal percentage and point production took hits. He was still the best player in the league, and he still won titles, but the Mikan Rule set a very important precedent for the young NBA: when a certain player or aesthetic becomes overly dominant, the NBA will intervene and change its rules in the name of diverse game play and competitive parity.

Imagine if *Jeopardy* changed its rules for Ken Jennings, or if the way pieces move in chess was changed because Kasparov was just too good. It would be crazy, but that's exactly what the NBA did to deal with Mikan—multiple times.

By the time he retired as a player, Mikan had completely revolutionized his sport. He became a template for the next generation of NBA aesthetics. The path to

basketball superstardom following Mikan began at the low block and ended at the rim. For the next 30 years, pro basketball was dominated by a parade of centers who extended the line that Mikan started drawing. Guys like Russell and Chamberlain became champions and MVPs, and the teams that had the best centers had the best chance for titles. The league's first superstars were almost all cut from the Mikan cloth, and the league kept messing with their dominance. Chamberlain was so athletic and so big that he could catch teammates' missed shots right above the rim and quickly turn them into put-backs. So the league outlawed "offensive goaltending." In addition, Chamberlain was so dominant in the post that in 1964 the NBA again widened its lane in an attempt to reduce his interior domination. That was over 50 years ago. Despite major facelifts in the league's first few decades, the lane is still the same size, even though nobody seems to

THE NBA COURT AFTER IMPLEMENTATION OF THE MIKAN RULE

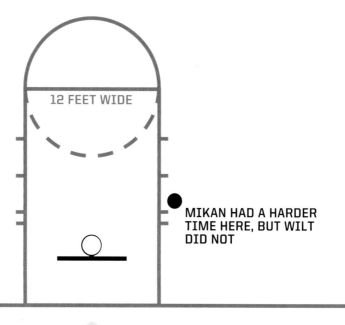

12 FEET WIDE

MIKAN HAD A HARDER TIME HERE, BUT WILT DID NOT

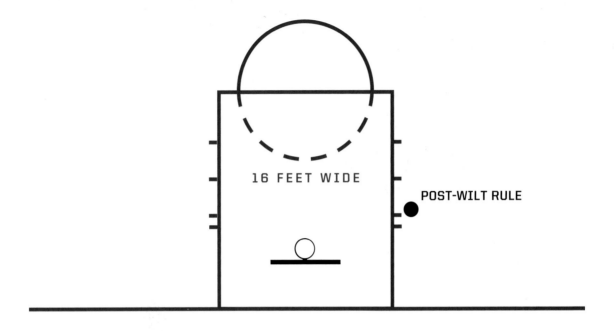

16 FEET WIDE

POST-WILT RULE

even try to post up anymore, let alone dominate from the post.

After the league introduced the Most Valuable Player Award in 1955, centers began to win the award almost every season. Of the first 24 NBA MVP Awards, forwards won only two or three (depending on how you classify Bob McAdoo), and guards won two. Centers won 19 or 20. You get the idea. It was a big man's league.

It was very clear that in the post-Mikan landscape, center was far and away the most valuable position on the court. Mikan had blazed the trail, showing a generation of big men how to dominate the sport. But he wasn't done reshaping pro basketball.

George Mikan the Commish and Abe Saperstein

In the 1960s, over a decade after his playing career ended, Mikan changed the game again, this time as a commissioner.

In 1967, Mikan became the first commissioner of the American Basketball Association, a brand-new pro hoops league designed to challenge the National Bas-

ketball Association. But the NBA was already popular, so Mikan's league needed gimmicks to get noticed and excite fans. Mikan came up with a few. First, he added a red-white-and-blue ball that he believed would look better than the bland orangish-brown spheres used in the NBA and the NCAA. The multicolored ball looked great, and kids loved it. But it wasn't enough. Mikan needed something that would affect every game in an exciting way. So he resurrected the bonkers idea of a "three-point shot," which had been unsuccessfully attempted by the American Basketball League in the early 1960s.

What in the world was the American Basketball League? The ABL was a short-lived pro hoops league that began in 1961 and folded up shop before it finished two seasons. It was the XFL of hoops, complete with its own Vince McMahon character. The commissioner of the ABL was Abe Saperstein, a man remembered much more for starting the Harlem Globetrotters than for running the failed ABL. Saperstein was part P. T. Barnum, part basketball visionary.

In the early 1960s, John F. Kennedy was president, the space race was just starting, and the Cuban Missile Crisis was keeping Americans glued to the news. Baseball was by far the most popular sport in the country, and Roger Maris was that sport's biggest story. He was igniting sports fans around the country by launching home runs at record levels. In the fall of '61, Maris broke baseball's most sacred record when he launched his 61st home run of the season, eclipsing Babe Ruth's legendary 60 home-run campaign of 1927.

Home runs were the most exciting play in America's favorite sport, and Maris became a household name by hitting more in one season than anyone in baseball history.

There was something about the long arc of the long ball that made baseball fans jump out of their seats. For those few seconds of the flight of the ball, everyone in the stadium—fans, players, announcers, and coaches—waited in suspense to find out just where the missile would land. And home runs weren't just gorgeous and suspenseful—they were potent too, the fastest way to score runs in baseball. They were the best thing in American sports.

It's no coincidence that Abe Saperstein's revolutionary idea came to basketball in 1961 in a country obsessed with missiles, long bombs, homers, and shots heard 'round the world.

Saperstein asked, what if we had home runs in basketball? What would that look like?

He pitched his crazy vision for a "home run shot" that would mimic the look and potency of a Maris homer, an impossibly long jump shot that would be the fastest way to score. Keep in mind, in the Mikan-Russell era—the first 20 years of the NBA—a vast majority of basketball shots were short-rangers. There was no reason to ever take long-range shots, which were harder and went in at lower rates. Wilt Chamberlain rarely shot from 10 feet out, let alone 25. To put it back into baseball terms, asking NBA shooters to shoot from 25 feet would be akin to asking Sandy Koufax to strike guys out from second base.

It was a wild idea, but after consulting with a few players and coaches, Saperstein conceptualized and delineated the three-point line. Where did he put it? Exactly where you see it today. Twenty-two feet in the corners, 23.75 feet along the arc. Crazy, right? It's been almost 60 years. What are the chances that the optimal place for the line in the time of Chamberlain is the optimal place for the line in the time of Curry?

Still, if it weren't for Mikan and the ABA, there's a very good chance that the three-point line would have been born and died in the same two-year span as the ABL. Steph Curry would have never become basketball's answer to Roger Maris if it weren't for Mikan and the ABA. In his book *Loose Balls*, Terry Pluto chronicles the ideation, implementation, and early days of Mikan's arc in the ABA—another alternative league to the NBA, but one that had more legs than the ABL. Pluto quotes Mikan reflecting about the three-point shot: "We called it the home run, because the 3-pointer was exactly that. It brought the fans out of their seats. It was first used by Abe Saperstein in the old ABL and we adopted the rule and their distances."

The ABA and its three-point shot changed basketball forever. Alex Hannum, who coached Chamberlain's 76ers to an NBA championship in 1966–67 and Rick Barry's Oakland Oaks to an ABA championship in 1968–69, described the early impact of the line and how it immediately resulted in more open game play: "In the NBA, we just clogged up the middle and dared teams to shoot from the outside. Nobody bothered to guard anyone 20 feet from the basket, but the 3-point play really did open up the middle. A guy starts hitting jumpers for three points instead of two and the coach has to change his thinking—and his defense. No other rule made the game more wide open and more fun to watch."

Hannum was right. Saperstein's line did more than just

add home run shots: it opened up the entire floor. It also made the sport a lot less crowded and a lot less physical. It made passes longer, and jumpers more exciting. The ball was in the air a lot more, and moving more, as were the players. Suddenly there was more space for the athletes to play in and more ways for teams to score. The ABA was on to something, and Saperstein's vision had come true.

Largely because of the three-point line, the ABA quickly distinguished itself from the NBA. The line affected almost every possession, even ones that featured no three-point attempts. Players spread out more, and ABA games were more fluid, more amusing, and more laid-back. While the NBA remained the more established and more successful league, compared to the ABA it looked prudish and conservative. The NBA was still dominated by brutish interior play, and the dichotomy between the two leagues would persist for about a decade before the NBA had no choice but to adopt the line.

In 1976, the two leagues merged. The NBA absorbed four ABA teams, while three others disbanded. A few years later, despite the protest of Celtics president Red Auerbach, the NBA adopted the three-point line, placing it in the exact same place where Saperstein originally envisioned it—22 feet in the corners, 23.75 feet along the arc. With the exception of three years in the 1990s, that's exactly where it's stayed while entire generations of players, from Chamberlain to Curry, have come and gone. Today everything about the game is different, except of course for the location of ol' Abe Saberstein's home run shot, which Mikan adopted for the ABA 50 years ago.

Maybe it's time for a change. Generations after Mikan

introduced the three-point line to the ABA to help give "smaller players a chance," it's the big players—the direct descendants of Mikan the player—who need a chance. In fact, big players may be less relevant in 2018 than small players were prior to the addition of the arc. During many of this decade's biggest NBA moments, centers were curiously absent from the games. For example, in the epic 2016 NBA Finals, both the Warriors and Cavs rarely even used their centers; both Andrew Bogut and Timofey Mozgov hardly got in games at all.

In the last decade or so, perimeter shooting has become by far the most important skill in the game; long-range marksmen have taken over the sport, and the only big players thriving in today's NBA are the ones who can shoot—and defend—on the perimeter. Guys like Bogut and Mozgov can't do either, so they're less valuable than ever. In fact, by 2018 Bogut, the big Australian center, the number-one pick of the 2005 draft, and one of the key figures in the rise of the Warriors, was out of the NBA entirely, at the age of 33. Mozgov wasn't doing much better. Although the Russian big man signed a massive contract with the Lakers in the summer of 2016, he spent the next few years as a financial pariah, bouncing from team to team, barely averaging 10 minutes per game for Brooklyn in 2017–18.

Between the major rule changes of the 1950s and 1960s, which neutralized post play, and the three-point line, the league gerrymandered basketball in a way that incredibly diminished the worth of traditional bigs. But while the early NBA was constantly changing its rules and moving its court lines around, today's NBA seems a lot like today's U.S. Congress—completely incapable of imagining, let alone legislating, any change.

This is a league where stretchy skinny dudes like Ryan Anderson and Channing Frye are more valuable than those silly dinosaurs like Al Jefferson trying to post up on the left block. This is a league where a guy like DeMarcus Cousins, arguably the most intimidating physical specimen in the game today, is shooting as many threes per game as guys like Reggie Miller ever did. In the 2017–18 season, Cousins shot 6.1 threes per game, a mark Miller eclipsed only one time in his 18-year career.

The two lane expansions, which dramatically devalued interior strength by resettling post-up players out into awkward areas we now call the midrange, were just the first blow of a massive one-two punch leveled at big men by the NBA. The second blow was the addition of the three-point line, which cartoonishly exaggerated the value of long-range jump shooting. This haymaker combination has effectively knocked the heavyweights out of the ring, forcing traditional big men to loiter in the awkward spaces between the analytically woke areas near the basket and beyond the arc. The redistricting of the court essentially forced traditional bigs into the areas that folks like Daryl Morey despise—spaces where you're too far off to muscle your way to a good look at the rim, but not far enough out to bask in the subsidized glow of the three-point line.

The last few decades have seen big men and their midrange post play become, unsurprisingly, "less efficient." Meanwhile, team tactics and personnel decisions are now increasingly focused on ways to post up less and spot up more.

While the lane expansions intentionally diminished the value of post play—and post players—the arc did the exact opposite for spot-up players: it wildly inflated the value of anyone who could drain jumpers from 24 feet away. An impossible back-to-the-basket, nine-foot jump hook over Joel Embiid's outstretched arms is worth two; another ho-hum Danny Green or Trevor Ariza open catch-and-shoot jumper is worth three. It is startlingly obvious to anyone who ever played *NBA Jam* that points no longer have a direct relationship with shot difficulty.

The quest for efficiency in the NBA is nothing new—indeed, Mikan and Chamberlain both were very efficient players in their time—but the current path to efficiency as dictated by the rulebook is threatening the diversity of game play in ways that we haven't seen since Mikan and Chamberlain. Chasing the efficiency dragon nowadays means chasing threes and forsaking entire swaths of the scoring area. Just like old times, a new, if different, kind of monocultural offensive landscape has taken hold in the NBA.

This is perhaps the defining idea of the sprawlball era: generations of rule changes have teamed up with a generation of players and coaches who grew up with the three-point line to redistrict the basic economic geographies that have guided basketball principles for decades. These same principles are the foundation ensuring that "greatness" and maximum salaries are reserved for those players who can most reliably perform the most impressive tasks at the highest levels. But as spot-up threes have become one of the most potent and frequent scoring options on the court, the men who can make them at the highest rates are becoming "great" despite the fact that this particular skill set is not exactly Jordanesque.

As teams, players, and coaches all find more and more ways to shoot more and more threes, the very nature of the sport is migrating outward, and it's taking some-thing important with it—namely, connections to the past.

The 1979–80 Houston Rockets took 4.6 threes and 86.8 twos per game.

The 2017–18 Houston Rockets took 42.3 threes and 41.9 twos per game.

The Current Aesthetic

If the 2018 NBA playoffs were any indication, the current aesthetic is dominated by three interrelated trends: positional versatility, perimeter shooting, and isolation plays. As Draymond Green became the dominant defensive figure for Golden State, the Warriors adopted the defensive philosophy of constantly switching defensive assignments on every ball screen, which diminishes the value of setting screens in the first place. Most of their players can defend multiple positions, but there are still some weak links in that Warriors defense. As Houston demonstrated in the 2018 Western Conference Finals, all that defensive switching could be used to an opponent's advantage. For instance, the Rockets weakened the Warriors defense by designing ball screens early in their possessions that forced Steph Curry to guard James Harden. Over and over again, Harden would end up isolated against Curry, the other Rockets would spread the floor, and the series became a glorified one-on-one contest pitting Harden on Curry, with the other eight dudes on the court watching from the best seats in the house.

Houston's coach, Mike D'Antoni, defended the strategy and suggested that such tactics are effective. "It's like, 'Oh my gosh, they ISO! That's all we do.' No, it isn't,"

D'Antoni said. "That's what we do best. We scored like 60 percent of the time on it. It's like, no, really? Like, 'Oh, they don't pass. Everybody stands.' Really? Have you watched us for 82 games? That's what we do. We are who we are, and we're pretty good at it."

He was right. Not only were these ISO plays successful, but they were a natural tactical response to the Warriors' "switch everything" defensive approach. That approach itself has only been made possible by the rule changes and regulatory failures that have greatly diminished positional diversity and the value of the size and strength of traditional big men in the NBA.

One of the key reasons why Green and the Warriors can switch everything in the first place is that it's become increasingly impossible for the Warriors' opponents to punish them for playing a miniature center. Simply put, we've reached a point where the best one-on-one advantages in the league are now gained in the matchups between a perimeter player and a slower, weaker defender out on the edges of the scoring area. This is a major departure from the norms that guided the sport for most of its existence. For most of NBA history, the league's best one-on-one advantages occurred in the post when the offense had a size or strength mismatch against a smaller or weaker defender. Like Mikan, Russell, Kareem, or Shaq on virtually any other player, they punished down low. But nobody plays that way anymore.

Houston achieved a huge advantage each time they got Harden ISO-ed on weaker defenders. That's why they went to that action over 150 times during the seven-game series. You know what they didn't do? They didn't try to exploit the size mismatch down low. Not

even once. The Rockets' Clint Capela, who is a monstrous 6'10" dunking machine, posted up only six times during the 2018 playoffs, and he never posted once during their series against the Warriors. Why? Well, why would he? The numbers are clear: post-ups are stupid; it's much more efficient to isolate Harden than it is to post up Capela. During the regular season, Capela's 55 post-up opportunities yielded an average of 0.92 points. Meh. During that same period, James Harden's 894 ISOs yielded an average of 1.15 points.

Lest you think these numbers are simply a function of Capela's lack of post efficiency, consider this. Of the seven NBA players who posted up more than 500 times during the 2017–18 regular season, Karl-Anthony Towns was the most efficient, averaging 1.05 points per post. That's good, but it can't hold a candle to either Harden's ISO number of 1.15 or the relative efficiency of even an average NBA three-point attempt, which in 2017–18 was 1.07 points. In other words, an average NBA three chucked up by, say, Trevor Ariza, Ryan Anderson, or P. J. Tucker is a better proposition than a post-up play by the league's best post player. It's no wonder the post game is dying, and the cause of death is inefficiency, the most dreaded ailment in the post-moneyball era.

With the rules tweaked to encourage perimeter play at the expense of interior play, as well as the non-enforcement of the rules that are in place, such as contact allowances in the low post, it's never been harder for players to exploit size and strength mismatches close to the basket. If players like Karl-Anthony Towns and Anthony Davis can't regularly punish much smaller and shorter players in the post—to the same degree that smaller, faster players can punish slower, weaker defenders on the perimeter—then why would they even try?

The entire aesthetic of the sprawlball era is driven by the realization of that discrepancy.

Although the league has essentially legislated against the big man's game since Mikan, maybe—just maybe—in the time of Curry, Morey, and endless ISOs and catch-and-shoot threes, it's time to reconsider. Perhaps as we reach a time when centers and post players are nearly extinct, we should consider enacting our own version of the Endangered Species Act. As we watch more and more games devolve into isolation fests or long-range jump-shooting contests, maybe it's time to throw the megafauna a bone or two.

Decades after Saperstein and Mikan, three-point shots are determining the outcomes of more and more games. Just rewatch the last few possessions of Game 7 of the historic 2016 NBA Finals. In the biggest moments of the biggest game of the decade, Golden State and Cleveland both just traded threes. There was barely any action at all in the two-point area. The pendulum has swung outward from the low block to the three-point line, and for some of us, the average NBA possession, marked by three stationary dudes loitering in the corners or along the wings, is already losing some of its majesty.

Saperstein's "home run shot" has become so commonplace that it hardly brings us out of our seats anymore. The 2017 Houston Astros won the World Series, and they also led major league baseball by averaging 1.47 home runs per game. Their NBA counterparts, the

2017–18 Rockets, led the NBA in taking 42.3 three-point attempts per game. Whereas three-point tries used to be novel events that happened a few times per half, by 2018 an average NBA game included over one per minute. Are threes still exciting if they happen every minute of every game? Are they still "home run shots" if they are as commonplace as a four-seam fastball? Are they still exciting when they are as common as two-pointers?

The rise of the three-point shot has also meant the decline of the two. Some of us miss the dynamics and athleticism required to score inside the arc. More specifically, some of us would like to see fewer P.J. Tucker spot-up threes and more of Jordan's fade-aways, Hakeem's dream shakes, and Abdul-Jabbar's sky hooks.

The increasingly homogenous aesthetic associated with late-era moneyball has less to do with geniuses reshaping the strategy of the game and more to do with a league that's fallen asleep at the wheel while the bus has slowly drifted toward a monocultural ditch of catch-and-shoot jump shots. The catch-and-shoot three in 2019 is about as unique and exciting as the post-up play was in 1978. The same factors that drove the lane widenings of the 1950s and '60s should drive future interventions in the coming years: aesthetics, tactical diversity, and entertainment.

Call me old-fashioned, but my favorite teams ever were the Heat and Spurs of the 2010s. For me, the ball movement and tactical diversity of the 2013 and 2014 Finals were incredible. Those series featured future Hall of Famers like Tony Parker, Tim Duncan, LeBron James, and Dwyane Wade—all phenomenal players who reached star status and won Finals MVP Awards without relying on threes. Their greatness manifested inside the arc. Those teams didn't exactly post up every trip down. The ball flew around at breakneck speed, and each squad featured some terrific long-range specialists like Danny Green, Shane Battier, and Mike Miller. The games were gorgeous.

But here's the counterintuitive part: if we like the way the game looks in this decade, we should be endorsing rule changes designed to slow or even reverse the league's perpetually increasing obsession with threes.

We should be supportive of changes designed to maintain the diverse aesthetic and athleticism that have lived in the heart of the sport since Bob Cousy and Russell suited up.

How much is too much, and when will this rising infatuation with threes stop? If present trends continue, the NBA will become increasingly bound to the three-ball and decreasingly bound to everything else. As a result of this major proliferation, threes will be even less exciting and even more routine than they've already become, while those gorgeous above-the-rim plays will become increasingly rare. It's a zero-sum game, you guys: every new three is one less two.

Going forward, the only players who will get playing time in the NBA will be three-point threats. The game will become a jump-shooting contest unless something changes.

But what could change?

Every time the NBA has faced an aesthetic crisis, it's changed its rule base to improve the look and feel of game play.

In a few more years, the aesthetic of those wonderful 2013 and 2014 NBA Finals will be a relic of the past, if it isn't already.

One reason the NBA is so sustainable is that it has constantly monitored and updated its rules. But in the midst of arguably the biggest stylistic upheaval in the history of the sport, it's curious that the league is suddenly sitting on its regulatory hands, exhibiting much more conservative tendencies about its rule base and the lines on its court. Maybe it's reluctant to make changes because the brand is doing so well. And maybe it's only grumpy old heads like me who seem to mind the rise of the three and the monotonous catch-and-shoot-and-repeat offenses it's brought us.

Regardless, this conservative era at the league office is still a departure from the open-mindedness and perpetual tinkering that characterized NBA regulatory behavior for its first 50 years. After all, it was a crazy idea and a willingness to adapt that led the league to conceptualize and then realize the arc in the first place, despite Red Auerbach's protests. It's hard to imagine anything nearly as drastic happening in the current climate. We're all Red Auerbach now.

The playing style of the NBA has never changed so much so fast, yet the lines on the court have never seemed so permanent. What would Abe Saperstein say? What would George Mikan say?

Commissioner Silver, at the very least it's time to *consider* some bold changes. In the spirit of Mikan and

Saperstein, let's look at some ways to update the game. How can we make it more fun? How can we make the sport more entertaining? Can we save the big man before it's too late?

Basketball is at its best when different kinds of players are able to thrive via different kinds of play. Since the inception of the game, five different kinds of positions organically emerged: point guards, shooting guards, small forwards, power forwards, and centers. One approach to NBA stewardship would be to protect each of these unique species going forward—to create a balanced version of the sport that ensures that each of these key characters can remain relevant to the plot as we turn the pages.

Current NBA oversight includes no such vision. Meanwhile, centers are vanishing from the league, wings are becoming power forwards—or more aptly, stretch fours—and post play, the dominant offensive tactic in pro hoops for decades, is going the way of MySpace. An average NBA game now features over 60 three-point tries (and still rising) and fewer than 20 post-ups (and still falling).

Albeit in a new way, the game is now as aesthetically monotonous as it was back when Mikan and Russell clogged up the interior. The moneyball monoculture is here, ladies and gentlemen, and let me tell you, it's not FAN-tastic. But as always, we're only one rule change away from making game play more diverse and more

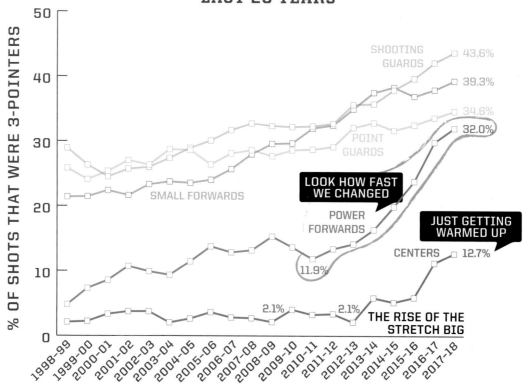

3-POINT ACTIVITY BY POSITION
LAST 20 YEARS

% OF SHOTS THAT WERE 3-POINTERS

SHOOTING GUARDS — 43.6%

39.3%

34.6%

32.0%

POINT GUARDS

LOOK HOW FAST WE CHANGED

SMALL FORWARDS

JUST GETTING WARMED UP

POWER FORWARDS

11.9%

CENTERS — 12.7%

2.1%   2.1%

THE RISE OF THE STRETCH BIG

1998-99 1999-00 2000-01 2001-02 2002-03 2003-04 2004-05 2005-06 2006-07 2007-08 2008-09 2009-10 2010-11 2011-12 2012-13 2013-14 2014-15 2015-16 2016-17 2017-18

entertaining. Is it time for a Mikan Rule to reduce the dominance of the spot-up man? If so, what would that look like? Let's look at some options.

Changes: Adjust the Line!

Mikan and Chamberlain both had their prime disrupted by a major rule change designed to weaken their scoring firepower. In both cases, the league made adjustments to the playing surface to reduce not only the efficiency of their post-up habits but also the frequency of their post-ups. The changes were just as much about aesthetics as they were about competition.

Let's explore how that same idea might work with spot-up players. What would some equivalent Mikan Rules be for the three-point era? Perhaps the most obvious change the league should explore is adjusting the size and shape of the three-point line.

First of all, why is the three-point line in the exact same place it's been since Abe Saperstein dreamed it up in 1961, almost 60 years ago? Back then, very few players could shoot from out there. Today, despite the fact that so many NBA players can now easily drain the shot that it's more like hitting a single than a home run, the line remains stuck in the same place.

So let's explore some ways to move the thing.

Move It Back to 25 Feet?

The simplest adjustment would be moving the line back. It's a logical idea with precedents in college basketball, in the WNBA, and even in the NBA itself.

Imagine a 25-foot line.

Back on June 23, 2014, I wrote a *Grantland* piece called "Is It Time to Move the NBA 3-Point Line Back?" It was just days after the Spurs had won the 2014 Finals over the Heat, and over a year before I ever worked in the Spurs front office. In case anyone thinks my line recommendation is based on some anti-Rockets or anti-Warriors agenda, let's revisit a short passage from that piece:

> Shooters are better than ever at draining 24-foot jumpers. Part of that is down to the way many teams design offensive sequences with the explicit goal of creating an open shot from that distance.
>
> Moving the line back, thus turning those 24-foot shots into long 2s, is one way to close the efficiency gap that currently is driving the league's obsession with 3-point shooting.
>
> If the NBA is interested in examining how moving the line would affect long-range shooting, it can refer to its own history. During three years in the '90s the league experimented with a shortened line (corners were basically the same). Unsurprisingly, 3-point attempts surged. By the end of that window—the 1996–97 season—21 percent of field goal attempts were 3s. The next year, the league moved the line back about 19 inches to its original position, presumably because that number was too high. The number plummeted down to 16 percent. Keep in mind, this year the league shot 26 percent of its shots from beyond the arc.

MOVE THE LINE BACK?

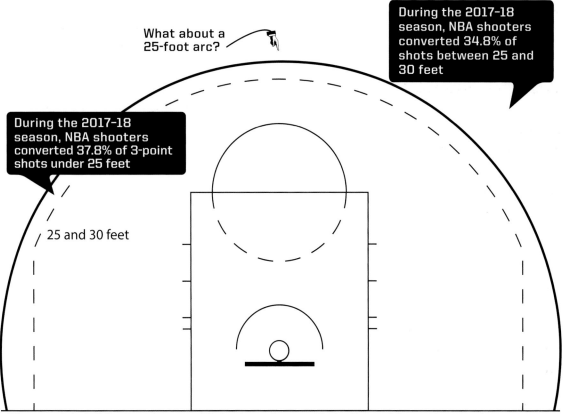

What about a 25-foot arc?

During the 2017–18 season, NBA shooters converted 34.8% of shots between 25 and 30 feet

During the 2017–18 season, NBA shooters converted 37.8% of 3-point shots under 25 feet

25 and 30 feet

The court is 50 feet wide, so a 25-foot arc is exactly half as wide as the court

We can also learn from the WNBA. Before last season, the league moved its 3-point line back 19.5 inches to correspond to FIBA's [International Basketball Federation's] line. The effects were immediate and significant. During the two seasons before that move, 25.3 percent of WNBA field goal attempts came from beyond the arc, and the league collectively converted 35.2 percent of those shots. When the line moved back, those numbers dipped to 21.5 percent and 32.7 percent, respectively.

In both cases the backward moves decreased both the frequency and efficiency of long-range shots, indirectly restoring more emphasis on the 2-point area. A move to a longer, 25-foot arc in the NBA would likely induce similar changes. During the 2013–14 regular season, NBA players attempted more than 52,000 3s. Just more than 25,000 of them were from deeper than 25 feet. As a whole, the league made 34.5 percent of those shots, compared to 38.4 percent of 3s closer than 25 feet.

As you can see in this graphic, the only time NBA shooters exhibited a decline in three-point frequency was when the league moved the line back out to its original position, from the shortened 22-foot version they experimented with for three years in the 1990s.

It's fair to expect a similar effect if we move it back again. Frequency would go down. Efficiency would go down. The value of spot-up men would go down. The relevance of twos would be resurrected, and the value of tactics that beget them would rise. The post-up man would get a bit more love.

The good news is that we can use those case studies to project how moving the NBA line back to 25 feet would affect shot behaviors in the NBA. The bad news is that a 25-foot line is still an arbitrary distance. Why 25? Why not 26? Why not 30? This is a fair question, and with the rise of analytics, we suddenly have the opportunity (and a responsibility?) to be a lot less arbitrary and a lot more thoughtful about the exact placement of the arc. Why don't we leverage all that fancy data the league collects to help us place the line at an optimal location? What about a data-driven line?

The Data-Driven Line

Here's an interesting fact: an average NBA field goal attempt is worth almost exactly one point. What a mag-

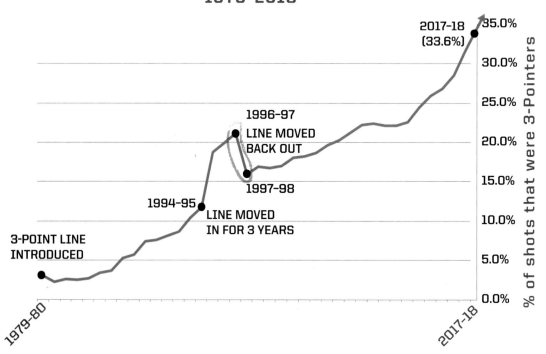

THE RISE OF THE 3 IN THE NBA
1979–2018

2017–18 (33.6%)

35.0%

30.0%

25.0%

1996–97
LINE MOVED
BACK OUT

20.0%

1997–98

15.0%

1994–95
LINE MOVED
IN FOR 3 YEARS

10.0%

3-POINT LINE
INTRODUCED

5.0%

0.0%

% of shots that were 3-Pointers

1979–80

2017–18

ical analytical convenience! This one-point average is very helpful as we compare and contrast holy efficiency across teams and players.

But what if we used that baseline to optimize the placement of the three-point line? What if the actual shooting and scoring abilities of NBA players informed the layout of the league's playing surface? It's something that Saperstein and Mikan never could have done. For generations, the league has adjusted its playing surface as a way to make sure the game remains as entertaining and competitive as possible. In the so-called Moneyball era, when every team in the league has begun to leverage data to strategize, the league itself has opportunities to do the same thing.

The invention of the three-point line made 33.33 percent a sort of magical number in NBA analyses. Anyone who can make a third of their threes can turn three-point shots into one point on average. It's the same as making half of your twos. But as a generation of shooters has warmed up to long-range shooting, NBA shooters are making 36 percent of their triples, and specialists regularly convert over 40 percent of them. That's the same as making 60 percent of your twos.

That slight increase in efficiency and the major increase in the population of players who can achieve that efficiency at high-volume levels are two defining drivers of the sprawlball era.

For individual players, these efficiency upticks may seem small, but at the league level they're massive. When a whole population of shooters are sinking 36 percent of their threes, the economic behaviors of shot selection at the population level completely change. There was a time when three-point shots weren't the

smartest jump shots on the floor for most shooters in the league. That time is gone now. Also, we now have data and analyses capable of mapping out with great precision where NBA shooters make and miss. These maps should inform how and where the league places its three-point line.

It's a logical approach based on the guiding principle that shots get harder with distance (duh!) and field goal percentage decreases with distance. Using contemporary shooting data, we can estimate where the line would have to be for the league to convert exactly one third of its three-point attempts.

Consider the 2017–18 season. By studying league averages at different shot distances, we can hone in on where the league as a whole made about one-third of its threes. As you can see in the following graphic, the shortest threes—those short ones in the corners—went in over 39 percent of the time.

This graphic reveals two key ideas:

1. There is a basic relationship between shot distance and field goal percentage, but it's not as strong as you might think.

2. League-wide, the shortest threes—the ones in the corners—go in almost 40 percent of the time. Given that two-point shots beyond 10 feet go in just 40 percent of the time, why in the world would you ever take a two-point jump shot?

But the graphic doesn't answer this key question: where would the line have to be so that the cumulative set of NBA three-point tries would go in 33.33 percent of the time? That's a hard question to answer, but by studying the nearly 70,000 non-heave three-point tries from 2017–18, we can make an estimate. During the 2017–18 season, excluding heaves, NBA shooters made exactly 33.33 percent of their threes from beyond 25.773 feet, a distance almost exactly two feet beyond the current line.

So why not place the line for the 2018–19 season at 27 feet in response to that analysis?

One cool thing about this approach is that we could refresh it annually. As shooters change, so could the line. Why not conduct this survey and delineation process after every season? Every summer we could look at the previous season's data and redraw the line based on empirical data. We could forever make threes worth one point around the league. Everybody's three-point percentage would suffer, but the league's best shooters would still be valuable. In fact, they might be *way* more valuable.

As the shot got farther out, players who could hit it 37 percent of the time would remain among the most prized commodities in the league. And make no mistake, Curry would still be among the most valuable

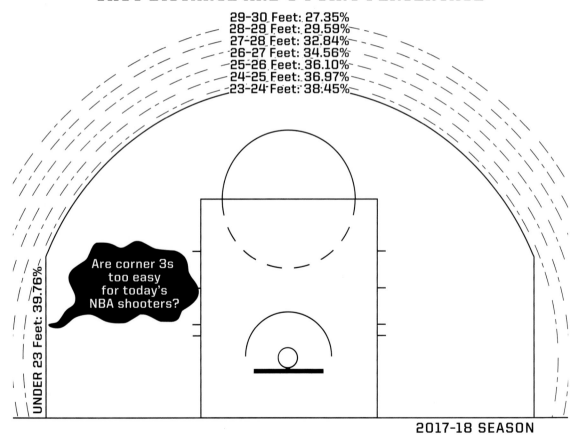

SHOT DISTANCE AND 3-POINT PERCENTAGE

29-30 Feet: 27.35%
28-29 Feet: 29.59%
27-28 Feet: 32.84%
26-27 Feet: 34.56%
25-26 Feet: 36.10%
24-25 Feet: 36.97%
23-24 Feet: 38.45%

UNDER 23 Feet: 39.76%

Are corner 3s too easy for today's NBA shooters?

2017-18 SEASON

players in the NBA. In 2017–18, 36 shooters tried at least 100 threes from beyond 25.773 feet, but only one converted more than 40 percent of them. Steph Curry made a ridiculous 43.6 percent of 172 threes from beyond that hypothetical data-driven line. His ability to be that good from that far out would make him stand out even more than he currently does in the sea of basic bros hitting 40 percent or better from the conventional distance.

Conversely, those whose fragile shooting abilities were most challenged by the new line would become less valuable, and their ability to "space the court" would be greatly diminished as the threat of their three-point shot waned. Andrew Wiggins, for example, converted just 22.8 percent of 123 tries from beyond our hypothetical data-driven line in 2017–18. At that rate, defenses wouldn't even respect Wiggins's long-range ability and could afford to play more aggressively.

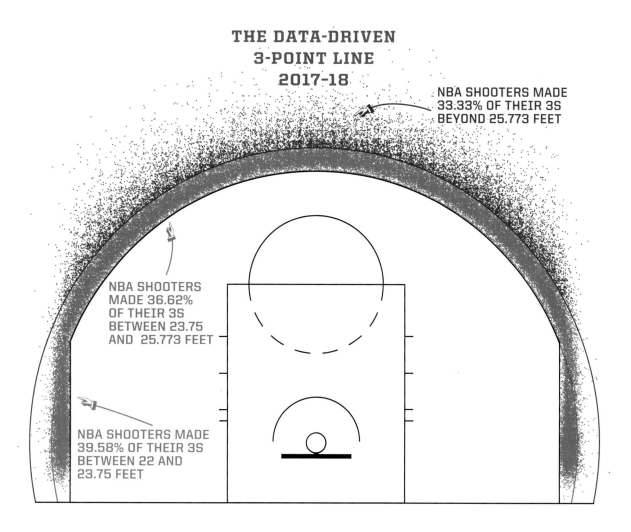

THE DATA-DRIVEN 3-POINT LINE 2017-18

NBA SHOOTERS MADE 33.33% OF THEIR 3S BEYOND 25.773 FEET

NBA SHOOTERS MADE 36.62% OF THEIR 3S BETWEEN 23.75 AND 25.773 FEET

NBA SHOOTERS MADE 39.58% OF THEIR 3S BETWEEN 22 AND 23.75 FEET

As it currently stands, many of the league's most active spot-up guys are only marginally efficient, and moving the line back two feet would make them even less so. Suddenly the population capable of making threes efficiently would decline, and the league would have to restore attention to the two-point areas and the players who could succeed there. Channing Frye would have to sweat again. Some three-point specialists would lose playing time, fadeaways would rise again, and the diversity of shot selection would surge. Midrangers would be cool again—at least for some players. Many three-point shots would be "dumb shots." And it would all be due to analytics. Man, Morey bitten by his own snake.

The very idea of the three-point line is based on the logic that longer shots are harder than shorter ones. This may have been true in the time of Chamberlain and Russell, but it's an idea that barely holds water in a league full of shooting specialists who grew up learning to shoot long-range jump shots. Virtually every NBA player can hit threes nowadays. Why not account for those population-level factors? Why not use facts to locate that line?

The basic economic geography of the current court is simple. But with the data and analyses available to us in 2018, we can survey it and manipulate it in exciting new ways. We can optimize game play and bring balance back to shot selection. It's a basic idea that could go beyond just the placement of the three-point arc. Where should the restricted area be? Where should the free throw line be, and why? How many shots should a player earn for drawing a three-point shooting foul? The league can use analytics to answer these questions—after all, the teams have been doing it for years.

The Corner Three

Ray Allen's incredible three-point shot in Game 6 of the 2013 NBA Finals was arguably one of the great shots in league history. Enough has been written about that shot and how Ray gently backpedaled into his sweet spot before receiving a perfect pass from Chris Bosh and releasing the sport's most brutal equalizer. But here's the thing: that place where Ray took the shot from—that little spot along the baseline where the three-point line is straight—is generally regarded as the "smartest shot on the floor." In fact, that place might actually be the stupidest shot on the floor.

Although the corner three has been the darling of the analytics movement for years, few people have really stopped to consider that, from an analytical perspective, the corner three shouldn't even exist. It's based on an analytical loophole, a seemingly minor decision in 1961 that now influences almost every half-court possession in the NBA. And why does the three-point "arc" have two big straight segments in it to begin with?

Let's make like Ray Allen and back up for a second. What is the corner three? The corner three is defined as the three-point shot along the baseline; while the lion's share of the three-point arc is 23.75 feet away from the basket, along the baseline the three-point line straightens out and is only 22 feet from the basket.

As a result of this configuration, some 23-foot jumpers are worth two points, while others are worth three. From most angles, 22.1-foot shots are worth two points, but along the baselines, for some reason, they're worth three. You don't have to be Billy Beane to know that doesn't make much sense.

The court is 50 feet wide, and the short corner arc is designed to leave three feet of shooting space for baseline three-point shooters. After all, NBA bros are big fellas with big shoe sizes, and they need enough space to catch and shoot. If the arc were 23.75 feet at all angles, that shooting space would be reduced to 15 inches in the corner area, barely enough space for Matt Bonner to fit his sweet New Balances in.

Even though corner threes make up less than 10 percent of NBA shots, they affect almost every half-court possession in the contemporary NBA. A seemingly minor decision—to shorten the arc near the corners rather than make a consistent 23.75-foot arc—has ended up reshaping the entire aesthetic of the NBA. Not only do teams and players constantly use that extra space to shoot, but they use it to "space" the floor. Used as a verb in the current NBA nomenclature, "to space" is to loiter, to stand still far away from the basket. It is the least athletic action any player can perform, but it is very valuable. In fact, while spacing is the least entertaining trick a player might perform, it is increasingly valuable, and nowhere is it more valuable than in the corners.

If you watch the game these days, you'll see almost every team station at least one, often two, players in the

GET RID OF THE SHORT CORNER?

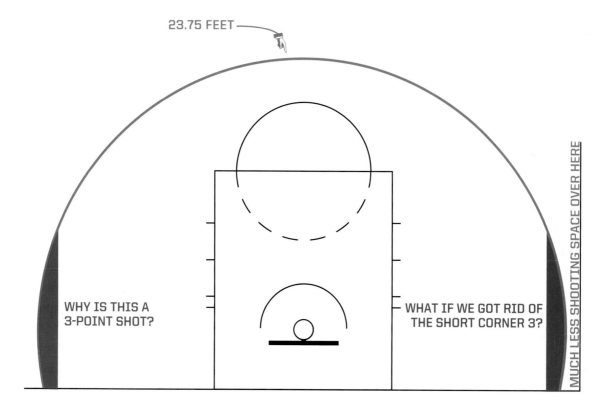

23.75 FEET

WHY IS THIS A
3-POINT SHOT?

WHAT IF WE GOT RID OF
THE SHORT CORNER 3?

MUCH LESS SHOOTING SPACE OVER HERE

remote corners of the offensive chessboard. The rooks in the corners are a signature part of the sprawlball era. All they do is stand around waiting for shot opportunities that usually don't come. So most of the time 20 to 40 percent of offensive players in the NBA are just standing around picking dandelions like little league right fielders. But unlike 10-year-old outfielders, who rarely affect the game, even when these rooks don't get a look, they influence most possessions by stretching out defenses and preventing help defenders from helping. They keep defenses honest, and they accomplish all of this by standing still.

As common as this loitering is now, it's important to note that no NBA teams ever did this before 1979. Why would you stash offensive players in the corners back then? Nowadays, every coach does it. Popovich, Kerr, and Carlisle all put two rooks in the corner of their chessboard. Genius.

Guys like Trevor Ariza, Shane Battier, and Allen Crabbe have earned millions of dollars not just because they can drain corner threes, but because by simply standing out there thinning out the opponents' defensive shape, they make their offenses a lot better, even in the possessions they don't shoot.

The corner three has made loitering a vital offensive tactic in the NBA. But this isn't the first time relatively stationary players have affected the aesthetic of game play.

Back before the Mikan Rule, the campouts were taking place near the basket, where defenders and offensive players toiled for prime real estate and were hesitant to leave once they got it. Rule changes like three seconds and illegal defense were specifically implemented to de-

ter loitering in the prime real estate and to encourage movement. These days, thanks to the three-ball, there's a bunch of new prime real estate out in the suburbs. But nobody seems to mind suburban loitering. Although the league was quick to outlaw loitering in the interior, they don't seem to mind it out in the corner three area.

It's yet another example of how hard the league has been on two-point fellas compared to their three-point counterparts.

The stationary rooks in the corners effectively turn many NBA possessions into three-on-three. The cornermen and their defenders are reduced to bit players—unless of course one of the rook's defenders dares to play help defense on a driving player after a ball screen. In that case, a future corner three happens via the drive-and-kick.

But is this interesting? Is it good for the league to place such a high value on two stationary shooting specialists camping out in the corners? Maybe, who knows. But one thing is for sure: outside of dunks and layups, rooks in the corners are yielding the cheapest points on the chessboard, and the numbers leave little doubt that the league is now chock-full of guys who can drain these shots at such high rates that teams would be crazy not to station them every time down the floor. Moreover, the ability to make that shot is now a prerequisite for almost every off-ball player in the NBA. But does anyone go to NBA arenas to watch these guys stand still in the corners?

One simple way to bring more movement back into the game and breathe more life into the two-point area is to make it a little harder on these loitering bros along the baseline. Drawing a consistent 23.75-foot three-point boundary wouldn't completely eliminate baseline triples, but it would get rid of the "short tees" currently being exploited by every team in the NBA. In 2018, the league was chock-full of incredible three-point shooters.

What's the loophole three? It's the corner three with a shot distance of between 22 and 23.75 feet. Everywhere else on the court it'd be worth two, but along the baseline it's worth three.

In the three seasons between 2013–14 and 2015–16, NBA shooters took over 44,000 corner threes, or 7.3 percent of NBA shots. Overall, they went in 39 percent of the time and yielded 1.16 points per shot, which is incredibly high efficiency for a jump shot.

But in the non-loophole areas in the corners—those spots at least 23.75 feet away from the rim—NBA shooters still connected on 36.79 percent of their attempts, which is right in line with league shooting efficiencies along the rest of the arc.

Loophole threes not only account for a vast majority of all corner tries, but they're also the league's favorite three-point shooting location by a landslide. In the same three-season span, loophole threes accounted for 91.4 percent of all corner threes, proving that NBA shooters love to take advantage of the "short tees."

If you divide the scoring area into a set of 2,000 or so one-foot-by-one-foot tiles, and then look at which tiles see the most shot activity, it becomes immediately evident just how "special" the loophole three is to the NBA right now. Between 2013–14 and the 2015–16, in the regular season, NBA shooters combined to take over 600,000 shots from all over the place, but a quick look at their 50 favorite spots shows that every one of these spots is either very close to the basket or in the loophole three area.

So what would happen if we eliminated the loophole three?

Four things would happen.

1. By shrinking the spot-up habitat for corner three shooters, we'd make their lives harder and their shots longer. In turn, that would disincentivize loitering. A consistent 23.75-foot arc would easily fit within the current court. However, it wouldn't leave much room for spotting up, and shooting space—at least three-point shooting space—would be much tighter. At the precise point where shooters would be straight in line with the basket, they would have just over one foot of three-point territory. And since these tall fellas have big feet, many of them couldn't reliably spot up in that tiny corridor; they'd have to slide up or down along the arc before they could find enough space to comfortably spot up, and even then they'd need more balance, more skill, and better offensive timing to generate corner threes. This simple change could make the game more exciting and the NBA's shot economy more fair.

2. We would see fewer corner threes. The most annoying side effect might be a lot more foot-on-the-line moments. Did he step on the line as he shot? Was his heel on the sideline? This

TOP 50 SHOT LOCATIONS
IN THE NBA

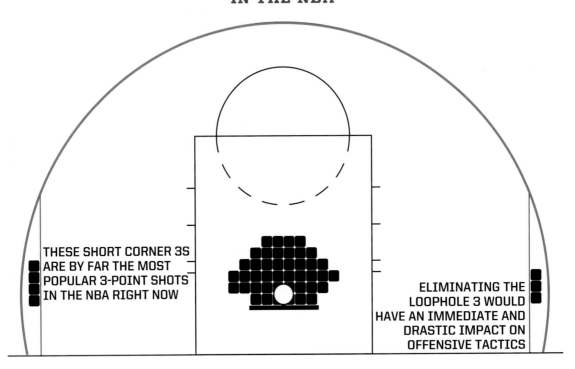

THESE SHORT CORNER 3S ARE BY FAR THE MOST POPULAR 3-POINT SHOTS IN THE NBA RIGHT NOW

ELIMINATING THE LOOPHOLE 3 WOULD HAVE AN IMMEDIATE AND DRASTIC IMPACT ON OFFENSIVE TACTICS

would mean more tedious reviews, which nobody would like. Incidentally, we could also widen the court from 50 to, say, 54 feet, but that would cause major nightmares for every arena manager in the league and force them to reconfigure their entire seating plan.

3. Regardless, if we got rid of the loophole three, we would see a slight reduction in shooting efficiency from the corner. As a general rule over the past few seasons, corner threes go in between 38 and 39 percent of the time. That number would decrease.

4. We would reincentivize other kinds of behavior on the offensive end. Fewer rooks, more bishops, knights, etc. How do we create the perfect blend of perimeter action, slashing drives, post-up actions, and fast breaks? That's a hard question, but one way to reduce loitering on the perimeter is to enact the same rules the league has applied to interior players. For instance, what if we simply added the three-second rule to the corner three zone? We could encourage movement on the perimeter and discourage all that standing around. If we painted the corner three area

and restricted the amount of time players could stand in that area—the same way we do with the paint—all those spot-up guys would have to be more creative with finding their shots, and timing would be a lot more important. Threatening the Arizas and Korvers of the world with turnovers the same way we threaten Dwight Howard and Clint Capela just seems fair.

Custom Lines

Warning: the following idea has often been ridiculed as the dumbest thing I ever proposed. However, a few people have told me it's brilliant. I present it again here, and let you decide for yourself:

What if every team in the NBA could draw the three-point line wherever they wanted?

Ever since the inception of the sport, basketball courts have been the same shape with equal dimensions no matter what city you played in. This consistency separates the sport from baseball and soccer, which both have different dimensions in different arenas.

When you walk into Fenway Park for the first time, you are greeted by the famed Green Monster, the left-field wall that is one of the most iconic images in baseball. Now imagine the same thing in basketball. What if different NBA teams had different dimensions on their three-point lines?

For generations, major league baseball teams have

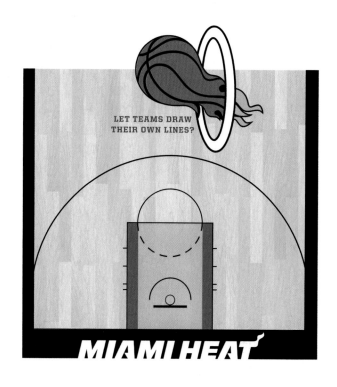

LET TEAMS DRAW THEIR OWN LINES?

MIAMI HEAT

accounted for "park factors" as they assemble their rosters. The Red Sox love right-handed power hitters who can take advantage of the Green Monster, and the Yankees love left-handed power hitters who can exploit the short porch in right field at Yankee Stadium. What if basketball teams could do the reverse? What if every season each NBA team delineated its own three-point line based on the strengths and weaknesses of its roster?

Where would Golden State put its line? What about Houston? You might think that Golden State would put their line closer in to get more threes; however, their shooters all thrive from deep. Curry, Durant, and Klay all hit from 25-plus feet with relative ease. By drawing their line at, say, 26 feet, they would emphasize their skills while challenging their opponents to swim in the deep end.

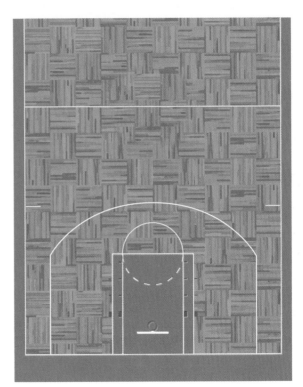

Other teams might choose to move the line closer or to feature asymmetries that keep opponents off-balance.

What if a team didn't want a three-point line at all on its home court? This might be the choice of a team with a dominant shot blocker, like Hassan Whiteside, or a team like the Miami Heat. Having no three-point line would force opponents to beat them near the basket rather than from beyond the arc.

That would be the most drastic option, and one the league would have to consider. But if dispensing with the three-point line altogether is too extreme, the league could easily institute some geometric constraints on the delineation of these lines. For example, the line would have to be no closer than 22 feet and no farther away than 30 feet at all locations, or the lines

would have to be symmetrical and identical on both ends of the court.

Regardless, different lines in different gyms would make every game a little more interesting and restore the relevance of home-court advantage in both the regular season and the playoffs.

Allow Goaltending on Threes

Many of the NBA's first major rule changes were aimed directly at George Mikan. Defensive goaltending was added in the 1950s to prevent Mikan from blocking shots right before they went into the hoop. Prior to Mikan, goaltending wasn't an issue, in part because no players could do it. But Mikan could do it, he did do it,

WHAT IF MIAMI DIDN'T EVEN HAVE THE 3-POINT LINE IN ITS ARENA?

MIAMI HEAT

a shooter got ready to release a three, there would be a flurry of activity near the basket as offensive guys and defenders toiled not just for rebounding position but also for shot-blocking position. Suddenly open threes would be much harder to come by.

Offensive bigs would have to position themselves to box out potential shot blockers. Catch-and-shoot specialists would have one more thing to worry about before they fired off a jumper. It would be exciting, and it would make catch-and-shoot specialists a lot less dominant than they are now.

Just as Tom Brady has to worry about a lineman deflecting passes at the line of scrimmage and free safeties intercepting them downfield, three-point goaltending would place a similar onus on Kyle Korver and immediately bring back the relevance of height and athleticism in the NBA. Bigs and other long athletes would be the free safeties of the NBA.

But would those three-point blocks be too easy? Some rules would have to apply, such as not being able to simply put your arm through the rim and block every shot that comes near it. Still, if the league found a decent way to sanction goaltending, how many threes would get swatted? Ten percent? Thirty-three percent? Seventy-five percent? It's hard to say. Maybe we could pilot the idea in the G-League to get the bugs out, but it's clear that such a change would add a lot of risk to every potential three-point attempt.

In today's NBA, catch-and-shoot guys are among the most potent offensive threats on the floor, despite the fact that their signature play is arguably the least athletic and least risky way to score. As revolutionary as three-point shooting may seem, from a basic eco-

and he quickly became the most ferocious defender the NBA had ever seen because of that ability. So the NBA outlawed it, and perhaps no rule change in the history of the game has done more to devalue big men than prohibiting defensive goaltending.

What if we revisited that rule change? What if we let defenders block three-point shots on their way down?

This may sound crazy—and it might be—but goaltending was legal before it wasn't. And speaking of crazy, so was adding a freaking three-point shot, which was yet another way the league intentionally devalued big men. By allowing goaltending on threes but not on twos, we would breathe some life back into the center position and into the two-point area.

It would be just like Kevin Garnett swatting those after-the-whistle jumpers, but in regulation. Every time

nomics perspective, it's actually very conservative. As of now, there is virtually no risk in a player like Korver or Ariza letting a three-ball fly, but if goaltending were allowed, suddenly these guys would feel real pressure and have tougher decisions to make. Suddenly they wouldn't just have to make sure the closeout guy wasn't going to block their shot on the way up; they'd also have to gauge whether the downward arc of their ball could beat the bigs in a race to the rim.

You could imagine an incredulous Jeff Van Gundy:

"What was Ariza thinking? He shot that ball even though Rudy Gobert was clearly in the basket area!"

Not only would the Arizas and Korvers have tougher decisions on their hands, but the value of athletic centers like Rudy Gobert, Hassan Whiteside, and Clint Capela would return. Smallball wouldn't make as much sense, and jump shooters wouldn't be so potent. The game would be more athletic and more above-the-rim.

Three-point goaltending would add even more suspense to the long arc of a three-ball by adding an additional possible outcome as an athletic defender swoops in to block an attempt right before the ball meets the hoop. The gaze of everyone in the arena wouldn't be fixated just on the parabola of the shot but also on the bigger players near the basket. Such a rule change would bring the spotlight back on centers and the lost art of interior defense in the NBA.

In addition, if goaltending were allowed only on threes and not on twos, it would restore a lot of the value of the midrange, where players could freely take jumpers without worrying about some monster swatting it away at the last second. Suddenly those long twos and elbow jumpers wouldn't be the dumbest shots on the floor anymore, and purpose would be restored to the post players and fadeaway artists long ago forsaken in favor of the catch-and-shoot bro currently dotting the edges of every NBA offense.

The goaltending proposal could be enacted without changing any lines on the court. But there are other ways to accomplish similar changes that also leave the three-point arc where it is. In fact, many of the best ways to bring positional diversity back to the NBA leave the line exactly where it is and make changes inside of the arc.

Fix the Two-Point Area!

In the heydays of Mikan, Russell, and Chamberlain, back when the three-point shot didn't even exist, post play dominated the NBA aesthetic. Virtually every trip down the floor looked the same. But when certain big men became too dominant and fans got weary of all the repetition, the league quickly rearranged the play-

ing surface to make post play harder and to forcefully diversify the look of the game. All of these changes occurred near the basket.

Now, after a generation of rule changes designed to fix that effect, the three-point line has done a lot to turn big men, especially big men who can't shoot threes, into an endangered species. Yet, despite the rise of the three-ball, the area near the basket remains the most important real estate in NBA basketball, and there's an opportunity to conserve the future of the big man by breathing some life back into his native habitat down by the basket.

Hardly any NBA teams are posting up right now. Nobody is dumping the ball down to the low post, as the Lakers used to do with Mikan and Chamberlain back in the day. However, if you look at the lines in the two-point areas, you'll see that they're still positioned as if teams were doing just that. The death of the post man has two causes: (1) the Mikan and Chamberlain rules, which widened the paint; and (2) the rise of the three-ball.

Now that over a third of NBA shots are three-pointers and it's clear that those long jumpers and their wild efficiencies are here to stay, why not reevaluate the Mikan and Chamberlain rules? After all, teams don't even use the post anymore.

What if we repealed and replaced MikanCare? What would happen if we turned the "lane" back into a "key"?

Like the goaltending proposal, narrowing the lane wouldn't be some arbitrary newfangled adjustment; it would honor the history of the game and add more di-

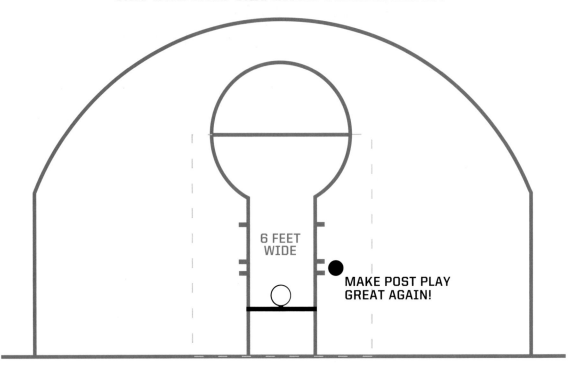

6 FEET WIDE

MAKE POST PLAY GREAT AGAIN!

verse action by restoring elements of the original rule-book.

Something very similar happened the last time the NBA made a major change to its playing surface. After experimenting with a shorter three-point arc for three seasons, when the league decided in 1997 to move the three-point line back, they moved it back to its previous location. It's like New Coke going back to Coke Classic. For many fans, rule changes are more palatable when they involve the possibility of going back to known precedents.

Now that almost every NBA player who suits up can knock down a catch-and-shoot three and almost every offensive stratagem is perimeter-oriented, wouldn't one easy way to restore aesthetic diversity to NBA ac-

tion be to encourage two-point offense? If we narrowed the paint area, we could do just that.

The lane is currently 16 feet wide. What if we thinned it back down to six or 12 feet? Recall that it went from 12 to 16 because Wilt was destroying dudes every trip down the floor. But here's the thing: there are no Wilts in the game anymore. We legislated them out of existence. Nowadays, it's easy to find Stephs and Klays and Hardens and Westbrooks, but there are no more Wilts, Shaqs, Mikans, or Kareems. Hell, there aren't even any McHales. Instead, there are guys like Draymond Green emerging as the most dominant "interior" defenders in the sport.

The big men who do make it onto NBA courts these days rarely ever post, and they are increasingly spotting

up from beyond the arc. But does anyone go to the gym to see DeMarcus Cousins shoot spot-up threes? Does anyone love to see Brook Lopez taking six awkward threes every game?

I sure don't. And perhaps one way to make the league becomes more diverse in the future is to look to its past.

The three-point shot and the army of shooters in the league aren't going anywhere, but maybe we can at least make teams think twice about starting a 6'7" center in the NBA Finals if we make him defend post players.

There are two main reasons why narrowing the lane would inspire more post play: first, it would obviously enable offensive post players to set up shop a few feet closer to the basket, thus making their shots a little easier, and second, it would require teams to defend the post with more gusto.

The arrival of smallball has just as much to do with the rise of the three as it does with the death of the post player. Smallball centers like Draymond Green and Kevin Love wouldn't have a prayer against Shaq or Duncan if those guys were able to get deep paint touches. But the current configuration of the paint, along with the enforcement of contact rules makes those touches virtually impossible to get. By narrow-

ing the lane, suddenly bigger, more physical offensive guys would be relevant again. If you didn't match them up with bigger, more physical defenders, the low post would become relevant again simply because post touches would quickly turn into drop-step dunks.

Now who doesn't want to see Draymond and Kevin Love get dunked on?

However, as it stands, the value of a big versus small mismatch on today's playing surface is too low to justify even trying to exploit it.

Contact Rules

Speaking of Draymond getting dunked on, aside from the antiquated size of the painted area, another reason why Draymond is so effective defending post players is that silly rules surround contact in the league right now. Again, the post man is an endangered species because his trade is "inefficient" relative to the trade of the man with the jump shot. The post man's two-point tries don't go in often enough. But why is that?

As anyone who has ever shot a ball can tell you, shots generally get easier the closer you are to the rim. But in the NBA there are two reasons why efficiency and shot distance aren't so simple. One is obviously the three-point line, which makes 24-footers worth a full point more than the 10-footers that post players often try. The other reason is defenders, the presence of whom greatly affects a player's ability to make shots. Duh.

While that's obvious, another reason why post guys are going the way of the dodo bird is that defenders are allowed to manhandle them. Anybody who ever watched Shaq or Duncan dominate Finals games knows that they did so by overcoming elbows, jersey pulls, and shoves.

The simple fact is that the NBA rulebook allows interior defenders to be physical in ways that perimeter defenders can't be. You can grab and push Shaq, and the whistle-blower will remain quiet as a mouse, but if you so much as lay a finger on Steph, that'll cost your team three shots—which, by the way, is the most punitive penalty in the game. Every time Steph or Harden get three shots, that averages out to well over two points per foul call. Shaq could dunk on Draymond and shatter the backboard, and he'd still only get two.

What if the league was more consistent about contact allowances across the court space? What if fouls were fouls across the board?

As it stands now, the geography of contact allowances is yet another driving force in the sprawlball era.

Again, I don't mean to demean anyone who believes that the current era has its roots in some kind of analytical awakening. That's certainly part of what's happened. However, today's aesthetic is more a result of a long pattern of legislative decisions that originally sought to disincentivize boring post play but have ended up greatly incentivizing everything else.

Any student of NBA history can easily find rule changes designed to make offensive life easier for guards and wings, but it's much harder to find any designed to help bigs. The three-point line itself isn't just the biggest rule change in the history of the sport; it has also been the most successful in a long line of rule changes—including contact allowances, three-second rules, and lane widenings—designed to make big men less relevant. They all worked. It's just that the three-point line continues to work more effectively with each passing season. As we move toward a league whose entire population can hit triples, we also move toward a league devoid of any big men who can't. But it doesn't have to be this way.

Here's an idea. What if we applied the same kind of analytical reasoning so lionized within the post-moneyball sports discourse to the rulebooks and the lines on the court?

What if instead of using fancy models to optimize shot selection or batting orders or defensive configurations

of outfielders, we used them to optimize our playing surfaces and our rules?

Ever since *Moneyball* came out, sports analytics has been framed as an activity that takes place in the front offices of team facilities. But the truth is, that's way too narrow a frame. We can combine analytical reasoning with new forms of data to enrich our understanding of sports from almost every perspective. To date, we have yet to really see this combination applied to optimizing the aesthetic of a sport. We've yet to see analytics used to engineer entertainment, parity, or diversity within the games themselves.

This is the opportunity to do just that.

Basketball is the best sport in the world for many reasons. One reason is that the sport lends itself to regular outbursts of athletic magnificence, which can take many forms. Ask anyone who has watched Magic, Jordan, LeBron, or Durant. Chances are, if you saw any of these guys, they'd blow your mind at least once. But chances are also good that those mind-blowing episodes didn't involve a catch-and-shoot three. Let's be real—catch-and-shoot moments aren't the most magnificent acts in the NBA. Compared to no-look passes, high-flying dunks, or impossible fadeaway jumpers, watching catch-and-shoot events can get kind of boring.

Basketball is at its best when different kinds of players— different sizes of players with different specialties—get together and make us swoon. But the sprawlball era portends a looming monoculture. The best league in the world is increasingly trending toward one form of play and one kind of scoring. Make no mistake, threes can be exciting as hell. But how much is too much?

The 2017–18 Rockets became the first team in history to take over half of its shots from three-point range. Many people don't think that looks good. It may be clever strategy, but I'd rather watch Barkley's fat ass toil and sweat on the block than watch Eric Gordon sit back and loft yet another 26-foot jumper. The latter is exactly what the current configuration of the playing surface and the rulebook is promoting. More Anderson, less Barkley. The Rockets aren't ruining basketball; they're just the most intelligent and visible example of a team aligning its strategies with the incentives and subsidies concocted by the NBA rule-makers. What if those incentives and subsidies themselves were as carefully crafted as Daryl Morey's rosters or Mike D'Antoni's offensive sets?

You can't be Charles Barkley anymore. You can't be McHale. You can't be Malone. You can't be Kareem. Hell, if Magic showed up as a rookie right now, the scouting report would be "big for the point guard position, outstanding court vision, great passer, willing defender and rebounder, but *not* a shooter. His range doesn't extend out to the line."

If Jordan were drafted in 2019, he'd spend a lot more time playing catch-and-shoot than playing rim-attack-dunk-on-fools'-heads. For those of us lucky enough to grow up in the Jordan era, almost all of us still will argue with anyone that he is the GOAT. He wasn't just my favorite basketball player, he was my favorite TV show. Jordan was must-see TV. He was the biggest star in America. But the two biggest shots of Jordan's career—the one to beat the Jazz and the one to beat Georgetown—were both the exact kinds of midrange jumpers that are deemed foolish these days. In fact, Jordan's entire arsenal of fadeaways and pull-ups would be labeled "poor shot selection" these days. For an entire generation of kids, the Jordan aesthetic defined basketball greatness and drove them to love the sport. "Air Jordan" propelled the league to another level by flying through the air on his way to the rim, making us all wish we could "be like Mike."

Over the course of Jordan's 15 seasons in the NBA, he averaged only 1.7 three-point tries per game; in contrast, he averaged 21.2 twos per game. He shot more than ten times as many twos as threes. Despite the fact that he was a shooting guard, Jordan achieved greatness by feasting on the meat of the defense, not by nibbling along its edges. By 2017–18, NBA shooting guards were taking over 40 percent of their shots from three-point range. Even as Jordan aged and the dunks became less frequent, he'd still score via athleticism and crafty footwork, relying on an endless array of fadeaways and jumpers, many coming via the low post.

O'NEAL, SHAQUILLE — X=250, Y=0
FIELD GOAL MADE

By 2017–18, none of the best scoring guards in the NBA could do that, or even cared to. Forget ten times as many twos as threes: both Steph Curry and James Harden would end many games with fewer twos than threes. They hardly ever spent time in the two-point area, let alone feasted there. But if you look at points per game and see that these guys seem to be on the same level as Jordan, remember, that's just an accounting trick entirely driven by the fact that three is greater than two. Jordan scored 30 and 40 a night countless times without hitting a three. From the guard position. Nobody does that now, from any position.

In other words, you can't "be like Mike" anymore. Actually you can—you can be just like Mike Miller.

If Kareem showed up at UCLA as a freshman right now, they'd be trying to get him to run pick-and-pop from the top of the arc. There'd be no skyhook. From Pauley Pavilion to Madison Square Garden, the best bigs in the game right now are posting up a lot less and spotting up a lot more. Between 2013–14 and 2017–18, all positional groups started shooting more threes, but bigs almost doubled their three-point activity. On a per-team basis in 2013–14, bigs were already shooting 3.6 threes per game; by 2017–18, that had swelled to 6.9 per game—a 92 percent jump in just five years. Bigs now live in the suburbs too.

If Dominique Wilkins showed up at the University of Georgia, he'd be put to work setting up shop in the corners or deep along the wings. There'd be no Human Highlight Film unless you love to watch YouTube montages of Channing Frye hoisting up forgettable threes.

We're not heading toward a world where the NBA is overly reliant on threes—we're already there. Almost all of the different offensive aesthetics of the game's bygone superstars would be out of place in today's game. This is a league where Ryan Anderson gets paid $20 million a year to play "power forward" and loiter 25 feet from the basket. His "power" is to shoot over 70 percent of his shots from three-point range and clear out space in the interior for his dribble-driving teammates.

Nowadays the paint stands as empty as it was full before.

The NBA is a league where scoring champions like Steph Curry are now scoring a majority of their points from three-point land. It's a league where incredible all-around players like Ricky Rubio and Andre Roberson get ridiculed for their inability to make jump shots, despite the fact that they can do almost everything else better than everyone else who plays their position. In the sprawlball era, jump shooting has become a pass-fail litmus test for every player who hopes to play NBA basketball, and the simple fact is that many of the league's most iconic Hall of Famers would have failed such a test. We're filling the league with more Channing Frye and Ryan Anderson types and fewer Kevin McHale and Charles Barkley types.

Still, as much as this report on the state of the league may sound like get-off-my-lawn or yelling-at-a-cloud ranting, the sprawlball era is just beginning. These are the good old days. If you love the game right now, then you too are an advocate of changes. Why? Because the massive stylistic upheaval is by no means complete. Every year the league pushes these trends further. There are no signs of slowing down, let alone stopping.

Championships, draft statuses, free agency values, All-

Star selections, and coaching reputations are all increasingly won and lost based on the ability to make three-point shots, and decreasingly won and lost based on the ability to make two-point shots. Left unchecked, the rise of the three/death of the two will continue to deform the sport and drive us further and further away from the goal and closer and closer to reducing NBA games to jump-shooting contests. And given the current rule architecture, that makes perfect sense. It's not Rocket science, it's basic finance capitalism.

In the time of flash boys and day traders, the quest for efficiency pervades everything in our culture. Nothing is immune. Not cinema. Not higher education. Certainly not pro sports. From Hollywood studios deciding which films to green-light to baseball managers deciding how to position their infielders, to NFL general managers deciding what players to draft, to NBA head coaches figuring out what lineups to start, decision-making processes across the culture are all beginning to look like the ones at Goldman Sachs.

You can see it on TV. ESPN looks more like CNBC every day. You can hear it in the discourse. *First Take* shouting matches sound more and more like *Mad Money*, and even the most casual observers are all evaluating teams based on offensive and defensive efficiencies.

The rise of statistical thinking, big data, and analytical reasoning has more to do with capitalism's perpetual yearning for growth than with any kind of newfangled enlightenment.

But the financial shrewdness lauded by Lewis doesn't end at Billy Beane's batting order or Daryl Morey's draft model. It manifests on the playing surfaces of the sports we love to experience, and poetically, it's unclear if that shrewdness will ultimately be good for the actual look and feel of the sports it's reforming. Financial thinking may be analytically superior, but is it aesthetically inferior?

What are the chances that the massive strategic and aesthetic differences engineered by financial thinking will actually beget aesthetic improvements on the field? Would you buy a painting from Warren Buffett?

Sports appreciation has never been less about aesthetics than it is right now. Sometimes I wonder when ballet will finally have its "Bill James movement." A lot of people actually think Baryshnikov was the best ever, but Sylvie Guillem had a much higher fouetté-over-replacement. And until Misty Copeland can put up a decent adagio efficiency rating, she shouldn't even be considered for MVP.

This might sound weird coming from the fella who made his name mapping out precise shooting efficiencies for every player in the NBA. But that obsession came from my desire to understand greatness in my favorite sport. It didn't come from a desire to direct it. And it certainly didn't come from a desire to derail it in the process of streamlining it.

So what now? The good news is that the NBA can easily leverage the same kinds of basic reasoning processes that have guided teams through the advanced stats era to help ensure that its product remains aesthetically pleasing going forward. In other words, while I think it's fair to say that analytics are threatening to distort the look and feel of pro basketball, I also know that they can help improve it too. Analytics and aesthetics can be best buddies.

The same methods that Morey used so well at the team level to find his revelatory offense can be used to ensure that we find ways to optimize the beauty of pro basketball at the league level. It's not up to me or anyone else to decide what beautiful or ugly is; however, the history of the National Basketball Association is littered with dozens of such judgments. Just ask the late great George Mikan.

ACKNOWLEDGMENTS

This book would not have been possible without the help of several people. I would first like to thank the good folks of Houghton Mifflin Harcourt, especially Susan, Mark, and Laura for all of their faith and their hard work. Y'all made this project possible.

Thank you Aaron Dana, for being so good and so professional. You gave this book a soul. Your art is inspiring. You're Keith, I'm Mick. Everyone knows Keith is better than Mick. I can't wait to work together again.

Thank you David Larabell, who believed in this project from day one, and also gave it life.

Thank you Ben Kalin for your professionalism, and your unbelievable commitment to correctness.

Thank you to Bill Simmons, who gave me my first big break in the world of sportswriting. You made writing a legitimate career for me and many others. What an amazing gift. You're Lorne Michaels for sportswriting.

Thank you to Chris Ryan who believed in me and helped me find a voice for the paragraphs in between the shot charts.

Thank you Shea Serrano, despite your height, you have inspired me so many times.

Thank you Nate Silver, for pioneering analytical discourse on the internet and also being so generous with your time and your support over the years.

Thank you to the San Antonio Spurs, especially R. C. Buford and Gregg Popovich. Although y'all have a few other accolades, you also changed the way I look at the game. You're both wonderful teachers.

Thank you to Connor Schell and the others at ESPN who have believed in my work and supported it for years, especially Hank who has helped me with data since 2012!

Thank you to jumpin' Matt Adams, who was one of the first people to collaborate with me on this crazy project.

Thank you to Luke Bornn, Dan Cervone, Alex Franks, Alex D'Amour, and Andrew Miller, who were the best academic collaborators I could've dreamed of back in 2012. All of you are geniuses and great to work with. What a wild ride!

Thank you to all of the great teachers at Penn State and UCSB that taught me how to make maps and visualize data, especially professors Cindy Brewer, Sara Fabrikant, Keith Clarke, Waldo Tobler, and Rob Edsall.

Thank you to the geography department at Michigan State University for giving me my first real chance to study and teach cartography in the real world. Go Green.

Thank you to Peter Bol and Wendy Guan at the Center for Geographic Analysis at Harvard for giving me a chance to teach at the best college on the planet.

Thank you Steve Hellemuth, and all the other visionaries at the NBA who saw the value of spatial data and brought it to the best basketball league in the world.

I would be a real jerk if I didn't thank some of my family. Without them, none of this would be possible. Most of all, THANK YOU to my beautiful wife, Adrienne, who has enabled me to map basketball players for the last decade. Your support and love means everything. Thank you to Rosie and Daisy, my hilarious daughters who bring me joy like nothing else I've ever experienced. Thank you to my Mom, who did so much for me it's ridiculous to even try and summarize that here. Thank you to my Dad, who among other teachings, put me in front of an Apple II when I was a kid and let me play around with Logo software, giving me early experience and interest in computer graphics. Thank you to the rest of my family and extended family. I love you all.

Thanks to basketball for being so awesome.

A
C
K
N
O
W
L
E
D
G
M
E
N
T
S

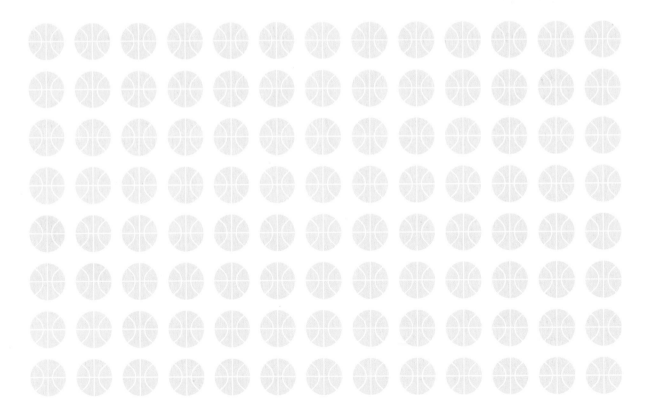

INDEX

Numbers in italics refer to text graphics

ABA (American Basketball Association)
    description, 196
    merger with NBA, 197
    multicolored ball, 196
    three-point line beginnings and, 197
    See also Mikan, George
Abdul-Jabbar, Kareem
    MVPs, 148
    as player/status and, 4, 34, 128, 130, 148, 165, 181,
        182, 201, 227
ABL (American Basketball League), 196, 197
Abrams, Jonathan, 93
Adams, Bennie, 101–2
Adams, Steven, 121, 182, *183*
Adu, Freddy, 130
Aldridge, LaMarcus, 4, 21, 23, 171, 178, 185
Allen, Ray
    Curry breaking record, 51, *52*, 53, 57
    James and, 71
    as player, 142
    scorers tracking, 23
    three-point shooting/records, 23, 49, *49, 50*, 64,
        64, 148, 157, 210
Allen, Tony, 55, 61

American Basketball Association. *See* ABA (American Basketball Association)
American Basketball League (ABL), 196, 197
analytics and basketball
    aesthetics/watching and, 109–11, 113–15,
        189
    beginnings, 19–20, 23–24, 77
    as evolving, 78–79
    exploiting rules and, 109–10
    skeptics, 20–21, *21*
    winning games/finances and, 111, 112
    See also specific components; specific individuals/
        teams; three-point shooting; updating the
        game
Anderson, Ryan
    background, 13
    contract/pay (2016), 11, 13, 14, 15, 19, 31
    description/as basketball player, 14, 20
    effects on defense, 15
    Harden and, 100–2
    Phoenix Suns and, 19
    "poster" and, 17, *17*
    Rockets/Spurs game (November 2016), 10, 11
    scouts ranking and, 13–14

Anderson, Ryan (*cont.*)

    three-point shots and, 10, 11, 13, 15, 114, 176, 225, 227

    value, 15–16, 19, 227

Anthony, Carmelo, 132, 134, 170

Area 31

    Jefferson and, 4, *4*, 5, 6, 178, 198

    map/description of, 5, *5*

    shooting efficiency/comparisons and, 5, *5*, 6

Ariza, Trevor, 114, 199, 200, 212, 215, 218

Art of War, The (Sun Tzu), 2

Auerbach, Red, 197, 202

Baer, Larry, 113

ballet, 229

Barkley, Charles

    analytics and, 20–21, *21*, 225, 227

    description, 31, 225

Barry, Rick, 197

Baryshnikov, 229

baseball

    analytics (moneyball) effects, 109, 111–13

    catchers, 74–75

    Gold Glove, 74–75

    home runs and, 196–97

    infield geometry, 75

    Moneyball (Lewis) and, 17, 111, 112, 115, 225

    "pop time," 75

    stadium dimensions and, 215

    stolen bases and, 74–76

Baseball America, 74

basketball numerical positions

    description, 186–87, 203

    "sixes," 187

basketball players

    diversity and, 161

    hype/expectations and, 130–31

    jerseys/two-point and three point comparisons, *224*

    "stars," 228–29

    uniqueness of, 23

    See also specific individuals

Battier, Shane, 71, 157, 201–2

Beane, Billy, 17, 111, 228

Bende, Dragan, 170

Bennett, Anthony, 150

Bird, Larry

    as player, 111, 131, 140

    threes (1987–88), 103

    traits, 131, 132

Blatt, David, 153, 154

Bleacher Report, 44

Bogut, Andrew, 33, 57, 187, 198

Bolt, Usain, 76

Bonner, Matt, 211

Bosh, Chris

    James and, 142

    as player/changes and, 170, 171, 188, 210

Brady, Tom, 217

Breen, Mike, 38, 72

Brewer, Corey, 62, 111

Brown, Kwame, 130

Brown, Mike

    before Cavaliers, 137–38

    as Cavaliers coach, 137, 139

    defense and, 139

Bryant, Kobe

    contracts/money, 60

    as player/status, 19, 55, 59, 131, 132

    statistics and, 19

Buford, R.C., 153–4

Capela, Clint, 10, 98, 100, 200, 218

Carlisle, Rick, 138, 212

cartographers in NBA

    first decade of this century, 23

    shooting data and, 23

Cartwright, Alexander, 75

Chamberlain, Wilt
    era of, 197, 210, 219
    as player/status, 9, 10, 128, 130, 132, 148, 161, 181,
        182–83, 190, 193, 196, 197, 199, 204, 220
Chriss, Marquese, 170
Cleveland Cavaliers
    firing/replacing head coach (January 2016),
        153–54
    James in Miami and, 150–52
    See also specific individuals
Cleveland.com, 123
Conley, Mike, 61, 173
contact rules and updating the game, 223
contracts
    cap-driven market place/zero-sum game, 16
    See also specific individuals
Cooper, J.J., 74, 75
Copeland, Misty, 229
corner three shot
    description, 28
    updating the game and, 207–8, *208*, 210–15, *211*,
        214
Costa, Brian, 113
Cousins, DeMarcus
    description, 198
    drawing fouls and, 92
    as free agent/move, 189
    three-point shooting and, 187, *187*, 188, 198, 221
Crowder, Jae, 101, *101*
Cuban Missile Crisis, 196
Curry, Dell, 42, 48
Curry, Stephen
    ankle problems/surgeries, 48–49, 60
    background, 42–43
    breaking Allen's record, 51, *52*, 53, 57
    Cavaliers/Warriors Finals (2016), 116, *117*, 119,
        120–21, *122*, 123, 124–25, *125*, 126
    compared to James, 142
    contract (2012), 60

descriptions, 28, 42, 55
DraftExpress scouting report, 43–44
evolution, 48–49, *48*
first shot/rookie year, 45–46, *45*, *46*, *47*, 48
game/three point shooting (February 2016),
    37–40, *37*, *38*, *40*
Jackson and, 54
jump shooting description, 52–53, 135
Kerr and, 57–58
MVPs/seasons, 28, 31, 34, 39–40, 41, *46*, 58, *59*,
    130
NBA draft, 43, 89
NBA Finals (2015), 63
NBA Finals/Game two (2018), *68*
other skills, 53, 57
parents (Dell/Sonya), 42, 48
as player/reputation, 88–89, 157, 178, 180, 199
playoffs/finals (2018), *68*, 106, 109
pop time, 80
relearning to shoot, 42–43
scoring near basket, 58, 61
scouting report/predictions on, 43–44, 58
shooting vs. Harden's free throws, 86, 89–90, *90*
three-point shooting (2015–16), *36*, 65
three-point shooting and, 28, 31, 34, *36*, 37–41,
    37, *38*, *39*, *40*, 51, *51*, 52–53, *52*, *53*, 57, 58,
    61, 63–66, *64*, *65*, *68*, 80, 140, 157, 161, 209,
    214, 223, 227
three-point shooting distances, 209, 214
traits as player, 28, 58–59, 61, 62
unassisted threes, 51, *51*, 53, 97
Under Armour/Nike and, 59–60
year three, *48*
year two, 48, *48*

Daniels, Antonio, 138
D'Antoni, Mike
    Morey and, 100
    Rockets/analytics and, 10, 100, 106, 199–200, 225

Davis, Anthony
    description, 179, *180*, 182, 184–85, 189,
        222
    development as player/three-point shooting
        and, 184, 188, 189, 200
    Green interaction (December 2016), 179–81,
        180, 182, 189
Davis, Baron, 150
defense
    components/description, 139
    two-point jump shot, 5
    See also fouls/free throws; *specific individuals*
Detroit Pistons
    playoffs/Cavaliers (2007), 140
    title/2003–04 season, 140
Diamond, Jared, 113
Dominique, 227
"Downside of Baseball's Data Revolution, The"
        (Costa and Diamond), 113
draft
    description/unfairness, 143, 150, 151
    team loyalty and, 142–44
    See also specific individuals
DraftExpress
    Anderson, 13–14
    Curry, 43–44
Duncan, Tim
    analytics and, 19
    as defense, 6, 31
    description/as player, *4*, 132, 165, 181, 201, 222,
        223
    James and, 148
    Spurs/Hornets game (March 2016), 4, 5
    Spurs wins and, 148, 149, 153
Durant, Kevin
    becoming Warriors player, 69, 76–77
    Nike and, 60
    as player/reputation, 59, 76–77, 148, 157,
        225

    playoffs/finals (2018), 106, 109
    three-point shooting distances, 215
Dylan, Bob, 173

efficiency
    in our culture, 228
    See also analytics and basketball
Embiid, Joel, 92, 198–99
ESPN, 130, 163, 228
ESPN: The Magazine, 42
ESPN.com, 13, 14, 109, 153
Eurostep
    description/fouls and, 93–95, *93*
    Ginobili and, *93*, 95
    Harden and, *93*, *93*, 95
Evans, Tyreke, 43, 46, 60

"fair play"
    sports and, 86
    See also specific sports
FIBA (International Basketball Federation),
        205
field goal attempts (2013–14 to 2017–18), 7n
field goal percentage
    as limited statistic, 28
    locations (2013–14 to 2017–18), 24–25, *25*
    media using, 19
    shot distance and, *7*
FIFA, 86
Fleming, David, 43
Flynn, Jonny, 43
football forward pass addition, 77
fouls/free throws
    concentration locations (2013–14 to 2016–17), *91*,
        127–28, *128*
    Davis/Green interaction (December 2016),
        179–81, *180*, 182, 189
    double standard/player size and, 179–81, *180*,
        182, 189

officiating/close-range vs. perimeter, 6, 103–5, 179–81, *180*, 182, 188, 223

player strategy and, 91–92

rules/automatic fouls, 181

on three-point shots, *103*, 103–5

on three-point shots/top players (2016–17), 103, *103*

value overview, 103–5

See also Eurostep; *specific individuals*

Fox Sports, 118

Frye, Channing, 198, 210, 227

Garnett, Kevin, 142, 171, 174, 188, 217

Gasol, Marc, 58, 61, 173, 174, 187

Gasol, Pau, 187

George, Paul, 13

Gilbert, Dan, 144, 149

Ginobili, Manu, *93*, 93, 148

Ginsberg, Mason, 188, 189

Gobert, Rudy, 218

"Golden Start" *Grantland* (Goldsberry), 57

Golden State Warriors

criticism of (NBA Finals/playoffs 2015), 63

February 27, 2016 game, 37–40, *37*, *38*

NBA Finals/playoffs (2015), 60–63

playoffs (2018), 106–9, *107*, *108*

playoffs loss to Clippers (2014), 53

record wins, 37, 40

three-point shooting importance, 65–69

Western Conference Finals (2016), 66–67, *67*, *68*

See also specific individuals

Goldsberry, Kirk

background/cartography, 24

background/playing basketball, 21–23

favorite teams, 201–2

NBA shot data and, 24–25, *25*, 26

shot/court location and, 21–23

Gooden, Drew, 136

Gordon, Eric, 10, 111, 114, 225

Grant, Chris, 149, 150

Grant, Horace, 19

Grantland, 57, 63, 71, 87, 166, 188, 204–6

Green, Danny, 199, 201–2

Green, Draymond

Cavaliers/Warriors Finals (2016), 116, 118, 121

Davis interaction (December 2016), 179–81, *180*, 182, 189

description, 171, 179

physicality, 121, 179–81, *180*, 182, *183*, 223

as player/changes, 154, 171, 178, 179

Griffin, Blake, 43, 62, 148, 188

Griffin, David, 153

Guillem, Sylvie, 229

"Hack-a-Shaq," 31

hand-checking

description, 55

league changing rules/effects, 55, 176

Hannum, Alex, 197

Harden, James

2017–18 statistics, 96, 97, 98

Curry comparison/fan response, 89–90

description/skills as player, 15, 18, 28, 31, *83*, 93, *94*, 97–99, 106, *110*, 161

draft, 43

dribbling, 98

Eurostep and, 93, *93*, 95

exploiting rules and, 101, *101*, 102, 105–6, 109–11, 112

fans views of/fouls, 102–3

fouls drawn/techniques, 92, 101, *101*, 102, 105–6

free throws/statistics, 84, *84*, 85–86, *85*, 90–91, *90*, 92, *92*, 93, *93*, 96, 97, 103, *103*, 104, *104*, 105

free throws vs. Curry's shooting, 86, 89–90

isolation plays and, 18, 98, 185, 199, 200

Harden, James (*cont.*)
    Jazz game/Western Conference Semifinals (May 2018), 100–3, *101*
    Morey and, *94*, *95*, *96*, *97*, 99–100, 106, 109–11
    MVP, 31, *96*, *97*, 106, 130
    November 2016 Rockets/Spurs game, 10–11
    as player/reputation, 82, 95, 114, 178
    refs and, 100–2, 105
    Rockets/Spurs game (December 2013), 82, 84, *84*
    Rockets strategy and, 95–99
    shooting foul locations (2013–14 TO 2016–17), *92*, *96*
    three-point shooting fouls drawn (2016–17), 102–3, *103*, *104*, 105
    three-point shooting statistics, 104–5, 114, 223, 227
    as unassisted three-point creator, 99–100
    unassisted threes and, 97–100, *98*
    Western Conference playoffs (2018), 108, 109
Harlem Globetrotters, 196
Harris, Lucious, 136
Haywood, Brendan, 139
Hibbert, Roy, 34, 178, 179, 187
Holiday, Jrue, 185
Hollinger, John, 20, 23
home runs in baseball, 196
Houston Rockets
    analytics/aesthetics and, 90–91, 109–12, 113–15
    basketball strategy/analytical reasoning and, 17–18, 95, 112
    Jazz game/Western Conference Semifinals (May 2018), 101–3, *101*
    Morey/analytics and, 11, 14–15, 17–18, 19, 21, 27, 95–96, 99, 106, 109–10, 111–12, 198, 210, 225, 228, 229
    playoffs (2018), 106–9, *107*, *108*
    three-point shooting fouls importance, 105, 106

three-point shooting importance/statistics, 18, 100
    See also specific individuals
Howard, Dwight, 58, 82, 182

Ibaka, Serge, 170
Iguodala, Andre
    Cavaliers/Warriors Finals (2016), 122, 123, *123*, 124
    as player, 37, 63, 106, 122, 123, *123*, 124
Ilgauskas, Zydrunas, 133, 136
Ingles, Joe, 102
Inside the NBA, 21
International Basketball Federation (FIBA), 205
Irving, Kyrie
    background, 150–52
    Cavaliers/Warriors Finals (2016), 118, 123, 124–25, 125, *125*
    injuries/missed play, 63, 116, 152
    Love and, 167
    as player, 53, 150–52
Iverson, Allen
    shooting graph, *44*
    as star point guard, *44*, 45

Jackson, Mark
    after Warriors, 124
    background/basketball's physical era and, 54, 57
    as Warriors coach/firing, 54, 57
Jackson, Stu, 55
James, Bill, 229
James, LeBron
    becoming "King James," 149
    Cavaliers capabilities and, 133, 136–37, 142
    Cavaliers/championship (2015–16), 153–55, *154*
    Cavaliers playoffs/finals and, 133, 137, 138–39, 142

Cavaliers/Warriors Finals (2016), 116, *117*, 118–19, 120, 121–22, *122*, 123, *123*, 124, 125, 126

changes (2011–12), 145–47, *146*

contracts/money and, 60

defense and, 138–39, 142

draft (2003), 130

free agency/moves, 142–43, 150, 156–57

Heat advantages, 142, 144, 153

Heat first year (2010–11 season/playoffs), 144, *144*

Heat move/response, 142–44, 145

high school, 130, *131*

his "snipers"/Goldsberry interview, 71

hype/expectations, 130–32, 133–34

jump shot and, 135, 144

Lakers and, 160

Love and, 167

MVPs and, 130

Pacers and, 179

peak/description (2012–13), 147–50, *147*

as player/status, 59, 60, 62–63, 121, 129, *129*, 135, 142, 154, 157, 187, 201, 225

playoffs/finals (2018), 109

playoffs/Pistons (2007), 140–41

pop time, 80

return to Cavaliers/first season (2014–15), 150–53, *151*

Rookie of the Year Award (2004), 134

rookie year/debut (2003–04), 133–35, *134*, 136

scoring champ (2007–08) season, 141, *141*

second year/close-range improvements (2004–05), 136–37, *137*, 138–39

third season/playoffs (2005–06), 138–39

as three-point creator, 155–57, *155*, *156*

three-point shooting effects and, 157

three-point shooting/game changing and, 141, 146, 156–57

traits/description, 131, 132, 133–34, 135–36

Jamison, Antawn, 139, 150

Jefferson, Al
after NBA, 18, 19, 34, 187
Area 31/left block success and, 4, *4*, 5, 6, 178, 198
description, 9, 114
March 2016 Spurs/Hornets game, 4, 9
three-point shooting effects on, 9, 10, 16, 18

Jennings, Ken, 193

Jeopardy, 193

jerseys/two-point and three point comparisons, *224*

Johnson, Magic
as player/reputation, 111, 132, 138, 161, 165, 225
rookie season, 161, 165
three-point shooting effects and, 161

Jokic, Nikola, 187

Jordan, DeAndre, 148, 161

Jordan, Michael
Bulls (1995–96 season), 37, 40
"hard fouls" and, 55, *56*, 57
as player/status, 19, 22, 34, 54, 55, 63, 111, 131, 132, 138, 140, 142, 187, 225–27
poster, *16*, 17
retirement, 132
rookie year/statistics, 133
traits/description, 131, 132

jump shots efficiency, 6–7

Kasparov, 193

Kennedy, John F., 196

Kerr, Steve
background, 54
as Warriors coach, 54, 57–58, 62, 118–19, 126, 154, 212

Kornheiser, Tony, 32

Korver, Kyle
accuracy/speed and, 78, 81
Cavs/Boston game (April 2017), 70, *71*, 71–72

Korver, Kyle (*cont.*)
    Millsap comparison, 73, 78, 81
    pay and, 77
    pop time, 77, 78, *79*, 80
    quickness/three-point shooting, 70, 71–72,
        73, 76, 77, 78, *79*, 80, 81, 114, 157, 217,
        218
    trade to Cavs (2017), 71, 72, 77–78

Lacob, Joe, 119, 181n
Laimbeer, Bill, 55
lane widenings/effects (Mikan Rule), 182–83,
    184, 190–94, *192*, *193*, *194*, 198, 201, 219,
    223
Leonard, Kawhi, 10, 15, 16, 125, 161
Lewis, Michael, 2, 17, 113, 191
Lillard, Damian, 98
Lin, Jeremy, 82
Livingston, Shaun, 116
lockout (2011–12), 57
Lombardi, Vince, 2
Loose Balls (Pluto), 197
Lopez, Brook, 221
Love, Kevin
    basketball skills/reputation, 34
    Cavaliers/Warriors Finals (2016), 118, 124, 126
    changes/three-point shooting and, 165–66, *166*,
        167–70, *167*, *168*, *169*, *170*, 171, 172, 173, 174,
        176–77, *176*, 187, 222
    on changing game, 174
    defense and, 174
    descriptions, *160*, 162–63, *163*, 165, *165*, 167–68,
        167, 171, *175*
    draft/rookie season (2008–09), 162, 163–66,
        164
    first season in Cleveland, 166–67
    injuries/missed play, 63, 116, 118, 152
    interview with Goldsberry, 166, 167, 168,
        174

    playoffs/finals (2018), 109
    trades, 151–52, 163, 166
Love, Stan, 162, 174
Lowe, Zach, 63
Lue, Tyronn, 124, 153–54
Lynch, Andrew, 118

McAdoo, Bob, 183, 194
McHale, Kevin
    background, 173
    as general manager, 163
    Love and, 163
    as player/description, 163, 170, *172*, 173, 174, 176,
        181, *221*, 227
McInnis, Jeff, 136
McMahon, Vince, 196
McMenamin, Dave, 122–23
Mahorn, Rick, 55
Malone, Karl, 22, 132
Manning, Peyton, 130
Maris, Roger, 196
Márquez, Rafael, 88, 89
Memphis Grizzlies
    by 2017–18 season, 174
    three-point shooting and (2013–14),
        173–74
    See also specific individuals
midrange defined, 29n
midrange shots
    decline/timing, 3, 4, 11, *12*, 13, 29–30, *30*,
        95
    See also two-point jump shot
Mikan, George
    as ABA commissioner/three-point line, 161, 171,
        183–84, 191, 194, *195*, 196, 197, 201
    description, 183, 191, *192*, 194, *195*, 229
    as player/reputation, 130, 148, 157, 181, 182–84,
        190, 191–92, 194, 196, 199, 203, 204, 216–17,
        219

Mikan Rule (lane widenings), 182–83, 184, 190–94, *192, 193, 194*, 198, 201, 219, 223

Miles, Darius, 133

Miller, Mike, 71, 157, 201–2, 227

Miller, Reggie

    speed and, 81

    three-point shooting/records, 34, 49, 57, 64, 169–70, 171, 198

Millsap, Paul

    Korver comparison and, 73, 78, 81

    as player/three-point shooting and, 72–74, 77

Mitchell, Donovan, 100

Moneyball (Lewis), 17, 111, 112, 115, 225

Monroe, Greg, 178

Moon, Jamario, 150

Morey, Daryl

    Anderson and, 11, 14–15

    background, 111–12

    description, *94, 95*

    Harden and, *94, 95*, 96, 97, 100, 106, 109–10, 111

    Rockets/analytics, 11, 15, 17–18, 19, 21, 95–96, 100, 106, 109–10, 111–12, 198, 210, 225, 228, 229

Morey's Law, 96, 97

Mozgov, Timofey, 33–34, 198

mural for NBA

    best shooters/by zones, *127*, 128–29, *129*

    overview, 126–29, *127, 128*

Murphy, Troy, 14

MVPs

    in 1990s/post-up moves, 22

    beginnings, 194

    list (2011—2018), 97

    multiple seasons awards, 148–49

    NBA mural and, *127*, 130

    player positions and, 194

players size change and, 161

three-point shooting changes and, 22, 28, 31, 161, 183, 184

unassisted threes and, 97

See also specific individuals

Myers, Bob, 154

Naismith, James, 39, 86

Nash, Steve, 55, 176

NBA

    comparison to U.S. Congress, 198

    current description, 227–28

    late 1990s, 54–55, *56, 57*

    merger with ABA, 197

    as sustainable/reasons, 202

    three-point shooting fouls drawn (2016–17), 102–3, *103*

    See also specific components; specific individuals; three-point shooting/NBA transformation; updating the game

NBA Finals/playoffs

    Bulls/Jackson (1998), 54

    Cavaliers/Warriors (2016), 116, *117*, 118–26, *119, 120, 122, 123, 125*

    Warriors and (2015), 60–63

    Western Conference and (2015), 60–61

    Western Conference finals (2018), 106–9, *107, 108*

    See also specific individuals/teams

NBA geography

    court space statistics, 2

    history/importance and, 2–3

    See also specific components

NBA transformation

    adjusting for specific players, 182–83, 184, 190–94, *192, 193, 194*, 216–17

    discrimination against big players, 178, 181–83, 184–86, 187, 188, 189, 191, 194, 198, 200–1, 217, 227

NBA transformation (*cont.*)
    double standard/player size and fouls, 179–81,
        180, 182, 189
    lane widenings/effects (Mikan Rule), 182–83,
        184, 190–94, *192*, *193*, *194*, 198, 201, 219, 223
    outlawing goaltending/effects, 182–83, 191–92,
        193
    reducing roughness/deliberate fouling, 190
    zone defenses end, 190
    See also three-point shooting/NBA transforma-
        tion; updating the game
Nessler, Brad, 133
New York Times, 93, 119, 181n
Newble, Ira, 136
Nike, 59–60
Nowitzki, Dirk, 144, 174

Oklahoma City Thunder
    Warriors game (February 2016), 37–40
    Warriors game (May 2016), 66–67, *67*, 69
Olajuwon, Hakeem
    era of, 111
    James and, 147
    as player, 22, 181
Oliver, Dean, 20, 23
Olynyk, Kelly
    Cavs/Boston game (April 2017), 70, *71*, 71–72,
        73
    description, 70
O'Neal, Shaquille
    as player/change and, *19*, 31, 130, 132, 142, 148,
        157, *165*, 181, 183, 187–88, 222, 223, *226*
    three-point shooting and, *187*, 188

Parker, Tony, 55, 148, 201
Parsons, Chandler, 60, 82
Paul, Chris
    injury, 106
    as player/star point guard, *44*, 45, 62

pop time, 80
    shooting graph, *44*
Paxson, John, 77, 188
Petrovic, Dražen, 42
Phelps, Michael, 76
Pierce, Paul, 142
Pluto, Terry, 197
points per shot
    distance and, *8*
    by location (2013–14 to 2017–18), 3, *3*, 25–26,
        26
    most common location (2013–14 to 2017–18),
        25–27, *27*
Pomeroy, Ken, 20, 23
pop time
    baseball, 75
    basketball, 76, *77*, 78, *78*, 80–81, *81*
Popovich, Gregg, 62, 138, 148, 150, 153, 212
Porter, Otto, Jr., 73, 78
possession value, 89
Powlus, Ron, 130

Rambis, Kurt, *172*
Randolph, Zach, 61, *90*, 173, 174, 176
Redick, J.J., 72, 77
Richmond, Mitch, 42
Riley, Pat, 142, 154
Rivers, Doc, 62, 63
Robben, Arjen, 87, 88, 89
Roberson, Andre, 227
Robertson, Oscar, 133
Robinson, David, 22
Rodman, Dennis, 19, 114
Rodríguez, Iván ("Pudge")
    as baseball catcher/awards, 74–75
    Hall of Fame and, 74
    stolen bases and, 75–76
Rubio, Ricky, 43, *44*, 227
Ruffin, Michael, 138, 139

Russell, Bill
  era of, 119, 181, 203, 210, 219
  as player, *9*, 128, 132, 148, 181, 182–83, 193
Ruth, Babe, 196

San Antonio Spurs
  NBA Finals and (2014), 148–50
  See also specific individuals
Saperstein, Abe, 196–97, 201, 202
SB Nation, 188
Scott, Dennis, 49, *49*, 51, *53*, 64, *64*, 171
Scott, Stuart, 162
shot distance
  field goal percentage and, *7*
  points per shot, 8, *8*
  three-point percentage and, *208*
shot locations
  2014–15, *24*
  changes with three-point shots, 11, *12*,
    13
  most common (2001–02), *12*
  most common (2016–17), *12*
  NBA tracking beginnings, 19, 23
  in zero-sum game, 29
shots (number) taken per year, 23, 30
Shumpert, Iman, 70
Shuttlesworth, Jesus, 49
  See also Allen, Ray
Silas, Paul, 137
Silver, Commissioner, 202
smallball, 34, 181, 182, 183, 189, 191, 218, 222
Smith, Josh, 62
Smith, J.R., 123, 124, 157
Smith, Kenny, 111
Smith, Stephen A., 162–63
Snow, Eric, 136
soccer
  arena dimensions and, 215
  diving/flopping and, 87, 88, 89

FIFA rules and, 86, 87, 89
  penalty kicks, 87, 88, 89
soccer World Cup (2014)
  description, 87–89, *88*
  Goldsberry and, 87–89, *88*
  shot attempts, 87–88, *88*
solutions. *See* updating the game
"spacing the floor," 15
Spoelstra, Erik, 154
Sports Illustrated, 130, 150
SportsCenter, 14, 22
sprawlball meaning, 10
Stern, David, 162
Stojaković, Peja, 174
stolen bases
  "caught stealing percentage," 75
  pop time, 75, 76
  positions/individuals involved in, 74,
    75
"stretch fours" defined, 14n
Suárez, Luis, 89
Sun Tzu, 2

technologies
  views of, 112
  See also analytics and basketball
testicle attacks, 121
Thabeet, Hasheem, 43
Thompson, Klay
  Cavaliers/Warriors Finals (2016), 116, 123, 124,
    125
  defending, 57
  Jackson and, 54
  reputation, 157
  three-point shooting, 57, *66*, 69, 215
  Thunder games (2016), 37, *66*, 69, 107
Thompson, Tristan
  Cavaliers, 120, 150
  changes in game and, 178

three-point line/shooting

    assist-dependence and, 49–51, 157–58

    average point worth (2017–18), 7

    beginnings/early impact, 8, 197

    catch-and-shoot threes rise, 76–81

    comparison to stolen bases, 76, 77

    corner three as analytical loophole, 210

    distances, *7, 8,* 41, 197

    efficiency, *7*

    environment and, 80

    history/home runs concept and, 196–97, 201, 204

    increase/timing, 3, *3,* 8, 28–30, *29,* 44, 190, 199, 201, *206*

    missed threes/effects, 106–9, *107, 108*

    NBA moving line (1996–97) and, *29,* 204, *206*

    players speed/accuracy, 79–80, *79, 81*

    players spotting-up behind line (beginnings), 10–11

    pop time, 76, 77, 78, *78,* 79–81, 80–81, *81*

    by position, *186, 203*

    pure catch-and-shoot threes/statistics, 76

    questioning value, 27, 109–10

    reasoning on points, 6

    record in single NBA season (after 2012–13), *53, 64, 65*

    record in single NBA season (before 2012–13), *49*

    shooting guards and, 70

    shot distance/3-point percentage, 207, *208*

    shots made (2017–18 season), 190

    speed/accuracy combination, 77–78, *79,* 80–81

    speed and, 70–72, 73

    tactics changing, 77

    top shooters, *39, 49, 53, 64, 65*

    unassisted threes, 50–51, *51,* 97–99

    unassisted threes created (2017–18), *99*

    Western Conference finals (2018) and, 106–9, *107, 108*

    See also Mikan, George; *specific components; specific individuals;* updating the game

three-point shooting/NBA transformation

    aesthetics/watching and, 109–11, 113–15, 189, 203, 212

    big players and, 178, 181–83, 184–86, 187, 188, 189, 191, 194, 198, 200–1, 217, 227

    center changes, 171–73, 182, 183, 184, 185–86, *186,* 187, 198, 201, 203, *203*

    connections to past and, 199

    continuing changes and, 34

    defense and, 15–16, 102–3, 174

    defensive switching and, 199, 200

    description, 30–31, *32,* 70, 73

    description if rapid change, 33

    effects on players/skills, 9, 11, 13, 15–16, 18, 19, 29, 30–31

    impacts (summary), 9–10, 11, *12,* 13, 18, 111, 114–15, 161–63, 198, 199

    isolation plays and, 199–200, 201

    MVPs changes and, 22, 28, 31, 161, 183, 184

    pay and, *77,* 199

    post play changes and, 176–77, 183, 185–86, *185,* 188, 198–99, 200, 201

    power forward changes, 162, 170, *171,* 178, 186, *186,* 187, 203, *203*

    power forwards becoming centers, 187

    reactions, 31–33, *32*

    shooting by position/changes, 186, *186,* 187, *187, 203*

    smallball, 33, 181, 182, 183, 189, 191, 218, 222

    value of players and, 157, 178

    See also specific individuals; updating the game

Tirico, Mike, 138

Towns, Karl-Anthony, 200

Traylor, Robert, 136

two-point jump shot

    decline/timing, 27–30

    defense effect, 5

    reputation of, 5

    three point shooting vs., 5, 8, *8*

    See also midrange shots

Under Armour, 59–60
updating the game
    aesthetics and, 225–26, 228–29
    big players and, 217, 219, 220
    contact rules, 223
    fixing the two-point area/lane changes, 219–22,
        220
    positional diversity and, 219
updating the game/adjusting the three point line
    25 feet line/effects, 204–6, *205*
    allowing goaltending on threes, 216–19
    corner three and, 207–8, *208*, 210–15, *211*, *214*
    data-driven line/adjusting annually and, 206–10,
        208, *209*
    team custom lines, 215–16, *215*, *216*, *217*

Van Gundy, Jeff, 218
Vucevic, Nikola, 187

Wade, Dwyane, 55, 134, 142, 201
Walker, Kemba, 4
Wall, John, 80, *81*
Wall Street Journal, 113
Webber, Chris, 174
Westbrook, Russell, 37, 119–20
Whiteside, Hassan, 216, 218
Wiggins, Andrew, 150, 210
Wilbon, Michael, *32*
Williams, Deron, 70
Williams, Lou, 103, *103*, 105
Williams, Mo, 150
Williams sisters, 130
WNBA (Women's National Basketball Association),
    204, 205
Wojnarowski, Adrian, 60
Wooden, John, 2
Woods, Tiger, 130

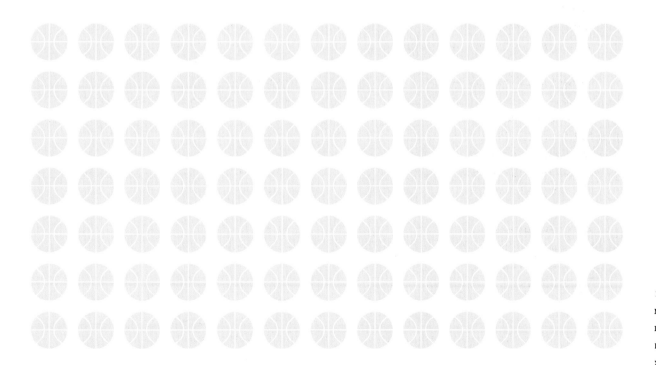